D0058319

My
Gorgeous
Life

The Life, the Loves, the Legend

Dame Edna Everage

SIMON & SCHUSTER

New York   London   Toronto   Sydney   Tokyo   Singapore

SIMON & SCHUSTER
Simon & Schuster Building
Rockefeller Center
1230 Avenue of the Americas
New York, New York 10020

1   3   5   7   9   10   8   6   4   2

Library of Congress Cataloging-in-Publication Data is available.

ISBN: 0-671-70976-3

In Memory of
Norm
and
For My Godson
Earl McGrath
Who Is
Very Much Alive

To one gone and yet remaining,
unrecognisable and without change.
A memory and presentment
of the eternal past.

Joseph Hergesheimer

Within every man there is the reflection of
a woman, and within every woman there
is a reflection of a man. Within every man
and woman there is also the reflection of
an old man and an old woman, a little boy
and a little girl.

Hyemeyohsts Storm

This little book is important to me and I
have written it as simply and as truthfully
as I can. How good it is I do not know
and in a sublime sense I do not care. It has
come into being *as* true art comes, with
absolute necessity and with absolute ease.

Iris Murdoch

All history is fiction, just as all fiction is
history.

Benedetto Croce

Not seldom to be famous, is to be widely
known for what you are not.

Herman Melville

Contents

CHAPTER I

My Roots

I AM PROBABLY JEWISH. Let's face it, Possums, shake anyone's family tree and, more often than not, a Red Sea Pedestrian falls out – and on his feet! Whenever I am anywhere a bit cosmopolitan, like New York or Los Angeles, people give me spooky looks as though I am a long-lost relation and, let's face it, I am a survivor: a fully paid-up, card-carrying survivor with a story to tell. And this is it.

It's a funny thought that there will be millions of people reading this best-seller, some voluntarily, many as a compulsory school or university text book, who have never heard of me. What a vain woman I would be if I thought everyone on the planet adored me.

Chances are you might run away with the idea this is just another showbiz autobiography written by a ghost for some stupid empty-headed glamourpuss. No way! This book is going to give new hope to zillions of men and women across the ethno-socio-economic board because it is the true story of one woman's journey from the kitchen sink to the corridors of power. A woman who has nonetheless remained natural, approachable and, let's face it, humble.

When I said I was probably a Red Sea Pedestrian, I should have said as well that I am *definitely* an Australian because that's where I was born a good deal less than a century ago. When you come from a wonderful country like mine, you don't delve into your ancestry too deeply, or you didn't until recently. You see, in the Olden Days, Australia was a dumping ground for British incorrigibles; now it is the other way around and we tend to send quite a few high-powered scallywags to England where they invariably set the cat among the pigeons, buying polo teams, newspapers, breweries and Van Goghs.

When you go to Sydney today, you could be sitting in one of its many up-market, internationally acclaimed, award-winning gourmet brasseries, surrounded by the cream of sophisticated Sydney society. However, you won't have to look very hard at your fellow lunchers to spy little tell-tale hints of convict ancestry. Even the way some of the menfolk in their Giorgio Armani plunging necklines jangle their Cartier chains gives you a spooky feeling of the bad old days when old-fashioned sex offenders were chained together – though hopefully *not too closely together*. Look at the womenfolk too in their Ungaros and Claude Montanas; those Toby jug faces and nutcracker smiles tell their own exciting tale of raunchy nights in the vice dens of old Sydney town.

No, in Sydney our chequered – or should I say arrowed – ancestry is only just below the surface so until recently no one asked you what your great-great-great-grandfather did for a crust. Most Australians, if they mentioned their convict past at all, generally claimed that their ancestors had been on the *staff* of some of those spooky old correctional facilities which would mean that the warden/convict ratio was about ten to one. Having a jailbird in the family was definitely 'not on' and everyone liked to pretend their ancestors came to Australia because they liked it. Certainly that was the case in my home town of Melbourne where everyone is descended from tourists who for various reasons – loss of luggage, passport problems, gastro-enteritis and snakebite – decided to prolong their trip Down Under a generation or two longer. (The colourful migrants who have flocked here since VJ Day are another story. The Greeks, Malaysians, Italians, boat people and Serbo-Croats, as well as the New Zealanders, are just a few of the ethnic minorities who made modern Australia the pulsating melting pot it is today. Meanwhile, we original Aussies are a good deal less coy than we were about our felonious forebears.)

I'll never forget the day when my wonderful mother locked me in the boxroom. This was a tiny room used for storage. I think I might have been 'naughty' that afternoon though some of my psychiatrist friends tell me there is no such thing as naughtiness any more and that I was probably portraying early signs of brilliant Megastardom when I gave my little playmate, Daphne, a Chinese burn behind the incinerator. Being a dreadful wimp, she screamed as though I'd really hurt her and my mother stormed out into our backyard giving a case-book demonstration, if only she knew it, of 'overreacting' (although I didn't know it then, she was probably at the middle, beginning or end of one of her famous nervous breakdowns). I can still hear her voice as though down a long tunnel, 'Leave Daphne alone,' as the boxroom door slammed behind me and I knew I was in for at least half an hour's solitary. I might even miss my favourite wireless programme, *Chums at Chatterbox Corner*, if that cry-baby got her way. There was no window in the boxroom, just a little green light leaking in through a high ventilator and a dead light-bulb, on which had once fried a daddy-long-legs. The cupboard, for it was more like a cupboard than a room, smelt of dust, Wundawax, Marveer Furniture Polish, old suitcases and hatboxes made of leather with a yukky smell, as though they were on the verge of turning back into meat.

Spookily enough, as I write these words, I can remember what leather tasted like, and pennies, ink and, I'm sorry, dirt. It is amazing the things kiddies put in their mouths and live to tell the tale. Luckily we grow out of it in most cases – Madge was always the exception.

I sat sobbing on the floor feeling resentment towards my mother, little knowing then that many moons later I would be locking her in the same room, but that's another story, an exciting and moving one too. Remind me to tell you about that.

Suddenly my childish eyes spied an old chest of drawers. Possibly a priceless old piece of furniture that had probably belonged to my gran. These days it would fetch squillions at Christie's, but then it was merely regarded as a worthless bit of junk. The wobbly old drawers were lined with the pink pages of the *Sporting Globe* and *Pix*, but the bottom drawer appeared to be locked. I gave the handles a yank and suddenly, in a cloud of dust, the old brass lock gave way and the drawer opened. It appeared to be empty except for what looked like a grubby old pair of pajamas and a rabbit trap. Remember, it was hard to see in there and my eyes were not as strong as other girls' (Dr Moss had just prescribed my very first pair of famous face furniture). Examining the jamas by what little light filtered through the ventilator, I noticed to my amazement they were covered with a spooky pattern – *broad arrows*! The so-called rabbit-trap was a short length of chain attached to a rusty orb. Although I did not fully comprehend the meaning of this discovery, I covered it quickly with a few sheets of old newspaper and slammed shut the drawer.

What could it mean? I wondered. My little mauve head buzzed with conjecture. It was only many years later that I unravelled the strange and terrible mystery that lurked in our family boxroom.

★   ★   ★

London's Somerset House isn't even in Somerset – actually it's somewhere off Strand Street near Australia House as a matter of fact, but it is a fascinating old place filled with history, pomp and pageantry and if you want to trace your family tree that's where you go. How could I forget the morning Madge and I set off in my limo for a little investigative probe into my ancestral roots. Frankly, Readers, I would be suffering from a severe case of Oldtimer's disease if I did forget that trip because it was only yesterday morning, and just as well Somerset House isn't in Somerset incidentally or we would only just have got there and it would probably be closed.

Luckily someone there recognised me from the telly which opened a few doors and cut a few corners. He was actually a tinted chappie but beautifully groomed and probably spotless. Madge certainly took a fancy to Denis as he was called, and when we left quite a few hours later she made a fool of herself buying more raffle tickets than she could afford from him, to raise money for Reggae Relief in Jamaica. I had brought along my great grandmother Beazley's birth certificate which we had found among my mother's effects the night we burnt her things, and after Denis had sweetly taken us into the bowels of the building on the top floor, a helpful lass (another fan incidentally) fiddled around with her computer and lo and behold the whole Beazley family tree started flashing across her screen. She said they have everything on microwave now, whereas in the old days it would have taken hours of digging through musty old papers.

'Are you sure you want to see this, Dame Edna?' she asked, looking at her screen with a little frown of embarrassment – and that's one expression I'm familiar with.

'Of course I do!' I exclaimed rather roughly. 'I happen to know my ancestors weren't saints, in fact they were probably scallywags, but whatever they got up to was the only way they knew of protesting against the gross social injustices which prevailed across the board in pre-Thatcherite Britain as we know it.'

Frankly this may not have been exactly what I said but it is certainly what I *think* and historians agree with me too. Modern research and carbon dating is proving that most so-called convicts sent to Australia in the old days were highly intelligent revolutionaries and intellectuals rebelling against ghastly conditions like the Plague and the Black Death.

'This is fascinating,' said the kind girl, pointing to a printout which had just curled out of her machine. 'Your namesake, Edna Beazley, was convicted for petty theft in London way back in 1770 and transported to Australia in a convict ship. I'm terribly sorry to have to break such ghastly news,' she added rather sweetly.

Strangely enough I didn't feel a bit ashamed because everything was falling into place. Hadn't I discovered that mouldy old convict nightie tucked away in Nana's chest of drawers? I knew it had belonged to a woman too, because the jacket buttoned on the left, and by the way it smelt of old-world toilet water.

'You're not telling me anything I didn't know already,' I said politely, 'but I'd just love to know what that poor waif stole to get her trip to Australia. Let's face it, these days the average English girl would *kill* to get there.'

My helpful archivist performed a few more arpeggios on her hardware and after a long electronic silence, her screen lit up with

amazing facts and figures. To cut a long story short, my poor
little ancestor was actually apprehended by a Bow Street Runner
stealing a gladiolus flower from a Covent Garden florist. (Probably, now I come to think of it, one of Audrey Hepburn's
ancestors. Remember *My Fair Lady*? I must phone Audrey and
tell her – I doubt if she needs to be ex-directory any more.) As if
that wasn't spooky enough, it appears she was one of the first
convicts to be shipped out of England and they were just going
to dump the poor things on some tropical island. Little Edna
Beazley, with incredible powers of leadership which I must have
inherited, was pretty soon running the ship and became friendly
with the bewildered old captain, who hadn't the faintest idea
where he was going. After he picked up a tummy bug and a social
disease on one of his layovers, little Edna practically navigated
the ship single-handed, and set a new course south where they
eventually landed. But she never got the credit she deserved.
What woman did in those days? The chauvinist old captain jumped
ashore and hoisted up the Union Jack. His name, incidentally,
was Captain Cook, and the land Edna Beazley had discovered
was Australia! Can I hear my Readers say, 'Pull the other one,
Edna?' I believe I can. But to those sneering cynics and chauvinists
who find it impossible to believe that a pretty little floraklept of
yesteryear was capable of finding a significant land mass, I would
refer them to the archives at world-famous Somerset House. I'm
sorry, but I would.

I'm naturally into reincarnation, in fact I would probably be
the reincarnation of Mother Teresa except that she's still alive.
Shirley MacLaine thinks I'm almost certainly the reincarnation
of Boadicea, Mary Queen of Scots, Lady Macbeth, Florence
Nightingale, Eleanor Roosevelt and Ethel Merman, and who'd
argue with Shirl on this particular subject?

However, we are all, to some extent, reincarnations of our
ancestors and that spunky little felonious forebear of mine certainly had a spooky influence on my life. Long before I ever knew
she had stolen a gladdy I had felt a strange attraction to those
gorgeous flowers. Once in the early sixties, I was on the stage of
a theatre holding an audience spellbound – a large vase of flesh-
pink glads sat on the piano – and as though in the grip of a

mysterious force, I felt myself snatch the dripping stalks from their receptacle and hurl them into the dusky auditorium; hands, like pink parrots, flew up and grabbed them and the front row of the stalls was soon waving their lovely floral tributes in time to my finale. I still end my shows the same way, but now of course I distribute zillions of gladdies every year, and poverty-stricken British florists have been known to buy front row seats in order to replenish their meagre stocks. But I'm sure the special relationship I have with gladioli – the fact that it is now Australia's National Flower thanks to me – is due entirely to my ghostly ancestor. Gladdies are very funny flowers in their private lives incidentally, and that is a horticultural horror story I'll be telling you later whether you like it or not.

CHAPTER II

Back to
the Womb

W HEN THE CONSORTIUM of international publishing tycoons flew into Geneva for a preliminary summit (or *Gipfelconfrenz,* as they call it) with my Swiss advisers to sound me out about a warts-and-all autobiography, I realised that once this deal was locked up, I would need a bit of help researching my infant years. Who could tell me intimate little things about myself as a bubba? A few folk sprang to mind, but were they still in the Land of the Living? Hadn't most of them been gathered, jumped the twig or caught the last ferry? And if a couple of them were still on the planet, how much would they remember of my infant antics and quaint, prematurely seminal sayings? Let's face it, when you're cuddling a kiddie or even trying to hold a reasonable conversation over a cup of tea while someone's tot chatters away in bassinette or playpen, you would be excused if you didn't get it all down on video and tape and have it biked off to the Smithsonian Institute. Most littlies, when it's all said and done, talk a lot of stupid twaddle and grown-ups could be forgiven if it went in one ear and out the other. If you are a child prodigy like Michael Jackson, Mozart and Mickey Rooney, your parents may be the last to know and chances are your toddler's tittle-tattle will never reach posterity. Who would remember mine? That was the big question – a question which would take me on a long journey across the VIP lounge of Geneva International Airport.

Incidentally, I have never bothered with élitist things like private jets or even bodyguards and minders, and if any sick troubled man from a broken home ever tried to make a sexual attack on me, my bridesmaid, Madge Allsop, has promised to throw herself between us. She has even begged for a trial run.

In no time at all, I was soaring high above the Alps. I pressed my brow against the chilly plastic porthole musing to myself, 'Somewhere down there in the midst of all those busy little people with their hopes and fears, tears and laughter, joys and disappointments, lies my money.' It was not a disagreeable thought. Here I was jetting back to Australia with my bridesmaid, Madge, tucked away about half a mile, fifty crying kiddies and five toilet lines behind me in Economy. I glanced at a few of the books I had brought with me for the journey: *The Life and Loves of a She-Devil, Women Who Love Too Much,* Lizzie Spender's scrummy book on pasta and the latest Jackie Collins.

Suddenly a rather plump, pink-coated steward plonked himself on my arm rest. 'Sockettes and slumber shades?' he enquired politely, plucking from a tray a little plastic sachet of in-flight accoutrements with his sanitised tongs.

I am not sure whether it was condensation from my air vent but a slight mist of moisture had engulfed me for a second, or could it be because it is difficult for a big macho cabin steward to enunciate *drily* the words "sockettes and slumber shades' at an altitude of 30,000 feet? I noticed he also had a lot of my albums, books and old programmes tucked under his arm so I could guess what was coming.

'I wonder, Dame Edna, if you would mind signing some of these for my flat-mate, Don? We never miss your wonderful shows.' I was glad he hadn't said 'sensational shows' or I might have had to have slipped swiftly into my showerproof Aqua-scutum!

Twenty-four hours and three Valium later my jumbo touched down at Tullamarine, Melbourne's world-class terminal. While Madge waited in the baggage hall for my Mark Cross and Louis Vuittons to come slamming and slithering on to the carousel, I was given the VIP treatment and whisked past the long queues of boat people (or jumbo people as they are now called since the devaluation of the Australian dollar) to the Arrivals Lounge, where I peered anxiously around for the person who was to meet me. There slumped on a tangerine Dralon sofa under a Rafis palm and a rare original, signed and numbered print by Sir Sidney Nolan (no. 3500 of 11,000), was my uncle Victor, well and truly off to bye-byes. How small and vulnerable he looked in his spotlessly clean duck-egg blue Aceytex shorts and his fawn poly-velourex 'I ♥ Australia' T-shirt, his gnarled old tootsies clad only in a pair of yellow rubber Taiwanese thongs. Gazing down at this little cicada of a man, with an imported digital around his ropy wrist, it was impossible to believe that he had once been called the Butcher of Borneo. It was hard to imagine him single-handedly castrating a battalion of Japs. Actually, I tried not to imagine it – unsuccessfully.

I was lost in my own thoughts when Madge came on the scene to announce my luggage had been packed into the limo. Uncle Victor must have smelt her Charlie because his old eyelids flickered.

'Ed!' he cried. 'It's little Ed.'

Flinging himself into my arms, I felt the brittle old bones of my mother's brother, the war hero, through my humanely culled acrylic Arctic fox.

'We've told your mum you're coming but I can't guarantee she'il rekonnise yiz. The staff out at Dunraven are looking forward to seeing you though, Ed. They'll probably roll out the red fatted carpet for you. No worries.'

I had decided to visit my mother's retirement facility as quickly as possible before the jet-lag set in. It was a miracle after all that the old darling was still with us and her Periods of Lucidity were, according to Sister Choate, becoming few and far between. But I knew there were jabs you could give confused oldsters which could make them chatty, or so I'd been told by my wonderful private doctor, Dr Balfour Gardiner, who works hand in glove with my gynaecologist.

As I sat rugged up in the limo with my wiry little uncle and Madge Allsop beside me, I was excitedly planning the questions I would ask my marvel mother. What were my first words? How long did you feed me? Was I avid at the breast? How young was I potty-trained? What were my early signs of brilliance?

It wasn't as though I *myself* was so interested in the answers to these questions but, with typical unselfishness, I was already thinking of you, my Reader – my millions of Readers – who would want to know it all.

It had been a year or so since I had visited Melbourne, Australia's nicest city. Peeping through the bullet-proof glass of my stretch limo, I saw the old familiar landmarks and new buildings too, typical of the exciting and innovative architecture which has made this city a hotbed of new ideas. We passed multi-storey advertising agencies, and instead of glass windows, yes, mirror, in which were reflected, you've guessed it, Possums, *other* high-rise advertising agencies faced with different coloured mirrors. The trams still rumbled down the wide streets not as yet veneered with mirror, but gaily painted by some of our internationally acclaimed award-winning artists. On the front of one of them I spied the destination 'Moonee Ponds', the suburb of my childhood. I felt my eyes moisten but there was no time for nostalgic detour if I was to get to Dunraven, St Peter's Close, before blanket-bath time.

Call me old-fashioned but I detest small talk. My wonderful old mother used to say, 'If you can't say anything nice, then don't say anything at all.'

As a matter of fact, that was one of my mother's many sayings which we found scribbled in a little pink notebook in the pocket of one of her old two-ply shell-patterned peach matinée jackets The Night We Burnt Her Things. One day I will publish some of her wise old words, probably printed by the Entity I use for all my charitable publications, the Prostate Press. 'A stitch in time saves nine' and 'Too many cooks spoil the broth' were also marvellous little philosophical phrases she used to come out with. Jealous types and smart Alecs have pooh-poohed this, saying they have heard those expressions hundreds of times before, and *they have*! Let's face it, my mother lavished her wisdom on everyone who crossed her path and, these days, her ramp. So is it any wonder that some of her pithiest sayings have spread around the planet?

One of the wisest things my old darling ever said was, 'You are as old as you feel,' and I must say those words were buzzing around in my head on the long limo trip from the airport.

Anyway, it's funny, but I, who can natter so fluently with the likes of George and Barbie Bush, Gore Vidal and Susie Sontag, found it hard to know what to say to my little uncle Victor. I knew how proud he was of me. Didn't he keep scrap books of all my doings, tape all my TV shows and dine out on my reputation? I use the term 'dine out' rather loosely, Possums, because I rather doubt if the poor old darling has ever eaten in a restaurant in his life and my little niece, Kylie, told me they actually never let him out in the daytime for fear he'd bump into a crocodile of Japanese tourists and experience a gruesome knee-jerk reaction. He was my mother's only surviving brother and I had tried to help him over the years in unobtrusive caring ways; the occasional Harrods hamper and odd manufacturer's samples for which I had no use, like compact discs of Swedish Chamber Music and last year's unused Filofax diaries. He may never have opened these prezzies, bless him, but Kylie told me he loved saying to his few surviving mates at bowls as he proudly brandished a copy of *French Provincial Soufflés,* 'Look what my niece Edna has sent me!'

'To the home of a friend the road is never long.' Yes, that was yet another of my mother's wonderful sayings, but I am here to tell you that the road to my mother's Twilight Home was the *dickens* of a long way considering I had flown across the world with ten pieces of luggage and a bridesmaid. I suppose I must have still been in the fast lane yet I knew the sands in life's egg timer were trickling away fast, and wasn't I researching the autobiography of the century? Supposing my marvel mother was gathered before I could extract her vital input, I would never forgive myself. And neither, I tend to suspect, would my Readers.

The internationally acclaimed lights of Melbourne were becoming few and far between and I realised we were about seventy miles from the city centre approaching the outer suburbs. Here, as part of the innovative and imaginative Greater Melbourne Plan, lovely new estates were being built where before there had only been farms and orchards. The new suburbs were being named after award-winning Australian sporting and cultural identities and my mother's Twilight Home actually lay near the boundaries of Keneally, Goolagong and Minogue.

Dunraven was a beautiful old period home built last century in the middle of nowhere by a famous bookie. The main reason it was not pulled down in the sixties was that no one wanted to build a petrol station there and the consortium of doctors who bought the old home for a song turned it into an up-market caring facility for the Confused Community. 'Let us cherish your Bewildered . . .' said the fully illustrated, colour brochure which showed a tanned doctor with silver sideburns and a stethoscope leaning across a desk, extending his hand to a refined and grateful gentlewoman, with a Zimmer walking frame, wearing a spotless cardigan and her late husband's Timex. There were also artist's impressions of cleanly dressed oldsters watching TV and Zimmering around in rose gardens, smiling all over their faces like those people you see on the Air Safety card as they slither down emergency chutes or calmly inflate each other's whistles. It turned out that the handsome doctor in the brochure was an actor in *Neighbours* and the real doctor was quite a different kettle of fish but that is another story, and a spooky one at that, which I'll tell you some other time!

As the new prestige homes of Minogue, Keneally and Goolagong pressed closer and closer around stately old Dunraven, the Consortium started to sell off bits of the garden, first the tennis court, then the croquet lawn and greenhouse, so that the old house was soon hemmed in by new developments and you would be lucky to get a Zimmer between the fence and the house. In my mother's case this wasn't too serious because she never had green fingers and was always happiest indoors. Sister Choate organised the occasional outing for the Partially Bewildered and once they all went on a bus trip to the TV studios to visit the set of *Prisoner – Cell Block H* where they were photographed with some of the stars. My mother, of course, received special treatment being mother of a world-famous Megastar and she was allowed to have a go at the ironing machine which is a feature of this world-famous mini series and is, I believe, the very same ironing machine on which Lizzie was tortured and gang-raped by Bee and the laundry-room gang. Sister Choate told me there was a bit of a problem getting her girls back into the bus since the bars and other security devices on the set reminded them so vividly of their habitual environment at Dunraven that they actually thought they were home.

At last our conveyance swung into St Peter's Close, the street in which Dunraven stands. It is not really a street but a cul-de-sac, probably once the driveway leading to the old home but now lined with prestige dwellings, all in total darkness since it was six o'clock on a winter's evening and the local community were all viewing in their family rooms at the back. The Melbourne sky was aubergine except for a little orange stain on the horizon where the sun had gone to wake up England. A crunch of gravel under the tyres and we were soon standing on the modernised porch. Sister Choate welcomed us in what must have once been a gorgeous nouveau-deco hallway. She attempted to curtsy as I entered but I nipped that in the bud. I know a lot of people feel like bowing and scraping when they meet me – in fact I can understand it – but like all Australians, I am non-élitist and I always like informality to be the keynote.

One of the main reasons why I hardly ever visited my mother was to spare her the jealousy of the other inmates. Seniors can be quite vindictive towards a privileged patient and I knew if I kept popping in and out with too many little luxuries such as *Harpers and Queen* and *Elle* magazines, origami kits, Walkmans or crystallised fruit, my mother could risk peer group persecution.

'I think, Dame Edna,' said Sister Choate with a little cough, 'that we should have a chat before you visit Mother.' I followed her uneasily into her office where to my surprise a middle-aged man in a suit sat smoking and viewing the News on a chipped ivory TV set. Although as I said, I despise élitism *per se,* I think a man ought to stand up when a Megastar comes into the room; I'm sorry but I do, call me old-fashioned. Ida Choate then muttered a rather offhand introduction and the 'man' turned out to be a female friend of hers called Fran Upjohn and a distinctly weird type if you ask me.

Ida Choate offered me a chintzy chair and a cup of tea. Then, like people only seem to do in films and mini series, she turned her back on me and said gravely, 'Yes, you will notice a big change in Mother. She is as strong as an ox and as fit as a fiddle but, with respect, I doubt if she is ever going to make a lot of sense, even with the intravenous Scopalamine.'

Frankly, Possums, I was irritated by this woman, who *I was paying a fortune to*, saying 'Mother' this and 'Mother' that, as though we were sisters for heaven's sake! I cannot bear people saying 'with respect' to each other either, as though we were all lawyers on a TV show.

I also did not much like my bridesmaid, Madge Allsop, plonking herself down on a couch and chatting away to Ida Choate's spooky girlfriend. For all I know, Madge probably thought she *was* a man. Still I am not a mind reader and in Madge's case, I am very glad I am not.

On top of that the tea was undrinkable, it tasted of swimming pools. If there is one thing that gets my goat it is eating food flavoured with cleansing agents. I have even been in quite grand places where the scallops tasted as though they had been marinated in Mr. Clean. I know that powerful chemicals are sometimes needed to fight infection in grubby kitchens but I prefer them *out* of my food thanks. I am sorry but I do. However, I was not too worried about anything I might nibble that night since I had heard that Dunraven, my mother's resting place, had very recently been raided by the Vermin Squad and heavily fined.

'I think I am the best judge of my mother's frame of mind, Sister,' I heard myself say rather sharply (she had asked me to call her Ida dozens of times but I have always pretended not to hear). 'Naturally I know my mother is no spring chicken, although she has got as many chemicals in her as one, but there are a few vital questions I have to ask her.'

Choate pressed an intercom buzzer. 'Nurse Ng, paging Nurse Ng. Dame Edna is here to see Mrs Beazley in the Sylvia Plath Suite.'

When I am jet-lagged, I do get irritable and my fuse is a good deal shorter. To think I had gone to all that trouble over the years keeping my mother's profile as low as possible and now here was Ida Choate broadcasting my arrival, not merely throughout Dunraven but probably within earshot of the whole street! The arrival of an adorable boat person in a crisp white uniform calmed me a little and I was led by little Nurse Ng, in *all respects* diminutive, in the direction of the Sylvia Plath Suite and the wonderful woman who had brought me into the world.

From time to time, I have given a part of my wealth towards the Dunraven Refurbishment Fund and they had, in a pathetic attempt to please me, named a ward after me. Once again my healthy hatred of élitism reared its ugly head and I persuaded them to name other rooms after famous female Achievers, hence the Dora Carrington Ward, the Virginia Woolf Incontinence Wing, the Diane Arbus X-ray Unit, and the Zelda Fitzgerald Fire Escape; all women who had *done* something with their lives.

No, I didn't like that Sister Choate; didn't trust her either. Going up the black rubber staircase I could smell the funny odour places like that always seem to have: a mixture of roast lamb, chloroform and little jobs. Not a combination I would go out of my way to inhale.

As I entered my mother's suite, I could see that Choate and her cronies had made a hasty attempt to tidy things up for my arrival. Publicity stills of me in glamour poses and snaps taken at lunches with Gore Vidal and Klaus von Bulow had been hastily stuck around the cheerless room, and not by Mummy I'll wager. You do not have to have a Mensa brain to see that a woman like Ida Choate had had her hand in the till, and if *she* was a member of my fan club then the Pope was a Red Sea Pedestrian. I suddenly remembered the David Hockney I had given Mother to make that bare room of hers prettier which had vanished within twenty-four hours. Although I could never point the finger, I have a shrewd idea that someone on the hospital administration maybe 'borrowed' it, judging by the brand new Jaguar XJS I spotted soon after in the driveway.

I do not think they had expected me to come straight from the Airport and Mummy was out of bed in her old pink chenille dressing-gown having her hair done. Another young madam, wearing little more than a skimpy green nylon overall and a purple love-bite, was busily painting my mother's toenails. The hairdresser was coaxing her sparse old locks around a spiky plastic roller and at the same time trying not to tangle with my mother's various conduits, tubes and drips which writhed about the room like a nest of pythons. To my horror I also noticed that the impudent young pedicurist had a ciggie hanging between her sulky lips.

Nurse Ng said a few brisk words and they scampered off, not without looking back and recognising me with eyes like saucers. My mother still sat motionless and I followed her gaze to the TV screen on which a woman appeared to be changing a baby's nappy. Mummy released an audible chuckle and Nurse Ng whispered in my ear, 'I think Mother's identifying.'

Curse that impertinent oriental miss! Why the dickens, I thought, do they all have to call my mother *their mother*? It sounded particularly stupid too coming from a *boat person*.

I positioned myself between the TV and my beloved oldster. Would she recognise me? I decided just in case to snap on my multi-directional Grundig in-purse tape recorder. My mother's eyes, the colour of lemon curd, narrowed and her gnarled knuckles tightened around her arm rests. To my horror, I noticed that one of those minxes had rouged up her cheeks and painted a silly mouth where her lips had once been.

'She knows you, she recognises you,' whispered Nurse Ng excitedly.

'Mummy,' I began.

'Hello, Bruce,' she said in a very clear, matter-of-fact voice. 'Have you turned off the sprinkler?'

Nurse Ng was getting even more excited. 'This is wonderful,' she said. 'She hasn't been as lucid as this for months.'

'Lucid my foot,' I said abrasively, trying not to be racist. 'My mother is talking twaddle; my name isn't Bruce. She is talking to her husband, *my father*. She thinks *I* am Daddy.'

'Daddy!' said my mother, throwing up her hands. 'Da, da, da, bub-bub-bub.'

Ng fell on her knees beside my mother, her glasses positively misting over with excitement. 'I am so happy, our treatments are working, this is the first intelligent conversation Mother has had in yonks.'

My fuse was getting shorter by the second. 'If you regard that as an intelligent conversation,' I snapped, 'then perhaps I have been away from Australia too long. My name is not Bruce and she is not your mother and I hate the word "yonks", it is completely uncalled for. Please leave me alone with Mrs Beazley and go downstairs and tell my bridesmaid Mrs Allsop she is needed up here. I have some important questions to ask my mother in private and I would like her to have her medication as soon as possible.'

After that speech the nurse scuttled away and I commenced the difficult interrogation, coaxing, caring. 'You must remember me, Mummy, it's Edna, your only daughter.'

My mother suddenly became very agitated. 'Quick, Bruce, quick,' she screamed. 'I think Edna's thrown her bottle out of the cot again and while you are in there, sprinkle a bit more citronella on her pillow or the mozzies will eat her alive.'

I pondered for a moment in consternation. A crafty ploy occurred to me. 'She *is* a thirsty kiddie isn't she, Gladys, did you take her off the breast too soon?' I said in a deep voice, changing tack and boxing clever.

Mummy thought for a moment and large tears started to roll down the irrigation canals on her face.

'Oh, Bruce,' she moaned, 'do you think Edna is really ours? Could there have been some mix-up at Bethesda . . . ?'

I felt suddenly old and tired, I was getting some answers at last but not the answers I wanted. I felt as though I was in some kind of a dream world and the voice of Madge Allsop came to me as though down a long, dark corridor. 'Where are you, Edna?'

In fact, she *was* calling me down a long, dark corridor. Words like 'Is she ours?', 'mix-up' tumbled around in my mind like undergarments in a Maytag drying cycle. My mother had opened a door into the past; perhaps a door I might have preferred to remain firmly shut.

CHAPTER III

Oldtimer's Disease

I AM NOT A saint. At least not yet, though I have had a rather flattering tip-off from my little Polish pal. However, Possums, it was pretty saintly of me, let's face it, to leap off a long international flight and then drive halfway across Australia in order to see a woman who thought I was someone else. Not many of my Readers would have done likewise I'll wager. Sometimes I think I give and care too much. In fact, my gynaecologist looked up the other day and said, 'Dame Edna, when will you ever stop giving?'

Come to think of it, it was a funny thing for a gyno to say out of the blue and it was the first time he has ever really looked me in the eye. But I had come a long way, not just to see the wonderful woman whose loins I had sprung from, but also to research this gorgeous book. My Readers would not have thanked me if I had walked away from Dunraven without jogging darling old Gladys Beazley's ropy memory. I know when up-market English people write about their childhood they interrogate their old nannies but in Australia we didn't have nannies – we had parents, I am sorry but we did, and my parent's memory was going to take some jogging.

I didn't much like that hospital but it was funny to think I probably owned it, or that it was owned by one of my wholly owned subsidiaries. (I must phone my Swiss advisers to see if I do and then make improvements accordingly; a wholesome replacement for Choate and her off-beat consort would probably be one of the first moves in a major staff reshuffle.) However, the staff had, if anything, spoilt my mother giving her special privileges. At night she used to be wheeled down to the electric fence at the back – Dunraven is a maximum security Twilight Home – to watch the traffic thundering past and occasionally she would throw Tupperware at the wires, producing showers of sparks which for a short time created a minor tourist attraction – quite an achievement considering that it is hard enough to inveigle tourists to Melbourne let alone the backwaters of its remotest suburbs. Now I was slumped more dead than alive on an aluminium chair trying to coax a few gems and reminiscences from this permed and painted doll who had once given me suck. Medication was the only solution. When would Dr Chamberlain arrive to give my mother her truth shots?

Instead of the handsome and innovative geriatrician, Madge Allsop entered the room and to my irritation went straight over to my mother and gave her an uncalled-for hug. Mummy looked up excitedly at my wizened New Zealand bridesmaid whom incidentally I have unselfishly supported for a quarter of a century.

'Edna,' she cried. 'I knew you would come to see me again today. Can you sign some photos for the staff, you know how they adore your TV shows?'

My mother had Madge in a vice-like grip and as I helplessly watched, a deep sob passed through my body and my eyes filled with scalding tears. Even if she were suffering from advanced Oldtimer's disease, it was too hurtful that Mummy could mistake a fawn-coloured, bristly old Kiwi fruit of a woman for her own glamorous daughter! And Madge was giving her every encouragement, the minx.

Suddenly my mother pointed a bony finger at me.

'There's your father over there, Ed,' she exhorted Madge. 'Aren't you going to give him a kiss?'

Oh, how Allsop relished her new role! She came simpering over to me and tried to give me a smack on the chops but I pushed her roughly aside. 'For heaven's sake, Madge, Mummy is delirious. Stop acting the goat.'

Madge whined, 'I am only human you know, Edna. After all,

I visit her far more often than you do, she has probably just transferred her affections.'

That kind of remark was typical of Madge and red rag to a bull. It was true that she might have popped out to see Mummy a little more often than me but then she had plenty of time on her hands. Did *she* have to entertain millions on stage, screen and television? Did she have to sit up half the night counselling famous friends or taking distress phone calls from the Queen, Mrs Thatcher and Elizabeth Taylor, to name but three? Did this frumpy woman, gloating over her mistaken identity, ever get asked to open the Harrods Sale, turn on the Regent Street lights or smash a bottle of Moët on the wall of a brand new Prostate Transplant Unit she had financed out of her *own pocket*? Not likely! People who feel sorry for my old bridesmaid and travelling companion are barking up the wrong tree, very much so. She is as cunning as a fox and I am sure she thinks that by buttering up my mother she is bound to get a mention in the Will. I know for a fact that she has had her eye on my mother's matinée jacket collection for years and when I once in passing said I wondered what happened to those old prosthetic devices in the estates of deceased senior citizens, Madge let it slip that she knew a way of turning a Zimmer frame into an attractive lamp. No wonder her beady eyes were devouring my mother's surgical hardware! In point of fact, Madge is the most selfish woman I have ever met and that docile mousy look of hers is one big *pose*. I dread to think of the disloyal things she says about me to others behind my back. This is a quality, incidentally, that absolutely sickens me.

The Sylvia Plath Suite was not exactly spacious, in fact there was barely enough room to swing a cat. That is why I chose it for Mummy. Not that to my knowledge she was likely to swing a cat *per se*, but in her last days at home she was starting to frighten the animals.

Anyway her accommodation at Dunraven certainly offered little room to house my mother's vast collection of knick-knacks and memorabilia; her old snapshot albums, doilies, talcum boxes, frocks and back numbers of Australian *Woman's Monthly* 1937–74. After Sister Choate and Dr Chamberlain and their team had

literally dug my mother out of her room at home and marched her
into the Dunraven courtesy van, we had the dickens of a job
getting rid of her effects but that is another story which I tell in
Chapter 22.

Because I can't help being a caring person, I always encouraged
my mother to think that she was coming home soon and that her
old room was exactly as she had left it with all her precious
possessions intact. This was partly true especially in the case of
her old brass bedstead which would not have fitted in the incinerator with the rest of her things and was also of great historical
importance since it was the very bed I was conceived in, I am
afraid.

Suddenly Madge exclaimed excitedly, 'Fran, Ida, come in.'

Sister Choate and her creepy companion needed no invitation
as they barged into the tiny room which was already overcrowded
with only three people in it.

'I hope you are not tiring Mother,' said the scrawny Sister in a
bossy voice.

I heard myself saying shrilly, 'I will tire my mother as much
as I like and would you mind asking that friend of yours wearing
a man's suit to take herself and her yukky cigarette out of my
mother's facility *at once.*'

I am always far too nice to people, even people who sicken me,
and I could not stand the sight of that spooky woman Fran with
her punky haircut puffing away at her king-size mentholated St
Moritz. Nor could I help but notice how Madge after only a few
seconds' acquaintance – *as far as I knew* – seemed to be as thick as
thieves with this queer couple. I heard my mother's voice. 'Lay
off Fran, you bully Bruce.'

She was looking at *me*, it was like a nightmare. With a smirk
Fran swaggered across to my troubled little mummy and with a
sickening wink to the others, gave her the rest of her barely
ignited St Moritz. Before I could intervene, my mother had
clamped it to her lips and in three drags had sucked it down to
the filter.

'Your mother enjoys an occasional cigarette,' said Choate in an
oily voice, 'especially with a drink. We don't believe in denying
our gerries their little creature comforts.'

'What seems to be the trouble?' said a man's voice.

Madge and Fran clambered on to the bed, Sister Choate flattened herself against the wall, my mother and I huddled in a corner so that Dr Chamberlain could half open the door and shoulder his way into the room. He was a large man and quite nice looking I suppose in a Burt Reynoldsy, Tom Cruise and Sellecky, Arnold Schwarzeneggery sort of way, if you like that king of thing. Personally I can take it or leave it though I know some women get 'turned on' by medicos, to use an expression I never use. Madge once told me in her sleep that she was longing to fall ill in the Outback of Australia so that she could be given an exploratory by the Flying Doctor. Knowing greedy old Madge, you could bet your life he would barely have climbed back into the cockpit before she would be demanding a second opinion.

Dr Daryl Chamberlain was what I would call 'acceptable' and he hadn't arrived a moment too soon.

'Heaven be praised you are here,' I said grabbing at his stethoscope.

He was not wearing one of those white coats but a lovely grey suit, hand-crafted in Australia with little pin marks round the lapels and a Rotary Club badge glinting in his buttonhole.

'I have come across the world to see my mother in a nursing home I probably own and I am fed up with the way I am being treated by that woman.'

I pointed a jet-lagged finger at Sister Choate whose sallow skin flushed a deeper orange.

'Stop it, Bruce. Stop it, Bruce,' cried my poor mother banging her Zimmer on the Pirelli rubber floor.

Madge and Fran tittered.

'Listen to her, doctor,' I adjured the physician, 'can't you hear her, she thinks I am her husband, *my own father*. It is awful. Can't you do something? A little jab? I want my mother back.'

I was sobbing now, it was too humiliating, all this in front of strangers. Daryl Chamberlain strode towards my mother and deftly shone a little torch in her eyes, those that the so-called beautician had done a pretty slapdash job on, and I noticed that although she had scrubbed a bit of peacock eye shadow on her lids, her Q-tips had certainly not touched Mummy's custard corners.

'How are we this evening, Mrs Beazley?' he said in a doctor's voice. 'Isn't it nice your daughter Edna has come to talk to you? I want you to get some sleep soon,' he said soothingly.

As he spoke he was rolling up the sleeve of her matinée jacket and snapping open an ampoule. Once again to my fury Mother's glance twitched adoringly in the direction of Madge. Soon the injection was over and my mother was tucked up in bed by little Nurse Ng.

'I'd like a word with you later, Sister,' I said as Choate and her friend skulked out of the door. Madge seemed about to join them but I put a stop to that.

'You'll stay with me and take notes,' I said.

'Is Dr Holbrooke still there?' my mother said from her pillow in a little voice.

Daryl Chamberlain looked at me with raised eyebrows.

'Dr Joseph Holbrooke was our kindly old family doctor when I was a kiddie but he has been dead for years. What does this mean?'

'Don't expect too much, Dame Edna. Mother is a very confused old lady but her long-term memory seems to be pretty sound. I have given her a shot of Scopalamine, the truth drug they used in *The Guns of Navarone*. Pretty soon she should be singing like a canary.'

Dr Chamberlain was beginning to sound a bit like Clint Eastwood or even Charles Bronson but I had given my nose a good old blow, patched up my make-up and prepared to ask Gladys Beazley a few sixty-four-thousand dollar questions.

'Mummy,' I whispered, 'were you proud of me when I was a little girl? Was I always saying clever things?'

My mother made little moaning noises and shook her head on the pillow. Daryl gave me a silent smile and gave the hypodermic another squeeze. I hadn't noticed before that it was still quivering in Mummy's spindly arm.

'That should do the trick,' he said with a wink.

'Do you remember when I was born?' I continued, hoping Madge was ready to take this down. She had once failed miserably at the Margaret Hosegood Academy for Secretarial Studies, Auckland, NZ.

Mummy's little face contorted like a dried apricot, her colour rose and she started rhythmically grunting. Frankly it reminded me very much of my old friend Shirley MacLaine at a Rebirth Day Workshop we did together in LA last year, though I can't remember who was giving birth to whom or whether indeed we had got it quite right.

'I think she is *having me*,' I said a little too loudly as I clutched Daryl's tanned yet tender hand.

'I think it may be something else,' the doctor said gently and then over his shoulder to little Nurse Ng, 'Nurse, two coffees and an incontinence pad at the double.'

I was a bit peeved to discover that I hadn't been born yet but then Mummy seemed to have thought so too for she was gazing happily into space with an expression of immense relief.

'What will we call her, Bruce?' she croaked. 'You know how I love the Talkies, can't she be Ethel or Dorothy, Elsie, Lillian, Claudette, Myrna, or even . . . ?'

This was really getting interesting and I barely noticed little Nurse Ng reappear with refreshments and absorbents. Madge scribbled furiously as deft Dr Daryl busied himself under Mummy's bedclothes.

'We're getting down to the nitty gritty now,' came his educated voice, muffled but excited.

'How about Tallulah?' my mother yelled. 'Or Marlene?'

A shudder passed through me as I thought what might have been, and it was spooky to think that I was nearly named after Marlene Dietrich who is still, at the time of writing, in the Land of the Living. I am almost ashamed to admit that I gave the magic hypodermic another wee little nudge.

'Hear her cooing,' my mother continued as she relived the most historic confinement in the history of the Southern hemisphere.

'We can't call her Edna, Bruce, just to please *your* mother, we cannot inflict our first born with a name like Edna,' she said with a little wince. 'What has she ever given us since we married but an earful – but shhhh, shhhh, I think she is trying to say something, it isn't just burping, it's words! It sounds like . . .'

Dr Chamberlain had resurfaced. He took a quick gulp of coffee and placed his firm yet clinically detached arm around my tense shoulders.

'What am I trying to say, Mummy?' I exhorted the oldster.

Suddenly my mother's eyes became dilated as she articulated something that sounded like: '*Mossop olleh!*'

'Write it down, woman,' I screamed. 'It must mean something.'

Could it be some foreign tongue? Shirley had often told me that reincarnated people talked a lot of rubbish most of the time and even got it published!

Dr Chamberlain was more cynical as he passed me my cooling coffee. 'Standard baby talk, I am afraid, Dame Edna,' he said sadly. 'Precocious certainly for a three-minute-old infant, but at least you have your first words – and from the horse's mouth!'

The other day when I was given a Doctorate of Culture at the University of Madrid, I told a clever old professor called Dr Frederico Mompou this story. He wrote my mysterious first utterance down on a piece of paper and with a secret smile said, 'Try reading it backwards, señora.' For the spookiest experience of a lifetime, I suggest my Readers do likewise.

Dr Chamberlain nodded towards the bed. 'What mystifies me,' he continued, 'is that if we are correctly reconstructing – with your mother's help – events in the Delivery Room at Bethesda Hospital in 1930-whatever, for some reason they seem to be delaying the moment of maternal confrontation, or "bonding".'

At that moment, my mother sat bolt upright in bed sending the hypodermic needle hurtling across the room where it quivered in the wall only millimetres from Dr Chamberlain's head. She was clutching her hot-water bottle and staring in horror at it as though it were a living thing.

'Yuk,' she bawled. 'The hair, Bruce, the hair! Look at her hair, *it's mauve*, where did we go wrong?'

CHAPTER IV

The Kid with Mauve Hair

M Y MOTHER'S BRUTAL words sent my mind scurrying down Memory Lane.

It is no fun having mauve hair, not when you are a school kid. I always felt different from the other girls anyway, somehow brighter, more on the ball. A pathetically skinny little New Zealand pupil with a crush on me had scribbled in my autograph book 'Dear Edna, you have that spark – magnetic mark.' Madge Allsop's words (for it was she) certainly summed me up. I was rebellious, yet far from naughty, prematurely intelligent, yet certainly no know-all. But the thing that set me apart most of all was my halo of bright wisteria curls. Apparently, Dr Joseph Holbrooke, who had brought me into the world and knotted off my little navel, is on record as saying that he had never seen anything like it before but school children can be so cruel, so cruel.

My earliest memories are of the country in the old township of Wagga-Wagga. My parents, Bruce and Gladys Beazley, had gone there from Melbourne as times were hard after the First World War and things weren't so pricey in the bush. Dad was a real veteran and had fought in the trenches in the first period of WWI. He had had a whiff of gas and had even been wounded. I remember as kiddies we were all intrigued by the shiny groove on his shoulder where the German bullet had nicked him. He still had a few souvenirs of the war. There were the brass shell cases which sat on the mantelpiece (my artistic son, Kenny, has them now with dyed maribu feathers in them) and he used to have a snap taken out of a dead German's pocket which showed a sad young woman sitting next to a soldier holding a spiked helmet. This snap was spooky considering the soldier had probably been killed by my father so the sad little woman in the snap was his widow. There was German writing on the back that no one could read. Little did I realise then that a few years later I was going to get mixed up with the evil Nazis but that is another story, an amazing story, which you will thank me for telling you later on!

Some of Dad's mates didn't get off so lightly; they either fell or lost an arm or leg and ended up as lift drivers. In my youth, the elevators in Australian cities were always manned by cheery ex-servicemen, either with one sleeve neatly pinned or tucked into a pocket or else balancing an abridged trouser on the little fold-out seat. As a nipper, I always thought these old Australian lift drivers lost their appendages in elevator accidents, as though from time to time the lifts themselves had recruited their own staff by some savage mechanical law.

Perhaps I am letting my imagination run away with me. That was another of my wonderful mother's sayings by the by: 'Edna, I think you are letting your imagination run away with you again.' That woman could have been a philosopher or even a TV personality. Yet, when you come to think of it, Possums, it would be a dull book indeed where the author's imagination did not from time to time run away with her.

My earliest memory is looking up through the flyproof net over my bassinette. I must have been plonked down in our back garden under the old peppercorn tree and the net was very important in case any of those big green quilted emperor gum caterpillars dropped off the tree on to my pillow. I was a beautiful baby you will not be surprised to hear and I clearly remember an enormous face looking down at me from the other side of the net with another big face over its shoulder.

'I think she is focusing, Glad,' said a loud voice (Granny's?). 'I wonder what she will be when she grows up?'

If only my little rusk-encrusted lips could have spoken I would have cooed one simple word – 'Megastar'. Instead, I distinctly remember smiling a gummy smile and releasing a thick dollop of curdled farina.

The thing I most remember about being a bubba is the discomfort of constantly being sick, falling over, dampening my nappies and not being able to coherently express myself. Imagine if these problems persisted into adult life; Australian politicians have got *all* my sympathy! You also spend an enormous amount of time on your back, a habit some women never seem to grow out of. The sounds I most remember are the sounds that woke me up in the morning, magpies or 'maggies' gargling in the bush nearby, the clop of the milkman's horse on the new asphalt road outside my parents' modest but spotlessly clean home and the silly clucking of our 'chooks' as they laid my breakfast 'googies.'★ In the time of which I write most Australians kept poultry, although by the fifties it was thought to be rather common. Now of course with the craze for free-range eggs, factories employ whole teams of boat people to dip eggs into yukkiness and roll them in chaff and feathers so they can be sold to yuppies for twice the price. Down the back with the chooks and past the clothes line was our spotlessly clean external toilet facility. In those days, few homes in country towns were sewered and our amenity backed on to a lane down which, in the hours of darkness, passed the spooky Nightman with his cart. To make his grim task easier there were little wooden hatches backing on to the lane from which he removed the brimming pails. I never saw him but there was a pale girl at school called Fay whose father was supposed to have been a Nightman but this was only said in whispers, to her face. Personally, I always thought Fay smelt perfectly clean, even sweet, of Lux and Palmolive, but I suppose if you were regularly cuddled by a whiffy Nightman fresh off the job you would tend to overdo the ablutions. Now I guess there will be a couple of generations of Australian kiddies who would look at you blankly if you ever said the word 'Nightman' in the same way as 'blotting paper' and 'clockwise' are lost on the Bic and digital generation.

Another early memory was of my mother in the laundry every Monday boiling sheets in the copper and prodding their white

★ Universal Australian usage for chickens and eggs.

tummies with the copper stick as they billowed out of the seething suds. When I was old enough I also helped her squash shirts and singlets through the wringer after they had been rinsed in the Reckitt's Blue. My mother was already wearing surgical stockings as she had just begun to have the first twinges of the Vein Trouble which was to plague her for the rest of her life. I was a big baby and I think I may have been the cause of the problem. Mummy must have said something once because I always felt a little stab of guilt whenever I saw those mauve knots and nodules creeping up her legs and blossoming like grape hyacinths behind her knees.

I attended a bush kindergarten where I showed early signs of the talent which has made me one of the most popular and envied women on the planet. I seem to be a natural leader and I can still remember how the other toddlers looked at me with eyes like saucers whenever I came out with something priceless. In my memory the little playground was always hot and dusty and I never liked to join the rough and tumble with the other children when I could be sitting on a little painted stool inside talking to my teacher, Miss Ely. I wish she was still alive so that I could ask her about some of my prematurely brilliant sayings. I heard that she jumped the twig over twenty years ago but I believe that up until the last she dined out on the fact that she had been my first teacher.

We always used to take a packed lunch with us and I still feel a little bit weepy when I think of my mother lovingly preparing my sandwiches – Kraft cheese and apricot jam, curried egg or Rosella tinned spaghetti. No polythene bags in those days. Our sambies were packed in greaseproof lunch wrap (where would you buy that today, Possums?). I remember a tot called Bernard at the Kindie who was rather slow or a bit of a 'droob'. As only children can, they set upon this unfortunate mite and rarely a day passed without him receiving a bloody nose or a Chinese burn. I can still see his mother, poor old Mrs Gifford, calling to pick him up, his garments torn, his knees crusted with scabs. They took him away in the end but not before his little lunch box had been kicked around the playground dozens of times by cruel bullies. Somehow the fate of his sandwiches was more poignant to me than the injuries those louts inflicted on little Bernie. It was awful to see one of Mrs Gifford's lovingly cut banana sandwiches stuck to the heel of a bully's boot. Packed lunches always make me cry. Mind you, Possums, banana sandwiches do get horribly brown and squashy on a hot day and the very smell of them used to make me violently sick. 'Better out than in,' said Miss Ely as she held my little tousled mauve head over the toilet, and it is an expression which has flashed into my mind at all kinds of odd moments in my life, including my wedding night, but that is another story, perhaps the most intimate story of all which you must promise not to skip ahead to read.

Our days at Wagga-Wagga were numbered. It was a sleepy old country town but my parents hankered for Melbourne, Australia's most refined capital and incidentally one of the most cultured cities in the world, if its inhabitants only knew it. Work for a man with my father's capabilities and War Record was not easy to find in Wagga either and my parents were Church of England in a small town which tended, to use a quaint old expression of my father's, to 'kick off with the left foot'. Not that I have anything against Roman Catholics. On the contrary, one of my best friends is Polish, single and lives in Italy. No prizes, Possums, for guessing what adorable old Left Footer I am referring to. But if our family did not exactly suffer religious persecution or discrimination as it would be called now, I was having a bitter taste of it at Pooh Corner, my Kindie. I have spoken already of the cruelty of children but bravely omitted to mention the treatment I received from a horrid element. I was always tall – I was a tall baby – and my mauve mop naturally made other girls, whether black, mousy, blonde or ginger, green with envy. My only friend seemed to be Miss Ely for somehow I never quite dared to tell my harassed and overworked mother of my nursery nightmares. With a spooky premonition of the future, Miss Ely comforted me. 'One day you will be proud of your height and your unusual hair,' she said soothingly. 'You are like a lovely agapanthus.' For years I thought she meant some star of the talkies called Aggie Panthus. It was only much later in life that I discovered these slender yet stately blooms topped with a crown of blue-mauve flowers. And indeed, I *was* a lofty agapanthus rising on my elegant stem above those other children who like puny lantanas, geraniums and phlox huddled far below amongst the weeds. I later learned to be proud of the crowning gift Dame Nature had given me when, as a teenager, I first started to grow hair that I could sit on.

CHAPTER V

The Friendly
Electrolux Man

MY FATHER ALWAYS longed to be in ladies' underwear. The retail side of the Rag Trade appealed to him and whenever my mother went shopping for a new frock (about once every ten years), he was always at her side. It is more than likely that my talented son, Kenny, got his flair for fashion from my dad's side of the family because let's face it, my husband Norm had no dress sense whatsoever, in fact he wore pretty much the same thing for a quarter of a century: a pair of fawn, striped flannel pyjamas and a brown and burgundy check woolly dressing-gown with a tasselled cord, saline drip and balloon catheter, not exactly the sort of thing you would see a Tom Selleck look-alike wearing on a knitting book cover. Most men get a bit twitchy when it comes to their own womenfolk's garments but if my mother was going out to a special occasion like a funeral or a flesh and blood stage show, Dad was completely at ease choosing her frock. Let's face it, when you have only got three frocks, choosing is easy.

I am afraid I am a bit of a down-to-earth old Megastar and I have not got a superstitious bone in my body though I do tend to believe in reincarnation and I think you will find some of the world's top brains and think-tanks do as well, I am sorry but you will. There is an exciting reference or two later in this book to reincarnation and frankly I wouldn't be a bit surprised if Calvin Klein and Karl Lagerfeld were not born again Bruce Everages. If they are reading this book, and they probably are, they will now understand why, whenever we meet for fun or a fitting, I give them a spooky old look.

Alas, my father's dream of affiliation to the Ladies' Garments Industry was never realised but the night my mother burnt his things, she found several items of feminine attire tucked away behind his masonic apron on top of the wardrobe, no doubt Mothers' Day presents he had forgotten to give her and poignant symbols of his thwarted ambition.

My father was a tall man with a prominent, almost pointed, Adam's apple, like most First World War veterans. He had a cracked rather wheezy voice on account of having been slightly gassed during the period of hostilities. Actually, I found out later from one of his mates that this had occurred while he was bravely performing kitchen duty at Puckapunyal (an Aboriginal word meaning something) Military Camp in Australia before he was actually shipped to France. Apparently he was peeling potatoes one day, completely unaware that the gas stove was leaking. when he finally lit a ciggie, it was a miracle that he was blown clean through an open window or I might never have been born and this wonderful best-seller might never have been written. He was 200 pounds in socks and hernia belt and like most healthy Australians, a keen spectator at football matches. He also loved animals, especially horses and not a Saturday of my childhood passed without the whole family listening to the races on the wireless. I can't say the constant whine and jabber of those racing commentaries by Eric Welsh and Bert Bryant were music to my childish ears but I knew it was almost a religion for my father and later for Norm. I can still see him huddled beside our overheated Radiola on a stifling Saturday afternoon, his face tense, his fists excitedly punching the air as the nags hit the home straight and the commentator's voice rose to a hysterical scream. My mother would always turn to us with a beautiful smile. 'Your father loves his sport,' she said tenderly.

I think I own quite a few racehorses today though I cannot be certain without faxing Switzerland but I am still slightly allergic to race broadcasts and, come to that, hot Saturday afternoons. Even when I am sitting out there at Ascot with little Blair, my

Bank Manager, in his VIP tent or in the Royal Box, I tend to tune out and be off with the fairies.

Daddy had had an assortment of jobs. At one stage when I was just a hop in his glass of chilled ale he was a Rawleigh Man. Rawleigh's were a wonderful old New Zealand firm who made all kinds of beneficial products from imitation vanilla essence to Goanna Salve, a marvellous, all-purpose ointment containing rare nutrients from the spleen of Australian reptiles or goannas. Rawleigh's also manufactured Ready Relief, a mixture of eucalyptus oil and the spleen of something else which my wonderful mother used to sprinkle on our pillows at night if we had the sniffles. These products were not sold in shops but from door to door by returned servicemen or 'Rawleigh Men' and the arrival of the Rawleigh Man was a big and exciting event in family life during the interbellum period, to use an adult education expression. I am afraid New Zealand hasn't given us anything else nearly as interesting as the Rawleigh range, in fact the only other things I can think of are the hot-air hand-dryer, the Kiwi fruit and Madge Allsop, all *very* overrated.

My father stopped being a Rawleigh Man soon after the birth of my youngest brother, Athol, following what I later learnt had been an 'incident'. Some foolish woman probably suffering from PW PMT (Pre-War PMT) had complained about my darling daddy. As far as we could tell later, there had been some misunderstanding when she had invited him across the threshold for a supply of Ready Relief.

The big event in my childish life was the move to Moonee Ponds, an unbelievable saga full of comedy, tragedy, humour and pathos, and one which I will be unfolding to you at a very early opportunity.

About this time electrical household gadgets were coming into their own. Even a lucky few had a Frigidaire though most of us still used ice chests and the Ice Man was a common sight scurrying from his horse-drawn cart up suburban sideways, shouldering a wet hessian sack and a dripping crystal cube. We kiddies would loiter behind his conveyance in the hope that he would give us a few chilly chips to suck though my mother always discouraged me from doing this. 'You never know where that has been,' she would admonish me – a favourite phrase and a wise one too when you think about it, especially in this day and age.

Australia has always been a spotlessly clean country and Australians welcomed the new technology, but our homes were mostly kept spick and span with old-fashioned carpet sweepers with little sprung gates underneath them from which we used to remove long grey sausages of gritty floor fluff. When the first vacuum cleaners were announced in Australia, they were given a warm welcome and housewives really rolled out the filthy red carpet. Soon the lovely homes of Australia swaddled in their peaceful morning hush were filled with the sound of wheezing and sucking as the womenfolk wielded their thrilling new appliances with their optional attachments.

Shortly after we moved into our new home in the Big Smoke at 36 Humouresque Street, Moonee Ponds, my father gave Mummy the gift of a lifetime, a brand new Electrolux vacuum cleaner complete with extension rod and two-way dusting tool. With her gleaming chrome extension rod she could reach awkward, dust-prone crannies like the curio ledge in dark stained wood which ran high up around the walls of our front hall and loungeroom. On this she sat her priceless collection of crockery; a Toby jug of Old King Cole, her antique Edward VIII coronation mug and her lovely plate with a picture on it of a coach arriving at an inn in the Olden Days. Tragically these were chipped and broken years later when my mother was high on tranquillisers – she must have also been pretty high on a stepladder to have been able to run amok on her own curio ledge. Goodness knows what those gorgeous knick-knacks would be worth today. I have seen ornaments *almost identical* fetch a fortune at Christie's (New York).

★   ★   ★

My memory of the Big Move down to Melbourne is vague. I was probably 'traumatised', to use an expression my daughter's therapist doesn't seem able to leave alone. There is a stupid school of thought which says that if you cannot remember certain things that happen to you as a kiddie, you have to spend an arm and a leg lying on a couch in some doctor's surgery tearing your parents to shreds. Twaddle! The fact is children have memories like

sieves and I am sure my readers will be grateful that I don't
remember every blessed thing that happened to me or this mega-
selling book would use up half the forests of Finland. There are
some very blank moments in my childhood, so what's new?
What I do remember were the trams clanking up and down
Puckle Street, Moonee Ponds' main thoroughfare. Walking
down it today you would think you were in a suburb of Athens
or Beirut unfortunately, but in the Olden Days it was one of
Melbourne's most fashionable streets; the Australian equivalent
of the Faubourg St Honoré or Madison Avenue.

Our new home was in the 'Federation Style' which is a bit hard
to describe but it is somewhere between art nouveau and art deco.
You would have to ask my son's flatmate, Clifford Smail, who
is 'into' that type of thing and has got a priceless lamp of a green
metal ballet dancer holding up a ball which he picked up for
nothing at a thrift shop. Number 36 had had one previous owner:
an old ex-serviceman called Russ Parker who had lived there
alone with a few stray cats before being whisked off to an Old
People's Home. Apparently he always kept the neighbours awake
in the wee small hours by noisily re-enacting some of the major
battles of the First World War, and if the truth be told, the poor
old thing had gone over the hill in more ways than one. This was
confirmed by our new next-door neighbour, Mr Whittle, who
described him as having 'a couple of kangaroos loose in the top
paddock.'

Even before the removal men had helped unpack our tea chests
and suitcases Mummy and I had scurried from room to room
exploring. There were still a few sad souvenirs of the former
occupant even though all his relations had descended like locusts
on the house seconds after the ambulance had taken him away.
An old Vaseline jar on the bedside table, a bottom set of teeth
beside the bath, a crooked picture of Menin Gate, the glass broken, in a corner behind the dining-room door and a brown slouch
hat with the side turned up on top of the wardrobe – a hat he
probably wore every Veterans Day when he marched with all the
other old Diggers – but now his marching days were over.

Any geriatrician will tell you that oldsters sometimes 'come
good,' in a big way too, and I must have known this instinctively

as a kiddie. It was spooky moving into 36 Humouresque Street, Moonee Ponds, knowing that old Mr Parker was still alive somewhere. What if he woke up one morning as bright as a button and decided to come home only to find another family living in his old dwelling and all his effects thrown to the winds? Call me old-fashioned but I do believe in ghosts although I have not got a superstitious bone in my body and I swear that one night I woke up in the early hours of the morning because I thought I heard a terrible thump and a man yelling, 'F—ing Huns, *skewer the bastards.*'

I hope it was just a ghastly nightmare and I can assure my Readers and my zillions of fans that is the only seven-letter swear word I have ever dreamed. Old Russ never did come back though I often wondered how he managed in that Home without his teeth.

In my wonderful stage shows, I often ask women in the audience to describe their homes to me and some of them find it a bit difficult. A lady once confessed to me that being in my company made the rest of her life seem like a dream as though I was the Only Reality and she really had to rack her brains to remember where she lived and who she was married to. Compliments like that don't grow on trees, do they, Possums? Now the boot is on the other foot and I am trying to describe to you the home in which I spent my girlhood and frankly it isn't easy, I am sorry but it isn't. As we slowly spruced the place up, putting down nice carpets where Russ Parker's lino had been, restained the curio ledge and installed a gorgeous lounge suite in fawn and burgundy uncut moquette, my parents little realised that the day would come in the eighties and nineties when the street outside would be choked with tourist buses and throngs of Japanese tourists would be filing from room to room, pointing their Minoltas and Toshibas at the home which their daughter had made so famous that it became a museum! I still get goose-pimples when I think that my parents' old lounge suite now has ropes across the arm rests and has been made into a postcard which has been sent around the world.

Soon after we had settled in and I had been enrolled at Moonee Ponds Girls' Grammar, my father began a new job with

Electrolux, travelling from door to door purveying vacuum cleaners. He would ring front-door bells and say to the wary Occupant with the lovely way he had, 'Good morning, I am your friendly Electrolux man.' It always worked like a charm, particularly after he had emptied a bag of filth on to their best rug and then given the lucky housewife a demonstration suck. Needless to say our own vac was thereafter always perfectly maintained and my mother never lacked the odd optional attachment. I will never forget the evening my father came home after a very successful day's sales, a hint of sherry on his breath and a little parcel tucked under his overcoat.

'What's that I can feel?' said my mother as she hugged him playfully. She was not kept guessing for long as her inquisitive hands come to rest on her very first crevice nozzle.

CHAPTER VI

My Ramifications

I N THE LAST chapter I meant to mention my three brothers, Roy, Athol and Laurie, and chances are it will come as a big eye-opener to a lot of my Readers to hear that I had, and to some extent still have, siblings. A lot of folk pick me for an only child and let's face it, I certainly am a bit of a 'one-off', but I have never made a big publicity thing about my wonderful brothers out of unselfishness. The fact that they have a Megastar sister with talent coming out of every pore and money to burn should never be allowed to interfere with their simple low-profile lives. Poor little Athol, my younger brother by about nine years, lives in a beautiful home in one of Melbourne's dress circle suburbs but the last ten years of his life have been a nightmare. Once the neighbours found out that he was my brother every Tom, Dick and Harry pestered him and his pathetic little wife Dawn (née Purdie) for my autograph. The priest asked him to open the church fête, and whenever I had a hit show on stage, film or TV, the paparazzi of Australia would hang outside his home for interviews. Athol doesn't earn much as a venetian blind repair operative (between you and me, in the privacy of this best-seller, I paid for his house and every stick of furniture in it) but to his credit little Athol has refused squillions from Rupert Murdoch and his ilk for his 'story'.

A Sunday rag recently ran a story – MY SISTER, DAME EDNA – and they even published smudgy snaps taken from a satellite of me visiting Athol's home in my limo. Athol swore he never told them anything but his wife Dawn whom I have never liked (nothing to do with Catholicism) piped up with some tale of woe about the cost of a swimming pool in the backyard, and how some gutter publication had offered to install one. In a weak moment I took the hint and in a short space of time Kylie, Damian, Bernadette, Shaun, Dermot, Kathleen and Nathan were all romping around in a ten-metre fully tiled free-form swimming pool with an inbuilt spa and travertine surrounds. No prizes for guessing who forked out for that little item. But Dawn has overplayed her hand if only she knew it and she'll get nothing more from me. Let's face it, just supposing I did call her bluff next time and she gave a press conference – MY SISTER-IN-LAW: DAME EDNA, or some such twaddle – she would be a foolish girl to say anything negative about me. I am such a popular, almost revered figure that the neighbours would tear her limb from limb.

I wasn't the first-born. I had a wonderful older brother called Laurie who I don't remember very well. He perished from a snake-bite before we moved to Moonee and I think the tragedy was one of my parents' main reasons for leaving the bush. As far as I can gather he had come home one day from school and casually told Mummy that he'd had a nip on the leg from a five-foot tiger snake in the blackberries down by the railway line. My mother immediately panicked, took out her teeth, nicked his leg with an old Gillette, and tried to suck out all the poison. By the time Dr Vaughan Williams arrived it was too late, and he told me many years later in the strictest confidence that I would ask readers of this mega-seller to also respect, that poor Mummy had spent an hour on her knees on the bare linoleum sucking the wrong leg.

My parents never mentioned Laurie again after the funeral but I think my mother had a bit of a nervous breakdown at that time; the first of many as it turned out. I remember she went away for a 'holiday' and Auntie Ruby came to look after me. She was a Captain in the Salvation Army and always wore her uniform including a navy-blue straw bonnet which looked old-fashioned then, although today people would think she had just strayed off the set of one of our internationally acclaimed award-winning nostalgia movies. Needless to say, when I was a kiddie, nostalgia hadn't been invented.

Auntie Ruby was a big woman with black hair in a bun, like everyone called Ruby (have you noticed, by the way, that everyone called Audrey has reddish hair?). She smelt of Fawldings lavender talc and, I'm sorry, BO. In those days BO, like nostalgia, didn't exist or at least nobody put a name to it. I don't remember when the Lifebuoy soap commercials started but I remember seeing them in the *Woman's Monthly* and leaving it lying around rather pointedly for Auntie to read. The ads were in the form of a comic strip showing a rather nice young woman (similar to the young woman with pimples in another ad) being shunned by handsome men at a dance, or strap-hanging in a crowded tram full of people with hankies clutched to their noses. The girl was usually rescued by a kind friend or medical adviser with a lamp on his head who whispered, 'BO,' and handed her a cake of Lifebuoy in plain wrappers. There was usually a tasteful picture of her later under the shower lathering her underarms followed by a romantic scene on her porch or at the pictures with a handsome Brylcreemed man giving her a bit of a cuddle. The man's balloon usually said: 'Thanks for a wonderful night, Joyce. See you tomorrow?' And her bubble said: (*thinks*) 'I'm the happiest girl in the world, thanks to Lifebuoy.'

I'm sure if 'Joyce' had been in full Salvation Army uniform my aunt might have identified, but as it was she didn't and I used to dread the moment every night when I said my prayers, kneeling on the bed with Auntie Ruby's arms around me pressing my frightened little face into her whiffy blouse. To this day I've always made a special point of personal hygiene though it has been an uphill battle getting Madge Allsop to toe the line. I made her use a roll-on deodorant almost as soon as they were invented though she used to squawk a lot in the bathroom, claiming that the ball jammed, pinching her pits. Madge can think of any excuse to avoid the normal habits of cleanliness and I have it on good authority that when she went to the New Zealand production of *Hair* and tried to leap on stage at the end to mingle with the cast, the grubby hippies on stage refused to dance with her. However, I forget that you haven't really met Madge Allsop, not on these pages anyway. She pops into my life quite soon though and, more's the pity, never pops out of it.

I suppose Auntie Ruby was a very kind person, which is what you usually say about someone you can't think of anything else to say about. Although I am one of the kindest women on earth as a matter of fact, I wouldn't like my epitaph in Megastar's Corner, Westminster Abbey to read: 'Here rests Dame Edna Everage, *she was kind*' – I'd rather die first.

My editor has told me not to mention too many people in this book who don't crop up again later, for fear they will confuse my Readers. To which I replied, 'Twaddle.' Who does she think she is, telling me how to write my incredible life story and remember the key figures of my past?

Young and impressionable as I was, Auntie Ruby planted something in my little wisteria head which was to give me nightmares for many moons afterwards. I don't recall how it cropped up, but she told me about a little boy down the street who was adopted by childless parents who then proceeded to have six of their own. It's a spooky old fact which my Readers will no doubt have observed for themselves. I felt terribly sorry for little Keith Henderson (my editor will hate me mentioning his name but my Readers aren't stupid); I am a softie from way back and my heart went out to that poor kiddie. I began to get the feeling that I too may have been adopted because I felt so different from my own family, a bit of an outsider if you like. I have since read biographies of Mozart, Shakespeare, Vlad the Impaler and Nancy Reagan and discovered to my relief, that they all entertained the same scary fantasy. Expressed bluntly it was: 'How could a brilliant and gorgeous person like me have been born to a stupid old boring couple like you?' It sounds awful, doesn't it, Readers? But that's how I felt and if this book isn't honest it is nothing.

I look back and realise how this fear planted in my mind haunted my early years. Supposing I *wasn't* adopted, there could still have been a mix-up at the hospital. What must the midwives have thought when my little mauve head popped out in marked contrast to my mother's mousy fibres? With all these little worries churning around, it's a miracle I never suffered from bedwetting as I have in more recent years. Madge Allsop's night sweats caused by a combination of the late-late movie and toasted cheese are forcing me to seriously consider the single duvet option.

Mummy came back from her mysterious 'break' full of beans and, as it happened, my brother Roy. In the move to Moonee her tummy got bigger and bigger and my father stayed at home a lot to look after her. I can't say I welcomed the idea of a new arrival in the family because I loved being the focus of attention, incredible though that may seem to people who know me today. But children, especially those with exceptional talent, are inclined to be a wee bit self-centred and I can still feel that little choking feeling I experienced as a pampered kiddie at the prospect of a rival under the same roof.

Since Laurie had been gathered, my parents had rather spoilt me and Daddy, as a special treat, would sometimes take me on his local Electrolux house calls. While he was demonstrating a new attachment or putting a new model through its paces on a client's burgundy and fawn art deco wall-to-wall carpet, I would sit quietly on the three-piece lounge suite reading one of my Nancy Drew books and feeling the scratchy uncut moquette upholstery prickling the backs of my mottled thighs. I would also be drinking in my surroundings, studying the framed snaps on top of the pianola, the brass shell cases on the mantelpiece, the galleon firescreen and the pictures if any, on the walls – usually, spookily enough, 'Daybreak' by Maxfield Parrish, a wonderful Australian colonial artist who painted pictures of people in flimsy underwear waking up on patios in the Botanical Gardens. I think these paintings were sold door to door during the Depression by limbless ex-servicemen along with *New World Encyclopedias* and honey. Other people's interior decoration always intrigued me as it does today, as anyone who has been able to beg, borrow or steal a ticket to one of my wonderful shows will heartily endorse.

My father thought I was his lucky mascot because I always made such a big impression on the clients. They would open the door a bit suspiciously, peeping through the crack first at me looking utterly gorgeous and then at the lapel of Daddy's smart double-breasted navy blue pinstripe from Wardrop My Tailor in

Melbourne then at his burnished Returned Serviceman's badge. Daddy would always say, 'Good morning. What a lovely home you have here. I'm your friendly Electrolux man and this is my little daughter Edna. I wonder if I could give you an obligation-free demonstration of our new Coronation Model?' If the client, usually a housewife in a kimono and butterfly hair curlers under a net, looked a bit reluctant, Daddy would add hastily, 'My youngster is thirsty, any chance of a glass of water?' That usually did the trick and within minutes I would be sitting at the kitchen table like a little princess with a delicious glass of raspberry vinegar in front of me. Once I even scored a scrumptious Spider (ice-cream squurged up with lemonade) in a pretty Kraft Spread glass with Hooey, Louey and Dewey on it – still my favourite Disney characters incidentally.

I got used to the compliments too as my father clinched a deal or demonstrated his crevice nozzle: 'What a fascinating child.' 'What beautiful eyes.' 'She doesn't miss a trick, does she?' or 'She's got our number', 'That kiddie will go far, mark my words.' If I had been a vain child all that praise would have gone straight to my head and only once did I overhear a horrid negative remark. If I recall aright, Daddy had failed to make a sale at this particular house and they hadn't even given me so much as a glass of water. As the front door closed behind us I distinctly heard the woman say to her daughter, 'Can't they read the No Hawkers, No Pedlars sign on the front gate? And wasn't that kid a *real little Madam*?' I never knew what a Madam was, not until much later in life as a matter of fact, but those cruel words stung my sensitive little nature deeply and I can't say I was sorry to hear the news a couple of months later that that woman's house had burnt down leaving them destitute. In my experience people always get their come-uppance sooner or later. A Sydney critic once accused me, one of the most left-wing radical women on the planet, of being 'a fascist and a racist'. I could have sued him for squillions or told Rupert or Kerry to give him the sack but instead I kept my dignity and said nothing. A few weeks later his rock opera flopped, his newspaper folded and his wife got bitten by a deadly funnel web spider. Why should I ever need the expensive services of my solicitors Fennimore and Gerda when Dame Nature sorts out very nicely in her own sweet time all those who are foolish enough to let their jealousy get the better of them?

Yet it was a jealous little Edna who peeped resentfully into the bassinette of baby Roy Beazley when he came home from the hozzie. Suddenly this red-faced little monkey lying there with a ribbon of white sick from the corner of his mouth to his ear made me want to throw up. I once overheard my father talking on our new black vulcanite 'Coronation Model' telephone. 'Gladys is tickled pink about baby Roy,' I heard him say. 'One girl in the house is quite enough.'

As you know we were living in the new home at Humouresque Street, Moonee Ponds, and I was forming new friendships, new attachments. Mummy would often be in the lounge with the blinds down when I came home from school. I must have been five or six at the time and Mrs Pritchard, Doris Pritchard's mother, would usually collect me from school and drop me off home when Mummy had her hands full. I peeped into the darkened sitting room. Roy was howling as usual and Mummy was fumbling with her blouse. I saw her pop one of her big white chests into his mouth and the noise stopped. I heard Mummy singing softly:

> 'Go to sleep, Mammy's little pet
> Mammy's little Alabama coon . . . '

It was the song she used to sing to me! I ran out into the backyard blocking my ears and quite frankly, Readers, I think that from that moment on I pretty well blocked little Roy right out of my life until recent years when I have been able to offer him financial succour. He certainly got plenty of succour from our mother and he had barely been weaned aged three and a half before Athol turned up on the scene.

Throughout my childhood I would look at those burly, almost ordinary, boys and at my own sensitive and fragile face in the mirror. 'Where do I come from?' I would ask Dame Nature, Jesus, Father Christmas or whoever cared to listen.

CHAPTER VII

Moonee Blues

I USED TO LOVE the walk home to 36 Humouresque Street from
Moonee Ponds Girls' Grammar. I must have been ten or
eleven at the time and the school uniform suited my lanky
looks; a wide-brimmed straw hat, orange blazer with brown and
purple braid (the school colours), a tie with a big knot (done by
my daddy from behind) and a short, pleated brown skirt brushing my mottled legs.

It was a hot summer's day as my best friend Phyllis Balderstone
and I, our school bags slung over our shoulders, mooched home-
wards. We didn't appreciate Victorian architecture then, though
thinking back, the old homes we passed, with iron-laced verandas,
have now made way for Safeway's and a big parking lot. Most
of the homes had hedges and white painted picket fences, and I
used to love popping the paint blisters with my thumbnail and
peeping into the dusty green privet for caterpillars, which Phyll
and I would drop into an old Clegg and Kemp jam jar with a few
gum leaves.

The asphalt footpath was buckled by the summer heat and by
the roots of the big plane trees with their piebald bark. When I
first came to the Old Country and stayed at the English-Speaking
Union in Berkeley Square, I noticed it was full of enormous
nightingale-infested plane trees as well, though the ones in
Melbourne streets peter out above the trunk since the council

regularly chops off all their branches so as not to interfere with the telegraph wires. The result is that our streets tend to look like avenues of hat-racks.

A few peppercorn trees dropped over the hedges and I jumped up to tug at their sticky fronds – like green feathers – trying to dislodge the chubby emperor gum caterpillars.

'Hurry, Edna,' cried Phyllis, 'or you'll miss *Chatterbox Corner* on the wireless.'

'I'm sick of that session,' I declared, in my prematurely grown-up way. 'It's mad and stupid.' 'Besides,' I said to myself as that foolish Balderstone girl disappeared through her front gate, 'I'm going to catch 'yabbies.'*

Ten minutes later I was in Moonee Ponds municipal gardens, strictly out of bounds for schoolgirls, but they were deserted anyway. Australians in those days hardly ever used their gorgeous public parks, since we all had our own lovely gardens at the front and back of our solidly built bungalows. Now of course, Australian public gardens are thronged with people, very few of whom were born on this side of the water.

The 'lake' was really more like a small swamp, probably one of the original Ponds of Moonee, 'billabongs', or cut-off meanders of the Maribyong River, as I later learnt in geography. More adventurous kiddies, older than me, used to attach worms and bits of meat to the end of a string and dangle it into the khaki water until a little tug announced that a 'yabby' or freshwater prawnie thing had taken an interest. Some nippers collected buckets of them and took them home and sent them crawling about the kitchen lino to scare their mums, and only recently have sophisticated Australians with BMWs and Originals on the walls taken to actually eating them with a glass of Tasmanian Chardonnay and a macadamia and kiwi fruit coulis.

But I was always a dreamer. In fact my aunties and teachers often used to snap their fingers at me and make little scissor movements across my eyes as I stared into a World Of My Own. 'Where are we now?' or 'Penny for your thoughts, Edna,' they would say. But I never told them because nine times out of ten my thoughts were worth a great deal more than that, as purchasers of this book are by now aware.

---

* Australian fresh water prawns.

I was daydreaming then, in a secluded nook amongst the reeds, my little skirt hitched up above my mottled thighs adorned with drawings. (As a kiddie, I used to love doodling on my thighs. I'm sorry, but I did.) I was peering into the murky water and three yabbies were already trying to scramble up the sides of my caterpillar jar, when I became aware of a horrible hand on my shoulder and a sickening smell of Muscatel. My blood froze and I felt the little mauve hairs on the back of my head stand up on end. 'You're a pretty little girl,' said a ghastly foreign-sounding voice. 'Can I help you catch something?'

Already a rough hand had glided down to my horrified hip. I swivelled my head around like the kiddie in *The Exorcist*. It was Mr Moshinsky, the Russian hedgeclipper, who rode around Moonee on an old Malvern Star pushbike, doing people's hedges for two and six a time.

'Not today, thank you,' I said with incredible presence of mind. 'My father will be here in a minute.'

He laughed horribly but his hand still gripped me tightly. 'Would you like me to show you something?' he said with an awful laugh. 'If you promise not to tell your mummy?'

Even then as an innocent child, I had a spooky feeling that if he was going to show me something it was not going to be a yabby or even a caterpillar, though it might very well bear a superficial resemblance to one. Things were getting blurry. I tried calling for help but my throat was parched and no words came. My knees seemed to buckle beneath me and my yabby jar slipped from my fingers and crashed against a stone. I made an attempt to run but it felt like going up an escalator the wrong way, as I finally collapsed on the footpath. Far off, a distant voice was saying, 'Wake up, Edna, look at this.'

'No, no,' I screamed. 'Never. Whatever it is, I'll never look at it.'

*   *   *

How long I wrestled with that pervert, Moshinsky – if pervert he was – I do not know, but I came to on the floor of my mother's little room at Dunraven, my hands around the throat of Dr Daryl Chamberlain. I must have been reliving that childhood terror in my jet-lagged dreams!

The doctor seemed in an agitated state and was yelling at me, 'I want you to look at something, Dame Edna,' and pointing at my mother's bed. 'You're tired and overexcited. You dropped off at your mother's bedside about an hour ago with a glass of water in your hand, but when you suddenly threw it against the wall and became delirious, we thought we should wake you. Besides your mother is coming out with some pretty interesting stuff.'

From where we sat, surrounded by broken glass on the floor of the Sylvia Plath Suite, we beheld the strangest sight. My mother sat on the edge of her bed in her fireproof combed polycotton nightie, holding her hot-water bottle to one exposed breast and crooning an old lullaby that seemed to open a floodgate of memory:

> 'Go to sleep, Mammy's little pet
> Mammy's little Alabama coon . . .'

It's a song you certainly don't hear much these days and if you did, most bubbas would be quite within their rights to report it to the Discrimination Council.

My mother gave her hottie a realistic hug and flapped it over her shoulder, beating it savagely. 'She's winding me I think, Doctor,' I said, still groggy from my ghastly nightmare. Interesting though this was, I could think of better things to do at three o'clock in the morning than sitting on the floor of a Sunset Facility in an outer suburb of Melbourne, watching a terminally bewildered loved one breastfeed a hot-water bottle.

'I'll have to get back to my hotel if I want to be human tomorrow for my nationwide press conference and my concert of Brecht/Weill songs with the Tasmanian Symphony Orchestra. Quite frankly,' I added, 'I'd be more interested in catching a spooky glimpse of myself a few years later, *at the talking stage.* Can't you press Mummy's "fast forward" button?'

Daryl Chamberlain helped me to my feet and helped my feet into my Maud Frizons.

'You're tired and emotional, Dame Edna,' he said, 'and you're hyperventilating. I'll ask Sister Choate to assist you into the car.

We've done enough work for one night. But I'm sure your mother has much more to tell us if I can find another vein.'

The thought of Sister Choate mingled with that dreadful nightmare brought it all flooding back. 'Where's Madge Allsop?' I cried, in a voice which probably didn't sound as though it had ever been overseas.

'I believe she's downstairs with Sister Choate and Dr Upjohn.'

'Don't tell me that creepy crony of Choate's is a doctor?' I exclaimed. 'I certainly wouldn't want her anywhere near me with a thermometer.'

'Oh no!' laughed Dr Chamberlain. 'Not *that* kind of doctor, Dame Edna. She's a doctor of Media Studies at Latrobe University. She's quite a character really. She and Sister Choate adopted an Aboriginal child a couple of years ago, but it went walkabout last month and they've taken it rather badly.'

I tried to kiss my mother goodbye but she was busy scrubbing the bottom part of the hottie with a handful of Wet Ones. You can't leave Madge alone for five minutes. She is a terrible judge of character and she is always making a fool of herself with the medical profession. She'll look for any excuse to get in touch with a doctor and every morning, without fail, she sits bolt upright in our bed and starts feeling for lumps. I wouldn't mind if only she felt for her *own* lumps. It is one of Madge's yukky habits that causes me seriously to consider single beds.

Sure enough, as I walked into Choate's smoke-filled den, I felt quite frankly as though I was interrupting an orgy. It was as if I'd stepped into an episode of *I, Claudius* – remember that? Who could ever forget it? It wasn't as though they were actually doing anything, but I knew by the faces of those smirking females that I'd been under discussion. Let's face it, when aren't I?

Daryl Chamberlain and I shook hands as Madge followed me sheepishly into the limo, and we travelled the hundred odd miles through the suburbs to the city centre in comparative silence. My old bridesmaid was asleep and snoring, so as you can imagine, the silence was only comparative.

Yet I couldn't sleep. Strange memories welled up in my mind. Once again I was running through the park, fearing to look back lest I catch another glimpse of the Thing which that old alien had wanted me to see. For some reason I never told my parents what had happened since, in point of fact, nothing actually had happened, but I had had a glimpse of something that my little brothers, Roy, Athol and Laurie, had hardly prepared me for. Something which, let's face it, no woman in her right mind ever needs to see.

On that traumatic night long ago, I had hardly been able to eat my mince on toast for the thoughts which raced through my little wisteria head. Mince, incidentally, was my mother's great speciality and it's funny to think that today grey is the most fashionable colour you can think of. In her own way, my mother was a pioneer of grey food: chops, potatoes, Brussels sprouts, soup – all emerged the same subtle shade of grey from my mother's oven, whatever colour they were to start with. She taught me many recipes, but that's another delicious story.

CHAPTER VIII

Allsop's
Fables

M Y BROTHERS, NOW middle-aged men and I fear almost like strangers to me, were very far from my mind as I sat in the back of the limo on the long journey to central Melbourne. After the exhausting flight and the ordeal of Dunraven, my mother's luxurious terminary, I was frankly a cotcase. My Readers may well remember that I had actually on one occasion passed out on the floor during the long and frustrating process of getting Mummy to spill the beans and sing like a canary about my infancy. Mark you, I had spent telephone numbers establishing that Twilight Facility and *I mean* telephone numbers with international dialling codes in front! Admittedly I hadn't personally interviewed Sister Choate; I had left that to Chris Bland, my thrusting young attorney at Fennimore and Gerda. He should have vetted the woman more carefully since she was definitely on the take – 'ripping me off' to use another expression I never use.

As if reading my thoughts, an adenoidal little voice with an unappealing New Zealand twang piped up at my elbow. It was Madge Allsop in that dreadful old moth-eaten tweed coat of hers throwing in her usual twopence worth of idle comment. 'Edna, do you think Sister Choate and her friend Dr Upjohn are a pair of lesbians?' I felt a groan of weariness and impatience rise within me.

'For heaven's sake, Madge,' I snapped nicely. 'I was dozing then, but since you've woken me up I'll thank you not to use permissive language like that with me. It's not a word I like. As a matter of fact lesbianism has always left a very nasty taste in my mouth.'

If Madge Allsop read books or indeed anything other than the New Zealand *Woman's Weekly* and occasionally, I regret to say, *Playgirl* magazine, I would not publish what I am about to say. However, and this mustn't go any further, I've always thought Madge had *tendencies*. When you share accommodation and more often than not a double bed with another woman you get to know them pretty well, I'm afraid. You get to know what makes them tick and Madge had more ticks than a bush mongrel, figuratively speaking. People who've seen her on my top rating television shows have written letters accusing me of cruelty to this woman, little knowing the true story of kindness and unselfishness which lies behind our friendship. Of course her apparent shyness and timidity is just a pose hiding a ruthless and ambitious minx. She is, I'm afraid, totally infatuated with me and certainly knows which side her bread is buttered. It's just sometimes she's rather too clingy for comfort and some of her role models are a bit on the creepy side.

She once suggested that we go to a fancy-dress party as Gertrude Stein and Alice B. Toklas. It struck me as odd at the time that a semi-illiterate woman like Madge could have heard of that American *rat-bag* and her spooky sidekick, but I checked them out with a Prof. in Eng. Lit. who told me that Gertrude and her crony were fully paid-up card-carrying deviants from *way back*. Madge has also got an unwholesome preference for male attire. Admittedly I gave her a lot of my husband's cast-off suits expecting she would at least exchange them at the Oxfam shop for a nice frock. No way! Behind my back, and on my account, she got the Emanuels to alter them all to fit her moth-like body. One of those suits she mutilated had sentimental value too because it was in this garment my husband Norm had his first urological accident. Suffice it to say that I'm a bit on my guard with Madge in some of the more intimate moments in our LTR.★ For example, if we lose the soap in the jacuzzi I insist on feeling for it myself. Need I say more?

★ Live Together Relationship.

'You certainly took rather a fancy to that odd friend of Sister Choate, didn't you, Madge?' I said in a whimsical voice. 'You were as thick as thieves when I came down to the office to drag you home.'

Madge pretended to miss the point. 'Dr Upjohn is a fascinating woman, Edna,' she twittered infuriatingly. 'Did you know she is descended from a man called Upjohn who was the hangman who finished off our world famous Australian outlaw, Ned Kelly?'

'How fascinating,' said I pretending to yawn and then adding rather wittily for four a.m., 'I would have thought a lot of people owed their descent to Mr Upjohn.' It struck me as sick that Fran Upjohn could boast of her grisly connection in front of an impressionable and immature creature like Madge. No wonder the Aboriginal kiddie she and Sister Choate had adopted had gone permanently walkabout.

The dawn sky was anaemia green when, dead on our feet, Madge and I tottered into our luxury hotel suite. I confess I flaked out pretty well fully clad, but with the nagging feeling that I had mislaid something somewhere, I knew not what.

The next day I was a write-off. I had to drag myself to Melbourne's internationally acclaimed award-winning Arts Complex for a rehearsal of Brecht/Weill ditties with the Tasmanian Symphony Orchestra conducted by my old chum Sir Charlie Mackerras, whom I adore! He said I had just the right husky intonation for those meaningful and socially relevant songs and I didn't dare tell him it was a mixture of jet-lag, Twilight Home coffee and emotional trauma. A fax from my publisher reminded me in an uncalled-for way about the deadline for this book and I realised that, weary as I was, I should have to continue my intensive research into those early years – the childhood that shaped a legend.

'Where are we off to now, Edna?' squeaked Madge excitedly as the limo swept us away from rehearsal.

'Back to Moonee Ponds,' I declared dramatically, 'though I doubt if I'll recognise it after all these months.'

Sure enough, Moonee's major thoroughfare, Puckle Street, was even more like the main drag in Istanbul. Bouzouki music reached us through the tinted bullet-proof glass of our conveyance and strange kebabby and falafelly smells percolated through the air-conditioning vents.

'Isn't it lovely, Edna?' wittered Madge with her face pressed to the window. 'It's so cosmopolitan now, not that dull old suburb we knew when we were little.' I turned away from my foolish bridesmaid, not wishing her to see the big hot tears which rolled down my cheeks. 'Where are you, Moonee?' I whispered to myself. 'Moonee of my girlhood, where have you gone?'

Thanks entirely to me, the suburb of Moonee Ponds is world famous. Let's face it, I put it on the map so that when people in far-flung corners of the planet are asked to name our best known landmarks they generally say Bondi Beach, Ayers Rock and Moonee Ponds – and *not* in that order. Tourists flocking there from all over the world to visit the Royal Edna Museum (my former home in Humouresque Street) would not notice how time has disfigured this once lovely neighbourhood. Like Madge, they probably think, 'How wonderfully cosmopolitan!'

Our conveyance swung into Humouresque Street and already I could see the gleaming coaches banked up in the street outside my modest old dwelling. The line of Japanese tourists stretched around the corner and I noticed the inscrutable darlings were already pointing their video cameras at my porch and avidly studying the full colour illustrated brochure about me and my home's history available from a booth on the front lawn – all proceeds to Prostate Relief. Whenever I am in my home town I pop in on my museum to boost the morale of the voluntary guides and National Trust personnel who caringly maintain what is, I'm sorry, *a shrine*. This time I decided to visit it later in the day because Madge and I had other things on our nostalgic agenda but my Readers may be sure that there will be a personally guided tour of number 36 later on in this publication.

The limo snuck unobtrusively down a few rather ethnic-looking sidestreets in the direction of Moonee Ponds Girls' Grammar and I felt wonderfully incognito behind the tinted glass knowing full well that to the predominantly Turkish and Lebanese population my numberplate, EDNA I, would have been Greek.

Have any of my Readers, I wonder, ever revisited their old school after many years? It's always spooky how *little* everything looks: the vast and dusty playground where bullies once held sway, the 'shelter shed', that sandwich-scented refuge flanked by crippled peppercorn trees behind which fast girls from broken homes smoked and played nurses or even doctors, all looked almost miniature. The shelter shed was a box-like structure on the far side of the playground and it was in its shadowy recesses that I first met Marjorie Kiri McWhirter.

I have an amazing memory, and I can meet someone I haven't seen for thirty years and remember exactly what they looked like. The remembered person is often just as real to me as their present day incarnation and I often find myself making comparisons, usually to the detriment, I'm afraid, of the person I bumped into. Let's face it, few of us are lucky enough to improve with age though I'm one of those lucky exceptions. Madge isn't. Fascinated I watched her push open our old school gate which neighed rustily. I saw an insignificant, middle-aged woman on the wrong side of unattractive yet simultaneously my mind's eye pictured, like a double exposure, Madge the kiddie: a wistful waif in an ill-fitting uniform with yukky scabs on her knees and a wet hankie pressed to her nose. I was Captain of my year and my chums and, come to think of it, early Edna-boppers, Val Dunn and Ann Forbes, introduced me.

'This is the new girl from New Zealand, Edna,' they said. 'She's hopeless at hockey and her nose has been bleeding *all morning!*'

'That's all we need!' I exclaimed with my hands on my hips and my head on one side as I gave this weedy Kiwi the onceover. 'What's your name, kid?'

'M-M-McWhirter,' she blubbed in a bloodstained voice, 'M-Marjorie K. McWhirter from New Zillan.'*

There are moments – momentous moments – in all our lives when we make a little decision which makes a big difference to our later lives. We open a door instead of closing it, we say no instead of yes, we turn right instead of left. Beware of Pity, Readers, because it was Pity which caused me to do a very odd thing on that fateful morning in the playground.

---

* Believe it or not, that is how New Zealanders pronounce New Zealand.

I opened the door of Compassion when I should have slammed it shut on Madge McWhirter's fingers. Old softie that I always was I felt sorry for the oozing scarecrow who stood stuttering before me. Taking command, I dismissed my chums Dunn and Forbes and put my arm around the shivering shoulders of the Kiwi wimp. IT WAS THE BIGGEST MISTAKE OF MY LIFE.

'This kid isn't well enough for the initiation ceremony today, girls,' I called after my retreating subordinates, 'I'll take her under my wing.'

Our school didn't have a matron like they do in traditional school stories, but Miss Godkin was good at first aid and McWhirter was soon lying wanly on a couch in the sick bay, her nostrils like two underdone miniburgers. She was wearing a ghastly and shaggy old twinset. I don't know how you would describe it: a yukky mixture of khaki and sludge that I would call 'squashed caterpillar'. It looked as though it had been knitted rather badly for someone else a long time ago from bits of wool found on a barbed wire fence. It had that homespun look full of burrs and grass seeds and, between you and me, little bits of lamb's poo. I'm sorry, but it did. I suppose today you would call it 'free range' or organically knitted. Anyway Miss Godkin wisely divested her of this nasty knitwear, but before tossing it on to the school incinerator, she had apparently given it a good shaking and we were all amazed a month or two later to see some little green shoots popping up in that arid corner of the playground. Those shoots grew into a kiwi fruit vine, the first in Australia! So Madge *did* bring something with her from New Zealand without knowing it. Actually it's a miracle she only introduced those stubbly little brown croquettes and not anthrax, foot and mouth, and Bovine Leptospirosis, as one might have expected.

Miss Godkin took me aside and whispered something to me which people have been telling me pretty well non-stop ever since. 'Thank you, Beazley,' she said. 'Do you only think of others, *never of yourself?*' What could I say? 'Keep an eye on this girl,' confided the kind teacher. 'She is an orphan with serious learning and co-ordination disorders, colour blind, sickly – the runt of the litter if you like – and . . .' Stella Godkin's voice dropped to an almost inaudible hiss, 'she's a New Zealander.'

The above snippets of information were about all I was ever to learn about my future bridesmaid's background. Not that I ever pumped her, but Madge never spoke of her early years, not even in her sleep when for a taciturn woman of Presbyterian origin, she did most of her talking. True to type she always cried poor and still does. It's got back to me that she has even whined to others about *me* being a tightwad!

Although I don't know it for certain there is every possibility Madge Allsop (her married name) is as rich as Croesus with money tied up in butter and kiwi fruit or whatever New Zealanders tie their money up in. I suppose I mean that Madge has a secret; something lurking there in her dingy depths – or shallows – which I'll fish out one of these days. But I'm jumping ahead . . .

My psychic powers are never wrong and I guess it was instinct that drew me to the Ugly Duckling of Moonee Ponds Girls' Grammar; the ugly duckling who would never turn into a swan. To be accurate Madge was really an *ugly Kiwi* making the odds even longer. Readers will recall that at the time of this historic meeting I had become Captain of my year. On the surface, confident, brilliant at my studies, without peer in sport and already the star of the debating and dramatic societies. I edited the school magazine *Tempus Fugit* and there was something about my exceptional looks and personality which drew people to me, staff and students alike. Yet it will not surprise anyone who has seen me on stage or television doing my wonderful shows to learn that I am basically a painfully shy person; the attractive extrovert the world sees and adores is a glistening shell within which lurks a soft and acutely sensitive organism.

Now that I am world famous it is amazing the number of people who approach me – and I *am* approachable – to ask for my autograph and tell me they knew me, or knew someone who knew me at school. The other day last year, I was minding my own business up-front in a jumbo when a frumpy crone from Economy tottered through the curtained class divider and announced, with a hint of duty free on her breath, that she had been at school with me and could I write a special message on a soggy Qantas coaster to her grandchildren Tamsin and Jake.

She didn't have a pen, these types never do, and while I

was rummaging in my Fendi clutch bag for my silver Tiffany Scribemaster I was also rummaging in my memory. 'Don't say you don't remember me, Edna,' shrilled this tipsy old lady. 'Jocelyn Kirby!' I froze. It was the Kirby girl, the school bully who had made my early years at school a living hell, the girl who had taunted me because of my unusual hair colouring, who had had the whole school chanting, 'There goes mauve-mop,' as I sobbed my way to prayers, the girl who had once sent my mother's lovingly cut sandwiches scattering in the playground dust. I had one of my double-exposures; I saw her then and now. The young tormentor, sallow-featured and mocking. And here she was now, swaying at my side, almost toothless, her sparse hair matted with Grecian Formula, her capillaried nose inches from me, a porridge-like pellet bobbing in and out of her left nostril as she breathed. Time had not been kind to this creature from my past I was not displeased to observe.

Graciously I sent my costly pen racing across the damp cardboard disc, 'To Tamsin and Jake, A Joyous Heart Always, from Dame Edna Everage. I knew your grandmother at school and I'm overjoyed to see she has turned out exactly as I hoped she would!' A careworn rheumaticky hand, trembling with gratitude, seized the coaster and she had just time to croak, 'Thank you, oh thank you,' before the stewardess bundled her back from whence she came. I felt a little glow, an old score settled in the lovely way Dame Nature sorts things out if you give Her time. I remembered Kirby had been the first girl I had ever met to come to school with a love-bite. She had stuck her neck out once too often.

'What has all this got to do with Madge Allsop?' I hear you cry, to which I answer, 'Nothing.' However, it gives you an idea of what I had to contend with in my early years. On the whole though, I was amazingly popular and only a few girls gave me a hard time. Never underestimate the power of jealousy. These days I wear a gorgeous ring studded with precious turquoises, given to me by a handsome Egyptian Prince, not unconnected with the world-famous shop Harrods. He told me it would ward off jealousy and I only wish I had had that ring at school.

Typically I showed Madge McWhirter a little of the kindness and concern – the TLC if you like – which I had rarely received as a new girl. I knew she would never survive the Initiation Ceremony. It was phase three that worried me since I doubted very much if Madge could swim and although even then she was the most unimaginative person I had ever met, I feared a night alone in the cemetery could unhinge a temperament already far from stable. In pulling a few strings and getting her excused from hockey I actually did myself a big favour, for Madge would have been a terrible liability in any team, and whilst we were out there on the pitch I saw to it the newcomer was gainfully employed whitening my tennis shoes and disinfecting my satchel.

Looking back, retrospectively, at the past, in hindsight, I am sure that Madge already had a crush on me and that I, frankly, encouraged it. I was, after all, the only role model worth copying and that pathetic young New Zealand orphan did all in her power to emulate me. Let's face it, she could have done a lot worse too with types like Jocelyn Kirby around. One morning Madge turned up at school bald. Well, nearly. Apparently she had soaked her mousy locks in some powerful household bleach – Clorox, I think – and then in a vain desire to resemble her idol, had tried to colour her hair purple using food coloring. When the clotted clump had dried she tried to tease it into something resembling my own lovely natural coiffure, but one flick of the comb through those rotted follicles practically scalped her. She had to wear a hat in class for months afterwards until her cranial designer stubble grew to a decent length again, and she became the laughing stock of the school.

Before you start feeling sorry for her remember Madge was, and still is, a very artful and calculating person who loves nothing better than the limelight, even if it takes the form of ridicule. My shrink, Dr Sidney Shardenfreude (whom I see for my children's sake – not mine) said Madge was a typical Compulsive Attention Seeker. Mind you, it didn't take a genius to see that, considering Madge had squashed herself on to the couch next to me. I don't mind her having a 'back to the womb' complex, but why does it always have to be mine?

As a schoolgirl she was less forward and pushy than she is now and it was almost touching the way she made herself useful to me. But when I saw *All About Eve* at the Moonee years later when my son Kenny and his flatmate Clifford Smail organised Australia's first Bette Davis Festival, I found myself riveted by little Anne Baxter's performance as the timid lass who comes to pay homage and then turns into a copycat and a back-stabber. I watched all her manoeuvres and sly infiltrations with a sense of mounting horror and pretty soon a spooky ripple passed across Anne Baxter's face and another face smirked out of the screen: the leathery face of Madge Allsop! As the lights came up, the full horror dawned on me as I saw Madge simpering at my side. I was Bette Davis and she was the scheming minx waiting for her moment of glory. I was so upset I couldn't concentrate on Cliff's lecture on the early films of Susan Hayward and Yvonne de Carlo.

Because Madge's parents were dead – or so the story went – she spent her schooldays living with distant relations in the nearby suburb of Pascoe Vale. She never let any of us so much as glimpse her down-market accommodation but my mother had a strong suspicion that it was *semi-detached*. Only once or twice did we ever see her auntie, Mrs Findlay, when she appeared at speech day wearing every colour of the rainbow. I remember at the time wondering in a nice way if there had been a power strike at Pascoe Vale; she looked as though she'd dressed in the dark. Incidentally, note that I was making perceptive yet caring observations about people even then as a teenager.

Madge had a funny smell about her too: a musty, stale lavender smell like the inside of old drawers. Actually, I have noticed the same smell on other kiddies who live with aged relatives or very old parents. In our classroom she had the awful habit of picking at her scalp and drawing big white sequins of dandruff down the mousy strands of her hair. Although I have slapped her wrist black and blue over the years, she still does it today, even at mealtimes.

CHAPTER IX

A Prisoner

'DON'T, DADDY! DON'T! Please, Daddy, don't don't *don't!*'
I screamed.
My father and I had always been very close, but this
was ridiculous. His calloused yet tender hand pressed against my
soft tummy, the other steadied my trembling chin whilst I gasped
and threshed around in the heavily chlorinated water. It was no
use, swimming was definitely not my strong point, I thought, as
I clambered out of our municipal pool into the rough embrace of
a beige war-issue utility towel.

Others seemed so much at home in the water, thwacking
themselves into the deep end, or bobbing up unexpectedly, snort-
ing and hawking and unashamedly 'milking' the frothy mucus
from their noses and recycling it into the swarming soupy water.
Sometimes I saw a kiddie move away from the others and get a
funny far-away look on its face. I knew enough to give those
common types a wide berth and even today the only public
swimming pool I can trust is in the basement of the Ritz Hotel,
Paris – off-season.

As I pulled on my clothes over my blue goosepimples I saw
Dad's little wince of disappointment. Hadn't he always said,
'You're not a real Aussie if you can't swim.' He himself was a
master of the 'Australian crawl' – our home-grown, award-winning, internationally acclaimed aquatic style, but somehow I
couldn't crawl in his footsteps.

All this is funny considering that Aquarius is my star sign

wouldn't you know and apart from swimming, I have always been drawn to watery things. Spookily enough, when Madge was a kiddie she had radical fluid retention. But I was never much of an amphibian.

Roy and Athol were already keen swimmers, real little water babies, and although we didn't live very close to the sea, the beaches of Mentone and Edithvale were only a hop, step and a jump away in our family's bottle green Hillman Minx. That was long before a Common Element had taken over our beaches. In those days when you went for a swim you only heard people talking Australian. It was when our ethnic minorities were in the minority – mainly greengrocers or fruitologists, fish and chip operatives and waiters. They were far too busy then to loll around on the sand as they do now, devoid of their customary aprons and getting far too confident and full of themselves. At least our Asian visitors know their place.

My pal Val had a comfortably off auntie with a beach home at Sorrento, a Melbourne seaside resort named after the song 'Come Back To Sorrento', by Beniamino Gigli. One Christmas holiday Val asked me down to stay for a week with her and her auntie. My new friend Madge wasn't invited – none of my old friends could stand a bar of her – so naturally Madge sulked but my mother was very excited. Sorrento and its neighbouring township of Portsea were the favourite resorts of Melbourne's 'silvertails' – people who had all been to the right schools, lived in the right suburbs, and drove English cars. On a Saturday morning outside the Portsea Hotel we once counted five MGs, two Jaguars, and twelve double-vented sports coats, worn with open-necked shirts and paisley cravats.

The house, called Pierview, was old and small and musty-smelling with salt-rusted fly wire doors, flaking kalsomine walls and sticky lino on the bedroom floor. It was furnished with things that had once been good from the family home in Flemington: a collapsed chintz couch, unravelling wicker chairs, brass ornaments and a few old Zane Greys, Ethel M. Dells and Elbert Hubbards on the bamboo bookshelf – no dog-eared paperbacks in those days. From the ceiling of the dark sitting room hung an alabaster-style dish, half full of dead blow-flies – art, if they only knew it, deco. These days yuppies pay a small fortune scouring thrift shops to make their homes resemble that shabby little dwelling.

Each morning Val and I would scamper down to the beach in our maroon Jansen bathers with shoulder straps and our white bathing caps. Val was into the sea like a shot but I always loitered under the umbrella, flattening my yellow towel and dipping into a favourite publication. Frankly I was a little afraid of those waves and getting my head wet. I always seemed to get sea water in my ears that wouldn't come out, and I would have to hop about on the beach with my head on one side with a horrible sound in my head like crumpling newspaper. Even in later life as a grown woman I always hated lying in bed feeling something hot gush and trickle on to the pillow.

I never cared for sunbathing. With my unusual colouring you have to be very careful of your skin, and I'm sure this applies to other people with mauve hair – admittedly a minority. My mother always put plenty of zinc cream on my nose and Kwik-Tan on my limbs which is probably why my wonderful skin is such a talking point today. I have actually been accosted by total strangers in the street asking if they can touch my skin and I generally let them if their hands are clean and the bit they want to touch is an acceptable distance from my erogenous zones, whatever they may be. Personally, I think they're a bit of a myth invented by *Cosmopolitan* magazine. The reason why most Los Angeles and Sydney women have faces like hand-tooled Spanish leather is due to the fact they have been shrivelling themselves since childhood. It is no exaggeration to say that by the end of summer most women I know look like mahogany tortoises with Colonel Sanders shoulder blades – dark brown and crumbed – hanging over the back of their sunfrocks.

As I lay on the beach trying not to get the sand in my crevices, slapping at the occasional March fly and listening to the distant squeals and splashes on the shore, I noticed one of our brave men in uniform a little further down the beach tastefully disrobing for a swim. Soldiers seemed to be everywhere in those terrible days in the early forties though the war still seemed a long way away to a child growing up in Melbourne. Admittedly they had begun to dig up our school grounds, building trenches and air-raid shelters, and we had all been issued with horseshoe-shaped rubber dummies which we were supposed to chew on when the bombs fell. At home my parents had stuck strips of Cellophane on our windows to make them shatterproof when Hitler bombed Moonee Ponds. On our hot brown Bakelite Radiola the Squadron-aires sang 'Berlin or Bust':

'We didn't want to do it, but we must Boys . . .'

and 'The Aussies and the Yanks are here . . .'

I am pretty sure the Japanese were in the war by then though children could not be blamed for getting Hitler, Musso and Tojo all mixed up. It was only when a Japanese submarine crept into Sydney Harbour that Australians really became aware that there was a war on. Nowadays of course Historians have come to look upon that little Japanese excursion as the spearhead of Australia's most lucrative industry. I doubt if we would have blasted that little sub out of the water if we had known then that they were only window-shopping in preparation for the big spree of the late eighties when they made the delightful discovery we were for sale.

I must have dozed off on the hot sand but suddenly I was wide awake, aroused by a sense of danger and panic. From somewhere out there beyond the waves I heard a voice calling, 'Help! Help! Edna, help!' It was Val, and she was in trouble. In a trice I was on my feet and running into the breakers towards that plaintive call. With no thought for myself, as per usual, I plunged into the aqua sea and struck out in the direction of my floundering friend whose little head in its bathing cap bobbed about like a ping-pong ball. Only when I was out of my depth with the salt water searing my throat did I remember that *I couldn't swim!* I was clawing at the water now, my chin straining upwards to avoid the waves which nonetheless washed over me. Val's head popped up a few yards away and I saw that she was swimming towards the shore and out of danger, whilst I was now in serious difficulties. I tried to make my life flash before me but it wouldn't. I remembered some of my favourite poems appropriate to the situation, 'The Boy Stood on the Burning Deck' and 'Not Drowning but

Waving'. How I wished I was only waving! On the beach I had been perusing, spookily enough, a book called *The Waves* by my idol Virginia Woolf. It was a bit above my head but not a patch on the real waves which were by then sucking me out towards shark-infested waters. Was Virginia a good swimmer? I wondered.

I must have blacked out, but seconds later I came to. Strong arms were around me, thrusting me upwards, ever upwards. The sky burst upon my vision like a daze of diamonds and I saw the face of my rescuer, lean, brown, concerned. 'You all right, kid? We'll be on the beach in a sec.' And so I was. My young saviour carried me in his arms and laid me gently on the sands. The beach was curiously silent as all eyes turned toward us.

'You were nearly a goner then, kid,' he said peeling off my tight cap and ruffling my damp mauve curls. 'Better get a few swimming lessons at the Herald learn-to-swim class in town or you could be history next time.' He gave me a wink and a pat on the cheek, and a strange sensation ran through my young body like a shudder. I looked up at him through my wet lashes taking in his lithe tanned physique, the gold hair mantling his chest and shoulders amongst which little rainbows danced in the sunlight. He was so close I could feel his warm breath on my cheek. He was naked, except for a pair of hip-hugging navy knitted swimming trunk with a rusty buckle and I could smell the musky oniony odour of his manly underarm. If I dared to look I could set right up his nostrils. Suddenly I recognised him; it was the young soldier probably no more than a few years older than myself who I had observed earlier on the beach, stripping off his uniform above my Virginia Woolf.

I wanted to say thank you, I wanted to say so many things, but no words came. I felt foolish and vulnerable and, yes, a strange yearning sensation in the uttermost core of me. At that moment I felt, and I'm not ashamed to confess this, as though that scantily clad young warrior could do with me what he liked: either take me to the pictures or buy me a double banana split with butterscotch topping, chopped peanuts and hundreds and thousands. I think it was at that moment that I first became aware of my hormones, though at that stage I didn't know what they were called. As for my handsome rescuer, he ambled back to his little pile of clothes, unaware of the new, thrilling yet scary sensations which were playing 'cat-and-mouse' in the tremulous young body he had snatched from the deep. I saw him sitting in the sand, rolling himself a ciggie from a packet of Havelock Ready-Rubbed Tobacco, a Boomerang cigarette paper fluttering from his lower lip. I wondered if I would ever see him again as I took that mental Polaroid of him on Sorrento beach. Little did I know what Fate had up her sleeve.

The Herald learn-to-swim classes were sponsored by a leading Melbourne newspaper and my father was most surprised when I decided to enrol. 'This is a turn up for the books, Ed,' he quipped. 'Thought you were a real little land-lubber.' My lessons went well at the municipal baths, largely due to my brilliant instructor. He was a charming Dutchman called Ernst Van Krenek who had been stranded in Australia by the war.

He must have been about forty years of age, but young looking with a cheeky mop of blond hair and piercing pale blue eyes the colour of bleached denim. Although still in my very early teens I think I must have been starting to notice the opposite sex without necessarily wanting to be opposite them. Ernst had a wonderful flashing smile and soon had me slipping gracefully through the water: butterfly, crawl and backstroke. Apparently he had been a champion swimmer back in Holland where his poor family still lived under the Nazis but whenever the subject of the war cropped up he fell strangely silent. I felt he nursed some tragic secret, and I was partly right. One afternoon in the middle of my lesson Ernst had a phone call. As a matter of interest I think the date was 20 April 1943. He came back to the poolside slipping on his Aertex shirt and looking apologetic.

'Sorry, Edna,' he said. 'I must urgently to my home go. I had forgotten already that tonight for a small party a few of my friends to my house were coming.'

I adored the quaint old Dutch way he spoke and he could have left his clogs under my bed any time he liked, I *would* have thought if I'd been a bit older.

'Don't worry, we will on your next lesson the time we are losing make up. Goodbye, little fish.' And with that my handsome instructor was gone.

Except for Madge, that incorrigible copycat who insisted on taking lessons as well, even though all she did was splash around the shallow end, the pool was deserted. Always conscientious, a perfectionist in everything I attempted, I did another few lengths of the crawl utilising the skills my mentor had taught me. How excited I was to think there was still a thing or two he had yet to implant in me.

'Hurry up, Madge,' I called out, and my voice echoed up and down the pool. 'Get out now or you'll go all crinkly.' Goodness knows why I bothered, for anyone seeing Madge today on TV or wherever would think she'd spent most of her life in a tepid bath.

'Oh look, Edna,' Madge suddenly exclaimed, pointing a blue-nailed finger at a glinting object on a poolside bench. 'Mr Van Krenek has forgotten his watch.' Indeed he had. For once Madge was right about something. In his haste to meet his guests Ernst had forgotten his beautiful solid gold wristwatch which I had often admired. He always took it off for the swimming classes and there it lay where he had left it. What was I to do? I could take it home and return it to him at our next lesson, but what if he came back to look for it and found it gone? The pool attendant who I'd never liked might easily tell him he had seen me stealing it. On the other hand, if I left the watch with him, none of us might see it again.

I remembered that Ernst lived in the suburb of South Yarra – a rather up-market area south of the river Yarra, a river north of South Yarra. Then and there I decided to return this valuable item personally, even if it meant a tram trip well out of my way – South Yarra was in the opposite direction to Moonee Ponds. Shaking off Madge was the problem. She dogged my footsteps and stuck to my heels like someone else's discarded Juicy Fruit. Then, as now, I couldn't move without that creature shadowing me like a private eye.

'Go home, Madge, quick sticks, get a message to Mummy and Daddy telling them I'll be a little late,' I adjured her brusquely. 'I'll be home as soon as I can.'

She gazed at me with that sullen poor-little-old-me look that I can't stand and slunk off into the gathering dusk without her usual protests and whining entreaties. At least she's gone quietly, I thought, turning the heavy gold object over in my hand. Won't Ernst be relieved to see me on his doorstep with his precious timepiece? I confess I entertained innocent visions of a hug of thanks, a grateful peck. Even . . . but the imagination of a healthy young schoolgirl is boundless.

My inquisitive finger moved down the Vs in a battered phone book near the tram stop. Not many 'Vans' in those days either, though Van Johnson was a rising film star, Van Heusen was sewing his lovely shirts and somewhere overseas, in war-torn Europe, Van Gogh was posting his ear to a waitress. Needless to say, none of these were in the Melbourne telephone directory. Suddenly there it was, just above and slightly to the left of my fingernail:

Van Krenek, E. 20 Walsh Street, South Yarra.

In the tram I stole another look at the lost property. There seemed to be some writing on the back, a bit like church writing, spiky, and in a foreign language, probably Dutch – and something else that made my heart miss a beat for a minute.

The tram seemed to take ages, and night was falling nippily. It was dark when the conductor put me off at Punt Road and a lady pointed out Walsh Street a couple of hundred yards away. Why did I now have such butterflies in my tummy? Shouldn't I have telephoned first? Why was it so important for me to return the watch in person? And had my parents been told of my whereabouts? Could Madge be relied upon?

Number 20 was a dark bungalow lurking behind a windswept hedge. As I opened the gate a huge Alsatian jumped out of the blackness and nearly knocked me over, but I must have smelt safe. Perhaps the chlorine from the baths which still lingered in my nooks and crevices reminded him of his handsome master, for he drew back growling and retreated to his position on the mat before the darkened front door. The house seemed without life or light. Funny, I thought, Ernst had mentioned a party – so where were the lights? Perhaps they were all at the back of the house? I decided not to ring the front door bell, for doing so would have meant an even closer encounter with that scary canine;

instead I pushed my way through the thick, scratchy bushes beside the house to where a back window shed a faint glimmer of light. Rising on tippy toes I could just look inside.

What I saw made my blood run cold. There was a large room, probably the dining room, and around the long table sat a group of men and women solemnly eating. The women had short blonde hair and wore formal evening frocks with low backs, cut on the bias. The men seemed to be in fancy dress of some sort. On the wall, directly opposite my window, was a large framed photograph of someone whose face rang a bell – it was not a nice face and the picture frame was draped with a red and black flag. The scene was slightly spooky because the only light came from the tall candles which flickered on the table. One of the men rose, I think on a signal, and prepared to blow out the candles and it was then that I saw he was wearing a black uniform with silver braid, and high black boots. As he turned I saw he had a red armband and on the armband was – horror of horrors – a swastika!

The instant I saw it the lights went out, but in the next second a glow appeared in the doorway, the pretty glow of an enormous birthday cake. It was being carried ceremoniously into the room by none other than Ernst, my swimming teacher, dressed as I had never seen him in the uniform and jackboots of a Dirk Bogarde lookalike. It was somebody's birthday, but whose?

The weird assembly suddenly stood raising their tankards and lifted their right arms in a stiff and sinister salute towards the picture on the wall. The penny dropped. All at once that little square moustache, that downturned mouth, those piercing eyes, that bang of dark hair across that evil brow meant one man and one man only . . . *but who?* I knew I had seen him somewhere before, at the pictures perhaps? In a newspaper cartoon? Perhaps they were all masons, like Phyllis Balderstone's father – and mine – who had little aprons on top of their wardrobes that they used to wear at secret meetings where they shook hands with goats and goodness knows what else? I strained to hear what they were saying but suddenly a rough hand clamped across my mouth and I felt a sharp stab of pain as my arm was wrenched behind me. A long way off a dog barked. I must have fainted.

'Vell, *meine Liebchen*, how long have you at our little fancy dress party been in looking?' I was on a hard chair and bright light glared into my eyes. I couldn't move either, for cruel ropes bound me to the chair cutting into my young flesh. I looked up squinting into the dazzling lamp at the circle of evil faces which peered questioningly at mine. I tried to speak, to explain, but no words came, my mouth just opened and closed like a fish. One of the most sinister-looking Nazis with a horrible scar across his cheek grabbed me savagely by the hair and hissed, 'How long have you on us spying been? Speak, Fräulein, or to punish you I will be forced.' Why, I wondered, hadn't he said he had ways of making me talk? That's what they always said in the movies, but this wasn't a movie, it was actually happening and young and inexperienced though I was, I knew this monster meant business by the way he playfully swished his riding crop against my naked, vulnerable thigh. The ropes were really hurting. Why didn't Ernst come to my rescue? Surely he couldn't stand by like the others and let me suffer?

It was true. My erstwhile swimming coach was not raising a finger to help me, not that he could since he was still holding the birthday cake which by now was dripping with hot wax.

'Vot vill we do with her, Krenek?'

Ernst's face hardened, suddenly he looked like a demon, no longer my kindly mentor from the Moonee pool. His lip curled mercilessly and he was about to speak when there was an enormous crash. The entire door of the dining room flew off its hinges and about six policemen stormed into the room. 'The game's up, Krenek, you swine,' said one of them dealing Ernst a sharp karate chop on the back of the neck which sent him face down into the cream gâteau. A woman with too much mascara screamed out something foreign in a foul language. The air rang with cries and blows, and as strong clean Australian fingers deftly loosened my bonds I saw that my uniformed rescuers had already handcuffed and bound my sullen captors and were marching them out at gun point to a waiting paddy wagon. The room was a wreck and the horrid picture draped with its Nazi flag hung crooked on the wall revealing a dark nook or aperture behind it. The chief of police strode up, and ripping down the foul photo stamped it on to the floor.

'You'd be too young to know, Miss, but it's 20 April, *his* birthday today,' he pointed down at the mess of splintered glass upon the carpet. 'This charming little bunch of bastards were giving him a party but your sticky beak certainly stuffed up their plans if you'll pardon my French.' I noticed Ernst, his uniform torn and splashed with cream, still sat slumped in an armchair, the nozzle of a rifle pressed into his neck by one of our boys in khaki.

'But . . . what about Mr Van Krenek, he seemed so nice, where does he fit in?'

'*Van* be beggared,' scoffed the Senior Security Inspector. 'If he's Dutch, the Pope's a Jew! We've been watching this unsavoury little outfit for a long time, Miss,' he said. 'Thanks to you we caught them in the act. Ernst Von Krenek is a top Nazi agent assigned to Southern Australia to monitor our wartime security arrangements in the suburbs of Melbourne. Look at this.' He showed me a Morse code transmitter tucked away in a cranny behind the picture and some papers printed with strange numbers. 'Anyone coming into this room would have just thought it was an ordinary, run-of-the-mill photograph of Adolf Hitler on the wall, little suspecting that behind it, those bastards – sorry, Miss – were sending back to the Fatherland top secret information about our all-night tramway services.'

'But he was such a nice swimming teacher,' I sobbed, dis-illusioned and heartbroken.

'That's for sure,' laughed the Inspector bitterly. 'He ought to be, he was a silver medallist at the Berlin Olympics in 1936. Teaching swimming and posing as a Dutchman was a perfect cover for him out here. You had a good time while it lasted, didn't you, Krenek?' he said to the defeated figure in the chair. 'You wanted the sunshine and the superlative living standards of Australia and you wanted to please your fiendish bosses back in Berlin as well. You wanted to have your cake and eat it too.'

Considering that Ernst was pretty well covered from head to foot with the gooey remains of Hitler's birthday cake the Inspector's last remark seemed rather apt.

'Take him away, boys,' he barked. 'This man is a disgrace to the Australian crawl.'

When Ernst and his cronies had been dragged away I asked Inspector Fenessy how he had found me.

'You're a lucky girl, Miss Edna,' he said, pouring me a nourishing cup of hot Bonox from his Thermos into a Bakelite cup. 'Lucky to have a good little friend like that McWhirter girl.'

'Madge?' I exclaimed. 'What's Madge got to do with it?' Inspector Fenessy smiled. 'She followed you here, Edna. She saw what happened and sprinted down to the station to alert us. I'd say you probably owe your life to that kid.'

As if on cue, Madge came in the door looking goodie-goodie. I suppose all the Inspector said was true and I gave her bony little body a hug which is more than most people would have done under the circumstances. I need hardly tell my Readers, however, that every time we have a little tiff, or I threaten to cut her already over-the-top allowance, Madge is at great pains to remind me of the night she saved me from the Nazis. Come to think of it it's pretty generous of me to have given her as much credit as I have in this autobiography.

In the interests of national security this incident never hit the headlines, though a lot of Melbourne kiddies wondered why their swimming lessons stopped in mid-stream so to speak. But for sentimental, and other reasons, I have always kept that golden souvenir of the night that was almost my last. Yes, Possums, I'm afraid I never gave Ernst his watch back and I sometimes even wear it when I'm in Sydney, where the womenfolk can never wear too much gold. There's a swastika on the back of it too, and an inscription. 'To Ernst from Adolf'. Spooky.

Not all that long ago, as a matter of fact, I heard that Ernst had been spotted in the Sydney suburb of Double Bay looking pretty old and fat and grey. Apparently he pretends to be a Hungarian now, *so what else is new*? And he sells second-hand BMWs to yuppies and orthodontists.

CHAPTER X

I Wash the Feet of Jesus

A LTHOUGH WE WERE never rich, I was fascinated by the poor – and still am! Whenever we were on a Sunday afternoon 'spin' in the car I would exhort my father, 'Pl–ea–se, Daddy, take us past the paupers.' He started it. Even if we had been up for a Devonshire tea or to pick up an azalea or two in Melbourne's world-class Dandenong Rangers (a lovely old Aboriginal word meaning something), my father would insist on driving back to Moonee via Dudley Flats. This was a ghastly slum, long since replaced, thank goodness, by condemned high-rise council housing. We would peer out of the car windows, our eyes like saucers, at the cramped terrace houses without nice front gardens like, let's face it, most of England. We saw the barefoot urchins playing knuckles and hoppo-bumpo on the scarred bitumen roadway, and the 'derros' – an Australian term of endearment for derelicts – staggering about in their tennis shoes and old army greatcoats swigging out of meths bottles. On one of my trips through a poverty-stricken part of Melbourne, I once glimpsed a woman about my mother's age with a beetroot-coloured face, squatting near a tram stop, enjoying a cork-tipped cigarette, and doing little jobs. It was one of those Polaroids a kiddie's mind 'snaps' that never seems to fade. That woman needed help though, in her case, help would have arrived too late.

'Look at that!' Daddy would say to us over his shoulder. 'You kids don't know how lucky you are.'

I have always counted my blessings, though I could be excused
for losing count, but it is so easy to get complacent and smug, so
that when I do my wonderful stage shows I always have a section
of the theatre – usually way way up high in the 'gods' where
sound and visibility is poor and upholstery rudimentary – for my
'paupers'. I adore them and they adore me.

Sometimes my dad would point at a poky little Victorian
building and say to Mummy, 'See that, Gladys, you complain
about Humouresque Street, but you could have done a lot worse,
darl.'

To which my mother would reply, 'It might be a slum, Bruce,
but look at that shiny door knocker and that gleaming brass name
plate – "Balmoral". The woman who lives there may not have
much of the wherewithal, but she has still got her pride. It costs
nothing to be spotless.' Incidentally that type of inner city home
which survived the great modernisation of Melbourne in the sixties is now being snapped up by yuppies for serious money.

Unless we went for an afternoon 'spin', I can't say Sunday was
ever my favourite day of the week. There always seemed to be
an atmosphere of tension about it and I think that had a lot to do
with the fact that it was the only day of the week when my parents
spent any time together. They never actually fought, though I
once remember my father chasing my mother round the house
and my getting very frightened. Looking back, I see this was
probably harmless horseplay, but parents never realise what a
scary effect their tiffs and tantrums can have on sensitive youngsters, especially when combined with indigestible roast dinners
and too many hymns. Even today I get a funny, empty, worried
feeling on the Sabbath; a spooky feeling of impending doom
which harks back to my childhood when my parents were forcibly
reminded that they were married to each other.

Call me old-fashioned, but I am a deeply religious woman.
That is to say, I firmly believe there is something Up There, and
I am sure most women feel the same from time to time. My
parents encouraged me to go to Sunday School and it was there
I fell in love for the first time – with Jesus.

My Sunday School was in a red brick hall next door to Holy
Trinity, Moonee Ponds, and we would sit on hard pews while

the superintendent, Mr Leonard Smithers, read us a Bible story. Mr Smithers spoke so quietly none of us could hear a word he said, but he was apparently a very 'good man' who did 'a tremendous amount of wonderful work for the Church'.

I remember thinking at the time that if I ever had to tell stories to people from the stage, I would make sure they heard every word I said – and manage to be a good person as well!! We used to sing 'What a Friend We Have in Jesus' and when the collection plate went around:

> Hear the pennies dropping
> Listen while they fall
> Every one for Jesus
> He can have them all.

At some stage every Sunday, the Reverend Tony Morphett, our young vicar, would pop his head round the corner and more often than not, lead us in a few prayers. He always had a kind word for me and I have to confess that he was one of the main reasons why I enjoyed Sunday School.

I suppose the climax of my theological studies was the annual Church Pageant when I made my first historical public appearance on stage. Mr Smithers cast me in the role of Mary Magdalene, that rather permissive friend of Jesus who, amongst other things, anoints his feet with various products (pre-dating Dr Scholl) and dries them off with her own hair. This would be an exacting scene for any young actress and it is an operation which requires a good deal of concentration and a good deal of hair. First of all you have to avoid tickling the feet of the actor playing Jesus or the credibility, not to mention the integrity, of the whole scene goes down the toilet. It's also much harder than it looks to kneel down in front of a lot of parents and restless kiddies in a hot hall, rubbing a mixture of Nivea cream and Vick's Vapour Rub off someone's feet with your own hair. I'm sorry but it is. (Unfortunately, the Sunday School budget did not run to frankincense or myrrh as recommended in the Bible.)

Because I had reached the self-conscious stage when I was ashamed of my natural mauve hair colouring, I had begged my mother to let me have it dyed brown. She had relented and it was only many years later that I let my own beautiful locks grow back as nature intended, as you see them today on stage or on colour television.

Imagine how I felt when we began to rehearse the scene and I discovered that Our Lord was to be played by none other than our handsome young vicar, the Reverend Tony Morphett. As a matter of fact, his feet were rather large and I never managed to get the anointing and drying done in under five minutes. A very long time indeed in which to hold the attention of an audience as professionals studying this book will know only too well. When at last I got up off my knees, having rubbed him off, and said, 'How was that, Lord?' I got my first round of applause. I cannot describe the effect that thrilling sound had upon me and it was still ringing in my ears as I shampooed Our Lord's stickiness out of my roots with a squirt of Clairol at a deconsecrated font at the back of the hall after our pageant.

'Well done, Edna. You are quite a little star,' said a familiar voice and a warm hand patted my shoulder. It was the vicar, my blue-eyed leading man, and he had called me a star! A thrill passed through me; a minor miracle if you like, and from that moment on, I knew where my destiny lay.

Needless to say, Sunday School took on a new meaning for me after that. I can't say I was able to concentrate much on those marvellous old Bible stories about Sodom and Gomorrah and the lepers who got turned into pigs, educational though they were. Frankly, Readers, I was sitting on that hard brown pew, half hearing Mr Smithers droning on like a blow-fly in a milk bottle, hoping against hope that Tony Morphett – my co-star – would pop his head into the hall. I suppose I had a crush on him but what, if anything, did he feel for me? A well-built prematurely gorgeous teenager who had had, let's face it, some intimate physical contact with his extremities, that was probably all. Sometimes he would turn up for the last hymn:

> Immortal, invisible, God only wise
> In light inaccessible hid from our eyes . . .

From the front row of the hall I could see Tony's Adam's apple moving up and down to the music, as I vainly tried to catch his bright blue eye, and another Heathen hymn, on the hit parade at the time, kept creeping into my head. I heard Chick Henderson croon:

'I dreamed of two blue orchids
Two beautiful blue orchids, last night
Oh what a big surprise . . . '

There was a war on and we had a soggy old air-raid shelter in the backyard to prove it. Mostly it was full of water – khaki water appropriately enough – so I couldn't help feeling that if the Japs or Musso did bomb Moonee we were less likely to be blown up than to drown as we scuttled to safety. Melbourne never was bombed and it was only after the war that most of it got knocked down to make way for service stations, car-parking facilities, shopping malls and precincts. The rest of our backyard was given over to silver beet and other useful veggies, and in the streets cars tottered around with cumbersome gas producers clamped to their backs to save petrol.

While we helped my mother preserve eggs by smearing them with Keepegg, my father would sit at our little kitchen table dunking Guest's Famous Biscuits and Butternut Snaps into his coronation mug of Glen Valley tea and frown at the front page of the *Sun News-Pictorial* which usually showed maps of third world countries covered with swastikas or sinister little Japanese rising sun flags. My favourite toothpaste at the time was Ipana which came in a yellow tube with a red and yellow rising sun pattern on it. It was quickly withdrawn in favour of a more patriotic package but I never thought it tasted the same after that. That was long before the chlorophylly fifties when all toothpaste tasted like grass.

My father wasn't called up because he was too old and had already done his bit in the Great War, where he got his 'groove'. I never understood why they called it 'Great' since no one ever had a good word to say for it! But Daddy would get into his uniform religiously every Veterans Day and march to the Shrine of Remembrance with a few old mates from his unit and in later years when his marching days were over he would still sit in front of our old wireless staring at the endless grey parade, tapping his frame in time to the band and singing,

> 'It's a long way to Wagga-Wagga
> It's a long way to go
> It's a long way to Wagga-Wagga
> To the sweetest girl I know . . .'

Once when the American fleet was in we had a US naval officer to Sunday dinner. It was funny to hear a real person speaking like they did at the movies and I think we were all too awestruck to exchange more than a few words with him, over my mother's tasty grey roast. Like all Americans then and now, he seemed very nice, polite and impenetrably foreign, as though he had come from Mars. Don't get me wrong, some of my best friends are American, but any country that can call a movie *Every Which Way But Loose* has to be a bit alien. Hank gave my dad a chunky bottle of green liquid called Mennen Aftershave which stayed unopened on the top shelf of our bathroom cabinet along with the Potassium Permanganate, a broken denture, and a funny red rubber thing, until the day we burnt my father's things.

They were terrible, dark days and many healthy young chappies were joining the forces. I wondered, with secret anguish, if our young vicar – my Tony – might be called up. One Sunday morning we were in the middle of 'All Things Bright And Beautiful' and as per usual another tune was playing in my romantic little top-knot:

> Mairzy doates and dozy doates
> and little lamzy divey . . .

It must have been September because the musty old hall was filled with the sharp fresh scent of daffodils which blew their yellow trumpets from a brass urn, arranged by the Ladies' Auxiliary.

> . . . a kiddlely divey too, wouldn't you?

There was a sudden kerfuffle and there on the dais with Mr Smithers stood Tony in the handsome khaki uniform of an army chaplain. He had come to say goodbye to us before going 'up

North' and to introduce old Canon George Lake who had come to take over. He made a little speech but I didn't hear the words. My eyes were brimming, and the vase of daffs was a blurred yellow blob which swelled, stretched and split into two, as my tears tumbled down. I felt Tony was looking straight at me as he asked us all to pray for his safe return.

I need not describe to my women readers, or indeed to more sensitive menfolk, my feelings of devastation in the days that followed. I certainly prayed for his return, but I must have prayed a bit too hard because he was back about eight weeks later having caught malaria in New Guinea. The poor thing was bright yellow and to make matters worse had even got engaged in his delirium to a fuzzy-wuzzy nurse. My mother said his family who were refined people with high hopes for him had been heart-broken that he had chosen a tinted bride though I suppose with his malaria, he was, to some extent, meeting her halfway.

But every night after that, for months later, I would wake up sobbing, my pillow wet, and I would not usually be able to nod off again unless I slipped into the kitchen for a slice of pineapple upside-down cake or one of my mother's scrumptious chocolate kisses.

CHAPTER XI

Hands Above the Bedclothes

'THE DEVIL ALWAYS finds bedclothes for idle hands to fumble about under.' That was another of my mother's wonderful old phrases though I'm not sure I've got it exactly right. These days it is fashionable to pooh-pooh the wisdom of parents as I know only too well from a lot of the philosophy I have tried to impart to my own youngsters. Water off a duck's back for the most part; in one ear and out the other.

But my heart had been broken once, and I was reaching an age when girls ask questions, and I needed a lot of answers. We were never taught biology at school; certainly nothing which could be applied to ourselves and it was only when one of my teachers – Miss Tumbey, a big woman with a bun – said something to me that I began to think pretty well non-stop about my female chemistry. What she said was innocent enough but it shocked me at the time because she referred to things I never felt able to discuss with Mummy.

'Noticed anything different about your body lately, Edna?' she asked. Let's face it, Possums, I had. I had noticed a couple of things, although they weren't getting as different as they should have been, fast enough. Some other girls in my class were already wearing 32A cups, and even larger, whereas my beautiful facial skin seemed to be developing the lumps that should have developed elsewhere. Many was the miserable morning I spent peering into the hole I had rubbed in our misted-up bathroom mirror, wrestling with my stubborn spots which never seemed to yield much more than a few drops of water. If I went to a dance or function I had to borrow some of Mummy's Cyclax powder to cover those little half-moon indentations my fingernails had made on my lovely face.

I have described, pretty fearlessly I hope, a few of the weird spasms that I was beginning to experience when I found myself approximately in the vicinity of an acceptable male. I felt sensations and desires which I could not put a name to. I had also at that tender age had yukky and traumatic encounters which could have undermined my fundamental normalcy, like that S and M nightmare in the Nazis' hideout where, quite frankly, I felt like Charlotte in *The Night Porter* after she'd been almost rampled to death by Dirk. (I *would* have felt like her except that gorgeous film hadn't yet been made.)

Other girls were beginning to go out with boys and even – horrible thought – trying to outdo each other's love-bites. Because I was always interested in the finer things of life, I turned up my nose at the antics of this Common Element, but secretly I tried to imagine them in the back row of the pictures or on dimly lit suburban porches chewing away at each other's necks and then looking to see if they'd inflicted a sufficiently impressive bruise. Call me old-fashioned, but that wasn't my way of spending a nice evening. I'm sorry but it wasn't.

But if biology bored me, I excelled in the cookery classes. I loved baking cakes and especially pavlovas, those scrumptious meringue and marshmallow desserts which were invented in Australia incidentally, and became so internationally famous that a Russian ballet dancer called herself after one.* My mother had been an expert cake-maker though naturally these days the authorities wouldn't let her anywhere near a Magimix. Not that we had such technology in our little cream and green kitchen in Humouresque Street. Mummy always whipped up her cakes by hand and if we kiddies were very good, we were allowed to lick the beaters, running our eager little pink tongues along the steel flanges of her whisk, digging out the sweet yellow mixture, sometimes spotted with scrummy raisins. Although my mother's meat and vegetable dishes were always delicate shades of grey, her colour sense ran riot in the cake department and when it came

* See recipe, Appendix.

to running up a rainbow sponge she never scrimped on the pink food coloring, though by then it was wartime and we were using Rawleigh's artificial essence made from goodness knows what. She was also being forced – by the Japanese – to experiment with butterless recipes but it was amazing what she managed to bake using all the wrong ingredients to help keep Australia free. A quick peep around any hotel lobby in the Southern hemisphere today might make you wonder why we even bothered.

'I got a gal in Kalamazoo-zoo-zoo . . .' sang the wireless.

At this stage of my life, I was putting on a wee bit too much weight: a combination of furtive little nibbles at cookery class, after school raids on Mummy's cake tin atop the ice chest, and the natural hormones in my organism which, as in any girl my age, were tending to go bananas. I was tall however, and there didn't seem to be anything so terribly wrong with being 194 pounds. Yes, Readers, looking back I can see that I was an intensely shy and frightened kid hiding inside a Shelley Winters body. I'm sorry to say that I think I might also have even been pining for the feverish form of the Reverend Tony Morphett, binge-eating to assuage my loss, as I imagined him in the arms of the fuzzy-wuzzy huzzey. A few snaps were taken of me at the time but none survive, not even in the Everage Archive of the University of South West Virginia who pay squillions for my old bus tickets. You may be sure that I have confiscated all records of myself at this troubled stage of my life, and I am happy to say that my porky period was mercifully brief. In fact, I trimmed down within months, thank goodness.

But remembering it certainly helped me cope with my daughter Valmai's foodaholic phase when it looked as though that foolish girl, for whom I have no sympathy, was digging her grave with her teeth. Yet even when I started tipping the scales at 150 pounds, I was still able to ride my Malvern Star bicycle down to the little shops to collect the groceries and other necessities. My bike was my pride and joy, a gift from my father who, in hindsight, I think may have hoped riding would give me some slimming incentive. My new friend Madge McWhirter would often accompany me for the run. In her case it *was* a run because naturally her poverty-stricken auntie could never have given Madge a bicycle; so she trotted along breathlessly on the footpath and usually got to the shops as I was speeding off home with the wicker basket on my handlebars, brimming with goodies.

I always meant to shout some word of encouragement to her but unfortunately my mouth was usually occupied with a Violet Crumble Bar or scrumptious Pollywaffle. For some reason, going shopping for your mother was always called 'doing the messages', an Australian saying which I have never heard elsewhere. Mummy always gave me her purse with an orange ten-shilling note crumpled up inside it with the ration books. The butcher and grocer would always clip off a few coupons with their scissors in exchange for chops, steak, eggs and butter. I always had a shopping list too, on which Mummy specified her requirements at the greengrocers:

> A nice lettuce
> 1lb of nice firm tomatoes
> 1lb of nice ripe bananas
> 1½lb of nice pumpkin
> A nice firm good-eating cauli
> 2lb of old potatoes

I wondered at the time if our greengrocer, Mr Cosmopolis, would have given us nice potatoes without necessarily being asked or whether all his merchandise would have been nasty had my mother not specified niceness.

Mummy didn't always buy her fruit down the street. Every week Mr Charlie O'Hoy, the Chinese greengrocer who, according to my mother, had longer fingernails than Myrna Loy in *The Mask of Fu Manchu*, would come clopping up Humouresque Street in his horse-drawn cart scuttling round to the back doors of all the homes with a basket of grapefruit, spring onions, lettuces and assorted berries. I don't quite know why my mother stopped patronising him; it could have been the war and not being absolutely certain that he was really a Chinaman, though I think also she once bought a quince from him that smelt funny. Horse-drawn vehicles were still a common sight in my girlhood and sometimes if I couldn't sleep due to some excitement or other, I would hear the milkman's horse making his slow progress up our block, the clinking bottles, jangling harness and other snorty, horsy noises. Now of course, you're lucky if a tradesman turns up before lunch or even once a week! The bottle collector appeared every now and then wrapped up in an old army overcoat atop his dray, drawn by a chestnut draught horse with a nosebag. You could hear him calling, 'Bottle-oh, bottle-oh' – more like a yodel really, from miles away. People would generally leave their empties in old hessian bags on the nature strip, or kerb-side, and I remember my mother once telling my father that Mr Warner had left two clinking bags out in one week. As she told us, she made a funny little drinking gesture, tilting an invisible glass. The postman, in a blue serge uniform and a peaked cap, always came by bike and blew a whistle if he popped anything in your slot. I wonder what happened to all those whistles that used to 'chirrup' so brightly through my childhood?

After one of her nervous breakdowns, I don't know which, Mother stopped baking overnight, so thereafter we procured all our cake necessities from a little home-made cake shop down the street run by the Misses Hidden. Their window was filled with little stands covered with paper doilies on which stood tennis cakes, passion-fruit sponges, rainbow terraces, lamingtons, pine-apple upside down cake, vanilla slices and lemon meringue pies. The shop was always filled with the comforting caramel aroma of my favourite food.

Everything was baked at the back of the shop by the spot-less Hidden sisters, yet with my ever-enquiring mind I wondered why their produce was called 'home-made' when it was so obviously 'shop-made'. Already I was showing the kind of intellectual curiosity and bracing scepticism which has notched me up honorary degrees in umpteen universities all over the planet.

Mummy always became evasive if I asked her questions about my body. So, like so many other lasses of my generation, I pretended to know all the answers in order to spare her feelings. Years later, the night we burnt my mother's things, I found, tucked away in her bookshelf behind a copy of Van Loon's *Lives* (another wonderful Dutchman), a little volume called *What Every Young Girl Should Know*. Inside it were tasteful diagrams of men and women showing how bubbas came into being. Actually the illustrations were so tasteful, it was impossible to tell which was the man and which was the woman. There was a picture of an unborn kiddie inside a balloon and a few other pretty uncalled-for diagrams which I only glimpsed as the yellow flames of our incinerator turned the pages with their long yellow fingers. So *that* was the book Mummy had meant to give me in my adolescence. She had either forgotten to, or been too embarrassed. These days of course, you can't go to the pictures or turn on the TV without seeing people committing gross acts of intimacy. But when I was young, we could only guess at the facts of life. One thing I knew for certain was that when people got married and went to bed, God knew they were married and gave them a baby. I wouldn't be surprised either if science wasn't coming around to that opinion today. Frankly, when all's said and done, it's the only theory that makes much sense or holds water, to use an obstetric metaphor. The only thing I couldn't understand as a youngster was how God managed to slip in and out of my parents' bedroom unnoticed rather like Santa did at Christmas time.

Naturally there were 'fast' girls at school, boy-mad, who whispered to each other behind the shelter shed about their activities, but I never listened or I might have got a very twisted view of something which I believe can be very beautiful. Well, *fairly* beautiful if you are extremely lucky and have no other interests in life. Contrary to what the menfolk think, we women hardly think about sex at all unless there's something radically wrong with us.

That is not to say that I never played 'doctors or nurses', but I always preferred to be the doctor and it's incredible the number of my young schoolfriends who wanted to be my patients. I suppose this was an early demonstration of my natural charisma which is so strikingly apparent in my wonderful stage and TV shows where all kinds of people are happy to let me do *anything* to them. My shrink, Dr Shardenfreude (who I see for my children's sake), says that my performances 'buzz with sexual energy' which I thought was a bit over the top. Yet it is fair to say that I give the menfolk in my audiences, and my male readers for that matter, something that they dare not ask their wives to give them.

CHAPTER XII

Norman Stoddart Everage

L ORD EVERAGE OF Moonee Ponds is one of the most famous
men in the world. Admittedly millions have never heard
of him; a bit of a paradox which it is not within the scope
of this book to explore. He never sought fame either before or
after our marriage but fame was nonetheless thrust upon him, or
more accurately, up him, in the form of the world's first moder-
ately successful prostate transplant.

We had met on the beach that scorching December day and as
I lay there on my towel squinting up at the lean young beau who
hovered above me in the sun, I little realised that his prostate
would be hanging over my head for the rest of my life. But so
many things were happening in my busy existence, that this
incident had got tucked away in the recesses of my memory.

The war was over and President Truman had taught the Japs a
lesson they would not be slow to forget. No more ghastly news
on the wireless, just gorgeous Doris Day with her bouncing
pageboy singing:

'Well, what do you know, he smiled at me in my
    dreams last night!
My dreams are getting better all the time.'

as I prepared for my first big dance. Time had passed since my
ugly duckling phase and I was a sparkling sweet sixteen, tall,
trim-waisted and with a lovely smile, my most endearing feature.

My mother knelt on the burgundy carpet in front of me, her

mouth full of pins, putting the final touches to my very first party frock, a full length lime and apricot floral crêpe-de-chine, with a soft crossover bodice, a slight cowl and a beaded snood. 'What's "to sum up", a three-letter word starting with "a" and ending in "d", darl?' asked my father, frowning up from his *Morning Murdoch* crossword. He was brilliant at them and I think it was from my father that I must have inherited my wonderful way with words. Mother didn't seem to hear. She was looking up at me, her eyes full of tears.

'Nnng nnt nnm nnnmnmm nmmm, nnmmv nmmf nnm nmmnmm nrrm. Nmms nm nmmnmm nmm nmm nmms nmmnmmnmm nmmnmm nm nmmmk nm nmm nrrrts hnnmd.' Mummy took the pins out of her mouth and began again. 'Look at your daughter, Bruce. You've lost your little girl.' She brushed a tear from her eye with a gnarled wrist. 'She is a woman now and she's certainly going to break a few hearts tonight.'

I glanced in our peach-tinted, scalloped-edge mirror, shyly touching my bodice where my mother had tucked a couple of pairs of tightly rolled tennis sockettes. Why? I wondered. So I was a little flat-chested, but my beautiful legs were (and are) my strong point and I had no quarrel with the way that Dame Nature had made me.

As if to remind me how fortunate I was the doorbell rang and I heard my brother Roy calling, 'It's Madge McWhirter. Wanna see her, Ed?'

Before I could say the forties equivalent of 'do me a favour, no way, you must be joking', a pathetic figure appeared in the doorway, in a fawn and brown net creation that looked like a chrysalis from which no butterfly would ever emerge. 'My date hasn't turned up,' whined Madge on the verge of blubbing. 'Can I come with you, Edna?'

'Your date will never turn up, Madge,' I replied with a pragmatism that most people have found helpful and caring. 'And where the dickens did you find that frock?' I enquired gently.

'It was my mother's,' said the orphan, plucking coyly at the brittle old garment. 'It is by a top New Zealand couturier.'

'That's obvious,' said I. 'If it was your mother's, it certainly must have been an old favourite.' And on a positive note I added, 'It will certainly see *you* out!'

Even in those far-off days, I was interested in clothes; no surprise that my youngest son Kenneth is now a household name in the world of high fashion. Funny too that as I gaze down at the ladies in my audience when I am doing one of my wonderful shows, I can't help making constructive comments about their frocks. Not that I ever get a word of thanks for my pains! Name another show in the history of world theatre, which goes out of its way to boost the morale of its frumpily dressed female patrons.

My mother came to the rescue. 'I'm sorry, Madge. Edna's date will be here at any moment and if you need a lift to the dance tonight you will have to ask him, though I tend to suspect two's company and three's a crowd.' (That was yet another of my mother's sayings which has since caught on like wildfire.)

I wasn't sure about my date. Actually I had only met him briefly at Ann Forbes's place. He was a burly Sydney boy in Melbourne for a holiday at his uncle's and there was something a bit 'ordinary' about him which wasn't just the Sydney background but seemed to run deeper. Ann said she'd seen him smoking and he smelt of the odd sherry. She said that he had also said something rather worrying to the effect that he wasn't much of a church-goer. *Not* the kind of thing you ever hear from the lips of a Protestant. But what did I care? When that slightly common voice on the phone said, 'It's Les, remember me? Wanna come to the big hop at the Town Hall nex' Saddy?' I heard myself say, 'Yes.' What if my partner *was* a bit older than the other spotty boys. He had promised to pick me up in a car, probably his uncle's, but a car all the same. There was nothing more pathetic than the sight of a girl in a balldress sitting in public transport. And now Madge was trying to spoil that. The doorbell rang again.

Once more, my mischievous brother bounded to the front door and Les was soon standing in our lounge holding out a gardenia and a scrap of maidenhair fern in a celluloid box.

'Thought you might like this to stick on your dress, Ed,' he said rather awkwardly. 'Mind if I use the lav?'

My heart sank. He was certainly a lot older than I thought and smoking too with the ash already sprinkled down the front of his slightly greasy dinner jacket. My idol in those days was Van Johnson but my date on this special night was a far cry from the adorable, beautifully mannered star of *Two Girls and a Sailor*. James Mason was another favourite who later became a close friend and my eyes were already prickling with tears as I compared him with the snaggle-toothed youth I now introduced to my parents. 'Daddy, I would like you to meet Les Patterson . . . from Sydney,' I added by way of explanation. My father clambered up from his recliner, hand outstretched.

'Pleased to meet you, son,' he said. 'I'll take you out the back and show you where it is.'

My mother's lips tightened and she spoke in the slightly lah-di-dah voice she always put on for company and shop assistants. 'How do you do? You'll find a clean guest towel by the wash basin,' and then to my brother, 'Roy, get our coronation ashtray for Leslie prithee, or he'll be ashing all over the carpet.' My mother always said 'prithee' when she was cross about something. 'Hark' was another Shakespearian expression denoting displeasure, as in the phrase: 'Hark at our daughter! Who said you could speak like that to your parents prithee?'

After they had left the room, we all sat aghast for a few seconds. I couldn't bring myself to look at Madge; I'd seen that triumphant smirk on her chops before. But I wasn't going to let her see how bitterly disappointed I was in the ill-mannered type who was to squire me to the ball. Instead I fussed over the gardenia saying how gorgeous it was and pinning it to my bodice with trembling fingers. My father came back into the room and went straight for the drinks cabinet producing a bottle of Penfold's Royal Purple port and a couple of glasses.

'Your Les seems a nice young bloke, Ed. Reckon he'd like a spot of this before he hits the road?' My mother looked daggers and was just about to put a damper on that suggestion when Leslie himself slouched back into the room, adjusting his dress. He took a glass out of my father's hand and to everyone's astonishment, helped himself to an enormous slug of port, some of which trickled on to his far from snowy shirt. He beamed around the room. 'Time to be goin', Ed,' he said, grabbing me roughly by the shoulder. 'Howsabout your little girlfriend Madge? Could she use a lift?'

Have any of my Readers felt that an evening was ruined, even before it began? That was how I felt that night. Madge had of course leapt at Les's suggestion and I had just time to shoot my mother a look of anguish before he bundled us both into the back seat of a clapped-out Oldsmobile Sedan and roared off into the night. I could feel my so-called girlfriend's gloating glow beside me as my evening's escort took his bloodshot eyes off the road and threw a packet of Camels into my lap. 'Either of you sheilas like a smoke? Promise I won't let on to your mum.'

'Thenks,' came a New Zealand voice from my right, and to my horror I saw Madge put a cigarette to her pursed lips and ignite it from a lighter which Les charmingly tossed over his shoulder.

'I didn't know you smoked, Madge!'

The McWhirter waif plucked the ciggie amateurishly from her lips, squirted a little jet of smoke into the air and coughed. 'Didn't you, Edna?' she replied archly. 'My aunt lets me have the occasional puff after dinner parties and on special occasions.' Again that giveaway cough. I know for a fact that Madge had had about as many dinner parties as the Pope had had meat on Fridays and the idea of special occasions occurring in Mrs Findlay's sad little suburban hovel was laughable – if I hadn't felt like crying.

We arrived at the car lot with a squeal of brakes and I could hear the thump of drums from the Hall, as we both scrambled out of that whiffy conveyance – unassisted naturally. Walking up the Town Hall steps my morale took a slight turn for the better as I overheard a few girls gasp and their young beaux whistle under their breath at my gorgeous appearance. Call me old-fashioned, and I am far from being a snob, but I did not want that admiring crowd to see my dowdy and unacceptable companions. No problem there fortunately, since Les Patterson had hurried on ahead, doubtless in search of liquid refreshment and Madge had been stopped at the entrance since she had no ticket, invitation or partner. I last glimpsed her over my shoulder, rummaging for coins in a funny little beaded bag that had seen more affluent days – and more beads.

I had been to 'socials' before but never a real dance and the Moonee Ponds Town Hall looked lovely that night. Balloons, paper streamers and decorations which must have been in mothballs throughout the long period of hostilities festooned the ceiling. From the stage came the music of Dennis Farrington's orchestra, a talented group which has since become world famous. They were playing the big hit of the moment 'Saturday Night Is the Loneliest Night of the Week', which, spookily enough, rather suited my mood, as I stood on the outskirts of the dancefloor watching the laughing, jitterbugging couples.

My heart sank as I espied Leslie weaving his way towards me through the dancers, clutching a glass of fruit cup and a large lager. I certainly wasn't thirsty and who knows what he might have slipped into my innocent-looking drink?! My mother had always warned me about accepting refreshment from strange men and Les was getting stranger by the minute. There was a well-known ladies' powder room in the heart of Melbourne's shopping centre called Milady's Lounge from which some girls had never emerged after accepting beverages from strangers. They had later reappeared in places like Hamburg, Beirut and Cairo doing the sort of thing that only air stewardesses would consider today. Les downed his lager in one gulp and dragged me on to the dancefloor still with a moustache of froth on his upper lip. In the hope that no one would recognize me I pressed my face to his soggy shirt front as he trundled me around the room pumping my right arm out of tempo. His other arm was locked around my neck and every now and then he would push his face over my shoulder and take a drag on the Camel he had going in his right hand. No single experience of pain and anguish in my life ever seemed to last as long as that sickening circuit; not even my son Kenny's difficult birth or the time I nearly poisoned Prince Charles. But they are dramatic stories I must remember to tell you some other time.

The music never seemed to stop and when at last it did I fled to the ladies' powder room where I locked myself in a cubicle, tore the already brown gardenia off my frock and flushed it down the toilet, sobbing my heart out. Would I go home now, I wondered, or see it through to the bitter end? But a little voice inside said, 'You're meant to be here tonight, Edna. Tonight is spookily *special.*' I also thought I could hear the voice of Lionel Barrymore uttering his famous phrase, 'Courage, Camille.' The band was playing a nice 'Pride of Erin' and I glimpsed Les on the other side of the hall at the drinks buffet, his arm around the pinched shoulders of Madge McWhirter. Someone tapped me on the shoulder.

'Excuse I, remember me?' said a soft voice behind me. I turned and saw a slightly built young man with a high tanned brow, fine wispy hair and alert, slightly prominent ears. He was not wearing a dinner suit, but a navy blue double-breasted suit with shortish arms which drew attention to his skinny wrists and large red capable hands. His shoulders were sprinkled with water as if he had only just given his cowslick a flick with a wet comb in that room off the foyer with a top hat, cane and gloves silhouetted on the door. He was nice looking, if not in a Franchot Tony, Jeff Chandlerish, Van Johnsonny way.

'I'm sorry,' I said. 'Are you talking to me?'

'It's just that you look like the girl . . .'

The shy young man carried on talking. 'Did you ever go swimming down Sorrento a couple of years ago?' I looked at him and suddenly I had a spooky flashback. The hot beach, the squeal of children, a cry of help, the big green waves sloshing over my face as I gagged for air. Then a firm yet tender arm around my threshing body and the faces looking down at me as I lay shivering on the beach. One face in particular, with water dripping from his wet cowslick, and a voice echoing, 'Are you all right, kid? Are you all right, kid? Are you all right, kid?'

'It's you! The young soldier who saved my life!'

'You were in a bit of strife that's all,' he said sweetly. 'You would've got ashore on your ownsome I reckon.'

'But you're too young to have been a soldier!' I exclaimed, suddenly sceptical. 'Yet you were in uniform, I saw you undressing on the beach.' I quickly bit my tongue realising I had perhaps gone too far.

'Just a trainee,' he replied apologetically. 'I only made Lance

Corporal in the quartermaster's office attached to the ninth divvy at Ravenshoe. The war was over before I could get in amongst it.'

We stood facing each other for a moment in silence, occasionally buffeted by other couples as they swirled past. Dennis and his band had just struck up a new number, 'I'm Beginning to See the Light'. I could see my lifesaver was trying to say something but the music was so loud I had to put my ear quite close to his lips to hear the words.

'Don't suppose you'd care for a dance, tho' I reckon you're already booked up?'

I don't remember what my lips said but all my other organs said yes as he swept me on to the pulsating dancefloor just the way he had swept me to safety nearly two years before. Quite frankly he was no Fred Astaire or even Donald O'Connor. Actually he was one of those dancers whose feet never dared leave the floor, but in his arms I felt safe and warm and yes, womanly. I didn't even care that we seemed to be always colliding, sometimes painfully with other couples or that the only word he seemed to utter was 'sorry'.

> 'I never cared much for moonlit skies
> I never knew love was such a prize
> But now that the stars are in your eyes
> I'm beginning to see the light . . .'

sang Marjorie Stederford, the pretty young vocalist on the bandstand. I couldn't have agreed with her more as my heart beat in time to the music and the warm odour of my mother's 'Evening in Paris' wafted up between us. From the corner of my eye I saw Madge standing forlornly near the bar with Les, a hankie scrunched in her right hand. It's funny isn't it how at every dance there's always at least one girl clutching a hankie – usually the wallflower.

By this time I was managing to lead my partner and I made sure that we swirled close by Madge so that I could give her a little 'thumbs-up' signal in case she was worried about me. Not something another girl would have bothered to do frankly.

It was then that I had one of my spooky Past Life flashbacks. I knew in the innermost core of my being that I had once been Salome doing a raunchy dance in front of King Herod, and that wasn't all I did either I'm afraid. My partner was looking into my eyes as though he had just asked me something.

'Salome,' I said dreamily . . .

'Come again?'

'Oh, my name's Edna. I was miles away. What's yours?'

'Norman,' he said huskily, 'my friends call me Norm.'

The music had stopped and hand in moist hand we moved towards the benches that lined the walls.

'Let's sit on the form, Norm,' I said, giggling at my own quaint rhyme. He brought me a refreshing fruit cup and a shandy for himself. He told me he was working in a clerical capacity at Ball and Welch, one of Melbourne's finest department stores and before the next dance had begun he had asked me to the pictures on the following Friday.

The band struck up 'One Meatball' and we were about to take to the floor again when I heard a slurred voice and smelt a boozy whiff.

'Mind if I cut in, Ed?'

It was Les, much the worse for a few sherries but still grinning from ear to ear and with a ciggie between his caramel lacquered fingers. He had grabbed my arm and I looked at Norman pleadingly.

'Sorry, mate,' he said calmly. 'The young lady's having this one with me.' And we brushed past him on to the dancefloor leaving Les gaping like a stunned mullet.

The night passed in a beautiful blur and when Dennis and his band played 'Goodnight Sweetheart', the lights dimmed and the mirror ball showered shimmering polka-dots of light over the smooching young couples.

'I'd love to come to the pictures next Friday night,' I heard myself say. 'What's on?'

He pressed his lips close to my ear. 'It's a double feature,' he whispered. 'It's Bud Abbott and Lou Costello *In Hollywood* and Esther Williams and Van Johnson in *My Thrill of a Romance*.'

My heart missed a beat and I glanced quickly down at my partner (Norman was just a smidgen shorter than me – in heels).

His hair seemed to grow fairer and mischievous little freckles were appearing one by one on his nose and cheeks. For a moment I was dancing in the arms of Van Johnson.

Norm took me all the way home in a tram and we parted gravely on our front porch without so much as a peck on the cheek. That night the mirror ball rotated in my dreams. I was a cross between Salome and Esther Williams doing the Dance of the Seven Veils under water. A horrible shark appeared with a face like Les Patterson that swam quickly away when my Norman appeared on the scene in a diver's outfit clutching a very long harpoon.

It was the happiest night of my life and I would often look back on it with gratitude in the eventful years to come. I doubt if Madge entertained similar memories of that evening but I heard from my chums, Ann and Val, that she had hardly had a dance all night and that at one point Les had tried to refill her glass from a big jug of fruit cup. Apparently all the fruit had got jammed in the top of the jug, Les had given it an extra tilt and the whole lot had gushed down her frock: a Niagara of pineapple chunks, cucumber slices, apple, orange and passion-fruit. She had been showing off so much puffing on those ciggies that by the end of the evening everyone said she looked pretty green around the gills. Madge was last seen on the steps of the Moonee Ponds Town Hall being violently sick into her beaded bag. When I heard this, I had to smile – compassionately; she would always learn life's lessons the hard way, that poor wee Kiwi lassie.

As for Les Patterson, he went back to Sydney and I never saw him again until many, many years later when the small print in a contract forced me to appear in the same show with him, but that's a horror story I will tell in a later chapter. I did hear, on the grapevine, that he had become a successful Australian politician – not, as the world knows, a profession demanding very high standards of honour, etiquette or personal cleanliness.

CHAPTER XIII

The Little Pink Streamer

I N THE BACK row of the stalls at the Moonee that Friday night, something happened that changed me from a girl into a young woman. Esther was opening and closing her legs with a lot of other underwater glamourpusses, making a beautiful chrysanthemum pattern as my idol, Van Johnson, waited for her on his poolside lilo. It couldn't have been a more appropriate movie; watching the story of a lady swimmer falling in love with a returned serviceman and Lauritz Melchior as the ethnic minority. How could I possibly fail to remember my own damp encounter with *my* warrior, Norman?

The picture theatre was warm and musky. Suddenly I was aware of my companion's steady breathing; he was attempting to press something strange into my hand. For a moment I froze, and then ever so slowly, my young fingers curled around it and I helped myself to a scrumptious Columbine Caramel, the first of many that night. It was as if he knew by instinct my favourite confectionery and I felt a wave of gratitude combined with an odd feeling of maturity. He was always thoughtful, buying me a copy of *Screen News* in the foyer and seeing me safely home in the tram without ever getting 'fresh' or uncalled for.

I was still a schoolgirl, the Captain of the school in fact, and although Val, Ann, Helen, Joyce and my other pals had boyfriends, they were all much the same age; certainly no one like my Norman who was at least five years my senior, and who had already fought for his country – admittedly behind a desk on Australian soil. But then I was always different, an Outsider if you like, a role model and a mould-breaker rolled into one. I was proud of my mature escort too when we met, week after week for our rendezvous at the movies and afterwards, perhaps some toasted raisin bread and a hot banana malted.

Daddy had just gone off on the trip of a lifetime. Some of his mates at the Returned Servicemen's League – Alf, Gordon, Sid and Bill – had organised a 'back to the trenches' excursion to the old battlefields in France and the Middle East where they had served their homeland in the First World War. It cost them all a pretty penny but the Club had chipped in and made up the difference, and Daddy was sending back wonderful postcards of overseas nooks and crannies and Third World views. My mother seemed to think it would be a good thing for him to see the old places again after thirty-five years – 'I hope it helps him get it out of his system at last . . .' she said with an air of a woman who had heard the same story once too often.

We saw them off one blustery morning at Port Melbourne. Norm came down to keep me company and even Madge turned up to wave a flag, for all the world as though my dad was going off to war again, the tasteless minx! Dad threw me a pink streamer and it was still stretched tautly between us when all the other coloured streamers, yellow and blue and red, had snapped into a tangled cat's-cradle, hanging over the side of the Lloyd Triestino vessel, *Castle of Udolpho*. The ship slid away but I could still see Daddy at the rail getting smaller and smaller.

Everyone was still waving and there were even a few water-works but Dad's streamer remained unbroken, my thumbnail whitening as I gripped my end. At last it too snapped and wriggled off into the wind, and I stuffed my remaining few inches into a blazer pocket as we all mooched back home.

Norman came to tea one evening and my mother's kid brother Victor was there who had fought in the Pacific. Uncle Vic (the Butcher of Borneo) really hit it off with Norm over my mummy's grey corned beef, beetroot salad, scones and apricot jam. It was man's talk about the war and sport and I was thrilled to see how naturally Norman seemed to fit in with our family, helping my brothers with their homework and correcting their arithmetic in his tiny neat handwriting.

It had been a dry winter and, because my father was away, Norman sweetly offered to water my mother's ferns. I joined him in the back garden and we chatted away like magpies while he untangled the hose, fixed it to the throbbing tap and directed its nozzle at the thirsty shrubs. It was an image that would flash back to me years later when I returned to Australia to visit Norm in the Royal Edna Prostate Foundation. Finding he had been moved to another wing, I managed to track him down the long corridors by following his ducting. Sometimes I think life has its own pattern, labyrinthine, spooky but exciting.

I suppose you could say – using a modern expression that I do not particularly like – that Norm and I became an 'item'. At the time, I didn't think of us as 'going steady' and all that that implied! But a friendship which had nothing to do with sex or acts of immodesty began to grow; a friendship which has sustained me over the years and helped me become one of the most mature and fulfilled female achievers on this planet. There are other men in history who have lent their quiet support to a prodigiously gifted partner. Just think of Len Woolf (Virginia's adorable hubby), Monsieur Curie, Prince Albert, King Boadicea and Harry Helmsley, if you don't believe me.

Norm didn't look all that much older than me. Admittedly his fine hair was receding fast which is why he Brylcreemed what was left into a Bing Crosby cowslick. But I had long since realised that I was a bit of a one-off. Boys my own age bored me and I craved a mature companion. But Norm always respected me and that was what I was looking for after some of the traumatic experiences I had had at an impressionable age.

Over the next few years we must have gone to the pictures hundreds of times, not just the stalls either, but sometimes the lounge where the seats were softer like my mother's Genoa velvet and sulky girls with trays supported by a halter strap sold Columbine Caramels, Dixie ice-creams and Old Gold Assortments. At one beautiful Melbourne picture theatre an organ rose up out of the stage and a blind organist played 'The March of the Toys' by Victor Herbert and 'The Teddy Bears' Picnic'. He then

turned, bowed a bit crookedly to the audience and sank down
into the darkness again, or what would have been darkness to us.
I loved the way the lights dimmed and the big burgundy curtain
mottled with light – green, pink and magenta. At last, after much
opening and closing of draperies, the screen was revealed on
which a lion roared, a globe revolved, Mr Universe struck his
gong or the Columbia lady held aloft her ice-cream cornet.

Victor Mature, Francis the talking mule, Carmen Miranda,
Trevor Howard, Barbara Stanwyck, Aldo Ray, Gloria Grahame,
Melvyn Douglas, Randolph Scott, Jane Powell, Jeff Chandler,
Jennifer Jones, Lassie and Rex Harrison were just a few of the
stars who gave me a little tantalising glimpse of life beyond
Moonee Ponds. I little dreamt that one day I would be a star
myself; that I would look down from a stage and see thousands
of little faces gazing up at me, grotesque with gratitude.

In my last year at Moonee Ponds Girls' Grammar, I helped
organise the school play. *The Mikado* by Gilbert and Sullivan was
suggested but the war had just ended and a lot of parents felt that
a Japanese show would not only be in bad taste but might even
lead to minor skirmishes and reprisals from disoriented veterans
in the audience. Instead our drama teacher, Miss Moira Jago,
chose *Macbeth*, one of Shakespeare's gorgeous shows and no prizes
for guessing who topped the audition for the leading lady. These
days I believe my old school now puts on co-ed productions with
Moonee Ponds Boys' Grammar but in my time the girls played
all the parts and, though I say so myself, ours was a production
that Hal Prince would have been proud of.

No show without punch, Madge insisted on auditioning and
Miss Jago told me privately, to my surprise, that Madge was so
good she could not decide as which of the three witches to cast
her. Certainly, having Madge in the show slashed make-up costs.
My opposite number was played by a rather 'butch' girl called
Deirdre Urquhart whose parents were Presbyterian, giving her a
wonderful insight into the character. She already owned a tartan
skirt and her hair was pretty short and tufty so she could more
or less stomp on to the stage as she was. I had thought a lot about
my character and decided that Lady Macbeth was, when all is said
and done, just an ordinary Scottish housewife trying to cope with

her husband's mid-life crisis and I am told that this is how it came across the footlights. I did the 'out damn'd spot' sleepwalking scene in a laundry setting like an early detergent commercial, and I think I brought the bard to life kicking and screaming into the twentieth century. I didn't know it then but I suppose I was a pioneer of Social Relevance.

That scene brought the house down and once again in my life I heard the sound of applause, the funny bang of theatre seats snapping up as an audience rises to a standing ovation, the occasional cry of 'bravo' from theatre buffs and the odd bouquet at curtain call. I have to admit Madge upstaged the other two witches, and mothers with young children in the audience actually covered their little eyes whenever she was on stage. It was a pretty mould-breaking production come to think of it which I would like to produce on Broadway one day, perhaps with music by close personal chum, Steve Sondheim.

Now that I look back it is not surprising that I had such a feel for Shakespeare because in a Previous Life I was once Ann Hathaway, the woman who helped Shakespeare write his wonderful shows. If you don't believe me, how do you explain this? When I visited the bard's quaint old-world style cottage at Stratford-upon-Avon *for the first time*, I went straight in the door, and much to the consternation of a large group of Japanese tourists walked directly to the kitchen and tried to make myself a cup of tea. Needless to say I didn't waste my breath explaining that I had once been Shakespeare's wife, but my little American friend Shirl was distinctly jealous when I told her this story. Now I am convinced that the 'out damn'd spot' segment was entirely written by Ann. Somehow it has a woman's touch so that when I made the odd mistake or 'fluff' reciting my part in the school play, it didn't seem to matter. Let's face it, Possums, I wrote it!

Yet when the applause had died and the bouquets had wilted I realised that in only a few short months my schooldays would be over and I would have to find myself a vocation. When you are superlative at almost everything it's very hard to decide which talent to utilise. I didn't want to go to university; I must have known that in the years to come I would be smothered by honorary degrees. I suppose I was waiting for Dame Nature to give me a sign and she did.

Spring had passed with its cool smell of jonquils and yellow wattle blossom, and the weather was warming up. Around our back veranda, the blow-flies buzzed like a chorus of kazoos as I came home from school one Tuesday.

'Anybody home?' I called, reaching as usual for the tartan cookie tin atop the fridge. Roy and Athol were in the next room listening to the wireless. Mummy, I knew, was out at an appointment with a Vein Specialist and the phone was ringing.

'Turn down the wireless, you kids, will you?! Can't you even hear the phone?' I yelled, as you would.

'Yes,' I said, when a crackly voice asked me if this was the Beazley home.

'Edna Beazley speaking,' I said. 'Who?'

The crackly voice said it was the Australian Consulate in Paris. I suddenly had an exciting picture of Maurice Chevalier, Charles Boyer and Adolf Menjou rolled into one. The line was awful. I pictured it as a long barnacled cable stretching under the sea all the way to France covered with seaweed and being nibbled by whales.

'I'm sorry,' the voice said after a particularly loud crackle. I thought he was apologising for the bad connection.

'We deeply regret that Bruce Clive Beazley met with an accident in the Somme Valley yesterday. He died almost immediately. We will be cabling in due course for instructions as to the disposal of his remains and effects.' We then seemed to be cut off.

I put down the phone, went into the kitchen and made a cup of tea. I then went out into our sunny backyard and gathered a few tea-towels and pillowcases off the clothes line, throwing the pegs into the old linen peg-bag. I went back into the kitchen with the basket of dry things and sat for a while at the kitchen table, sipping my tea and eating a Butternut Snap. The boys' radio programme droned on and on from the next room. It was getting on my nerves. I stormed into the lounge. 'Can't you kids keep that racket down? Do you think the whole street wants to listen to that stupid twaddle?'

'Gee, look at Ed, Roy!' said Athol grinning. 'She's cryin'.'

*   *   *

My mother's veins were no better for the bad news. A cable then a letter confirmed that ghastly phone call with the information that Daddy had tripped on a grassy mound whilst trying to take a snapshot of his old battlefield, and had fallen backwards into what had once been a trench. The shock had been too much and he had passed away in roughly the same place where he had come so close to being killed all those years before.

In due course, his mates, poor old Alf, Bill, Sid and Gordon brought back his ashes and a sad little band they were when we gathered at Melbourne General Cemetery for the interment. Those weeks since I answered the phone had been rather dreamlike since Daddy's postcards kept coming and it was hard to believe the world was one friendly Electrolux man the less. We would wander around the house with the funny sensation that he had just been there.

I stood with my family, Norm's arm tightly around my shoulders, watching the little casket draped with the colours of the Australian Infantry Forces, being lowered into the grave as Canon Lake recited something suitable:

> 'He shall not grow old
> As we that are left grow old
> Age shall not weary him or the years condemn
> At the going down of the sun
> And in the morning
> We will remember him.'

Old Bill put the bugle to his nicotine-stained lips and bleated a wobbly lament. I noticed Mummy glancing down rather proudly at her new surgical stockings. Athol was picking his nose and I fumbled in my pocket for a hankie but there was nothing there, only a little bit of twisted pink streamer.

CHAPTER XIV

Sparks
in the Sky

I N SPITE OF her bereavement, my mother looked well, even ruddy in the firelight. It was dusk, and a nippy night lay ahead as Roy, Athol and I helped her feed our big incinerator down by the fowl-house behind the clothes line. From that blackened old forty-four-gallon drum, orange flames jumped high into the indigo sky and red and yellow sparks jostled the pale stars as we threw on another cardboard box of old clothes and papers.

'Your father was such a hoarder,' Mummy said lifting Daddy's old khaki army jacket out of the incinerator on the prongs of a garden fork. It was busy with blue and yellow flames. 'No wonder the home was always full of moths and silverfish,' she added, forking it back into the blazing drum and sending up another tall plume of yellow sparks. Funnily enough, most of Daddy's clothes, particularly his pyjamas and undies, burnt very well, but paper things like his war diaries, books and old Sunday-School prizes took a lot of prodding and a splash of kerosene to really catch alight. At first they even seemed to put the fire out. When the blaze was really roaring Mummy suggested we toss in his teeth and shoes.

It was hard work heaving those boxes down the backyard in the gathering darkness. Daddy was one of those people who kept everything, old cigarette tins, magazines and especially the packaging things had come in, 'in case they ever came in useful', which of course they never did. These days I suppose he would have collected all those styrofoam moulds that come with radios and Magimixes. Then of course there were all his bits and pieces in the toolshed like the bookends he'd been making for years.

In the nick of time the doorbell had rung. It was old Gordon Gibson who'd been my father's army mate in the third division and who'd been with him when he'd had his accident, dropping in to pay his condolences. He arrived not a moment too soon, and we quickly 'roped him in' to help us stoke the incinerator and clear out the toolshed where he sweetly asked if he might souvenir the odd item. Atop the wardrobe in my parents' bedroom Athol found the black box Daddy used to take when he went to Lodge. He was about to chuck it on the fire when Mummy stopped him angrily. Opening it up she tenderly removed my father's masonic apron.

'You can burn the box now, Ath,' she said, 'but not my lovely new oven mitt!' she added with a girlish laugh.

I sometimes think Mummy invented recycling.

Naturally we had given what we could to Mrs Chesterman and Miss Hoadley at the Church Opportunity Thrift Shop, but they said they had 'no call' for most of Daddy's left-off effects, and that books, shoes, and old snapshot albums were very 'slow movers'. I think Mummy would have given a lot to the Salvation Army except that she wasn't talking to Auntie Ruby that month. Auntie Ruby and Mummy were having a tiff about something.

The incinerator was still warm in the morning, full of fine white ash, and smelling sour and bitter, like the breath of someone who has been eating the wrong things. Beside it was a charred copy of R. M. Ballantyne's *The Young Fur Traders* which must have bounced out of the fire. It was one of Daddy's Sunday-School prizes and would probably be banned today. Near it, in the buffalo grass, was half a carpet slipper still smoking. I picked it up, doused it under the tap and kept it for years in an old Willow cake tin, because I always remembered Dad in those slippers. Call me sentimental if you like, but we are a sentimental family – I'm sorry but we are.

Norman was wonderful through all those bad days. Mummy told him he could pop in any time he liked, and it was nice in the evenings when we all listened to *Martin's Corner* sponsored by Kellogg's Cornflakes followed by *Dad and Dave* brought to us by Spearmint, PK and Wrigley's Juicy Fruit Chewing Gum, to have another man sitting in Dad's squeaky recliner. I knew Mummy liked him too, though she once said to me, 'He's nice, Edna, but you can aim a bit higher than that.' Then she added wistfully, 'I wish I had.'

Who or what could be higher than Norm? I asked my young self.

It is true that he was beginning to occupy a very important place in my life especially now that Daddy had jumped the twig. But the strong feelings I had once experienced at Sorrento when he scooped me out of the water and flung me dripping on to my towel never really came back.

Yet he was so thoughtful, so polite, unlike the rough crude boys my girlfriends were dating, and the so-called physical side of our relationship didn't seem to interest him, thank goodness. Sometimes after we had been to a particularly romantic movie and we said goodnight, he would give me a little peck on the cheek accompanied by a funny lunge which wasn't quite a hug. Since this is a brutally frank publication I have to say that I half wanted Norm to go a little further than he did, but I always pretended that I didn't, encouraging him sometimes and then turning inexplicably cool so he never quite knew where he stood with me.

'Always keep the menfolk on their toes,' said my wise old mother once, 'or they'll take advantage of you and use you to the hilt.' Whenever she said 'hilt', she would always make a stabbing gesture, which didn't seem very appropriate – at the time.

Norman was even pleasant to Madge McWhirter which really wasn't necessary. 'She's quite a nice kid underneath, Edna,' said Norm, old softie that he was. 'She's had a rough trot – no parents and that. She's not even a bad looker when she smiles.' Norman wasn't talking about the Madge I knew, that's for sure, and I felt a twinge of anger to think that that artful creature had already got to work on my boyfriend.

If I had been worried about the future a few months before it was all settled now. Mummy was far from well – mentally – and my brothers were a handful and just entering the pimply stage. Someone had to hold the fort, and that someone wouldn't have time for university or finishing school or any of those nice things which my headmistress, Miss Tolley, had told me I deserved. My last speech day was a tearful affair as I trotted up to the dais time after time to collect my prizes: speech and drama, singing, art, Bible studies, history, domestic science, biology, geography, poetry, hockey and animal husbandry. I was Captain of the school which I have only mentioned once before due to modesty and I will not mention it again for the same reason. But I was the most popular Head Girl in living memory according to our old bursar, Miss Bunce, who went back a long way. Miss Tolley made a short speech saying how everyone expected me to go on to great things – or words to that effect – and how well I had done at my exams in spite of Daddy being gathered at an awkward moment in my studies. My eyes were monocled with tears as I stood stiffly listening to these tributes, for I knew that the 'greater things' that I would be going on to would be no greater than the kitchen sink, my mother's demanding bedside and a laundry trough full of muddy football shorts and soiled jockstraps.

Even Madge's prospects were better than mine for her auntie, Mrs Findlay, had scrimped and saved to send her to ballet lessons at the church hall given by Olga Ballaratova, a once fairly famous Australian ballerina from the town of Ballarat. Actually, I found out later that her real name was Fay Chubb and she was about as Russian as my foot. Heaven knows what kind of ballet Madge ever hoped to appear in. We had been to see *The Red Shoes* and she was certainly no Moira Shearer though there were a few creepy parts in the repertoire which she would probably manage like the monster in *Swan Lake*.★

If I was to become a household drudge for the foreseeable future, I had one thing going for me. In one of my Past Lives I had been Cinderella.

I didn't know it then, but as a child whenever the story was read to me I felt a strange sense of identification, no more than that. Naturally I never mentioned it at the time, though today reincarnation is a scientific fact. So even during the years of boredom and selfless family devotion which followed I knew, deep down, that one day I *would* go to the Ball!

★ Footnote for adult education students: Von Rothbart, the evil magician, father of the black swan.

Our family were quite poor though we owned our own home and the Electrolux Company had been generous when my father had finally hung up his crevice nozzle before leaving on his fatal trip to the Continent. Mummy still received his small war pension and my brothers did paper-rounds and collected bottles. Our house was always a hive of activity. During the war it had been a 'Fat for Britain' depot and all the neighbours used to leave their old dripping in farina tins and other receptacles on our front porch, taking care to first strain out old string and charred parsnip chips. My mother used to send it all off to a central depot where it was shipped to England and turned into goodness knows what. Unfortunately, we heard later that most of the 'Fat for Britain' ships were sunk by the Japanese before they reached their destination and it is funny to think that at the bottom of the Pacific there still rests the pinguid residue of thousands upon thousands of Australian Sunday roasts, a kind of gigantic drippings slick. Old Miss Whittle who lived at number 37 still thought the war was on for many years after the cessation of hostilities and continued depositing her fat on our doorstep. So one of my brothers' many chores was to return Miss Whittle's dripping and give her an historical update. It meant nothing since a week later another greasy old jam tin would appear on the porch.

My mother was becoming a bit of a handful. By now I was doing most of the cooking, cutting the boys' lunches *and* cleaning the house. Mummy was spending more and more time in her bedroom, pottering about and, I'm afraid, becoming a bit of a hoarder herself. Just to what extent, we never fully realised since she never let me in there with a vacuum cleaner and I never saw it until fifteen years later when we practically had to dig her out with a bulldozer to get her into the Dunraven courtesy van. The only thing she ever took an interest in was her garden and particularly our gladioli plantation which was the pride of our street. 'Imagine as many as fifty six-inch blooms from one bulb and a foot square of ground; if you need to imagine this, then you have never grown a really good gladiolus.' So says David Laidlaw in his wonderful book *Growing Gladioli*. Gladdies can grow in their giant size to six feet high with florets eight inches across in every colour of the rainbow and we won prize after prize with our blooms. Even today since our old home has become a museum, the glads still flourish under expert care and I have the spikes harvested and flown around the world for distribution to my grateful audiences.

Several years passed like a kind of dream. I was not unhappy because I knew Dame Nature had something up her sleeve but I was impatient to know what it was. The boys sprang up like wildfire, Norman was always helpful and attentive and incidentally, doing very well for himself in the accounts department at Ball and Welch. Incredibly, my old school friends Ann and Val had got married and were 'battling for a home' to use a period phrase. A cream brick veneer bungalow was every young girl's dream dwelling in those days, preferably with a sandblasted reindeer on the glass doors between the lounge and dining room. It was at Ann's wedding that two momentous things happened. I met Pixie Lambell, one of the most beautiful women Australia has ever produced, and apparently a good friend of the Forbes family. She had been a top model, appearing regularly in the magazines wearing glamorous frocks and furs, and her green eyes, flaming red hair and gorgeous bone structure were on an advert in all the trams where she pressed her cheek against a man's chest and said (in a balloon), 'It is *indeed* a lovely shirt, sir.' Miss Lambell kept staring at me all through the service and afterwards she came up and took me to one side. 'Have you ever thought of modelling?' she said to my surprise. 'With your height, legs and bone structure you could be world-class.' Overwhelmed I replied that it frankly hadn't crossed my mind and where would I begin?

'I have started a school of fashion and deportment – the first in Melbourne,' continued my gorgeous admirer. 'If you could come a couple of nights a week, I would groom you personally at no charge.' I blushed, not knowing what to say, my fingers and thumbs seemed to be all fingers and thumbs.

'You have great potential,' she went on, 'and I am *never* wrong. Please let me take you under my wing, Miss Beazley.' Her words I must confess were like music to my ears and she smelt lovely too, of something sweet and fragrant and duty-free. Already I could see myself on the cat walks of Europe and on the covers of *Harpers*, *Vogue* and the Australian *Woman's Monthly*. I would have to change my name to something more glamorous like hers. 'Bambi' Beazley appealed because I had once been described as doe-eyed but there was already another Melbourne beauty of that name. I tried to think of other Disney characters, but somehow Dumbo Beazley or even Pinocchio didn't quite hit the spot. Miss Lambell and I stood at the foot of the steps of Holy Trinity, Moonee Ponds, as Ann and her new husband, Murray Inglis, emerged in a shower of confetti. She kissed her lovely bouquet of carnations, grape hyacinths and gardenias, and sent it flying high into the air. I raised my hand and the bouquet fell into my grasp. Everyone laughed and a couple of the girls gave me a hug. 'I caught Ann's bouquet,' I said, turning to my new benefactor. 'That's lucky, isn't it?'

'Lucky for some,' replied Miss Lambell with a knowing smile, 'but not for all.' She drew a little pink card with a scalloped gold edge from her leopardskin clutch bag and pressed it into my hand. 'Give me a tingle, Miss Beazley,' she said and was gone.

For the next year I managed to visit the Lambell Academy of Poise at least twice a week. It meant a tram trip into the city where Miss Lambell rented a large suite high up in an office building in Little Collins Street. Like all elevators in Australia it smelt of sausage rolls and pasties for some reason, but once the doors opened on to the sixth floor, one was on soft mushroom carpet where an attractive receptionist with glasses resting on top of her head and cyclamen lipstick talked on a white phone. On my first day Miss Lambell (we were not on first name terms until some years later) took me into her office where there was a leopardskin couch and a lovely original of her by internationally acclaimed, award-winning Australian artist, Charles Eltham. It was the most beautiful painting I had ever seen, Miss Lambell was wearing a strapless leopardskin sheath and holding a ciggie in one long black-gloved hand. Her fiery locks were scraped back in a chignon and her lips parted in a sophisticated smile. Her eyes followed me all around the room.

'I see you're admiring that young glamourpuss on the wall,' said Miss Lambell laughing. 'It was many years ago, but Charlie caught something I think. You must meet him, Miss Beazley. He adores beautiful women and *he is itching* . . .' Miss Lambell flicked her intercom. 'No calls for the next thirty minutes please, Cynthia,' she murmured and then continued, 'He is itching to paint someone new, the face of the future, if you like.'

If my morale needed a boost, it was getting one. Miss Lambell took me through all her exercises and shared with me all the secrets of a fully paid-up, card-carrying glamourpuss. At home I would practise walking around with a book on my head and the speech exercises she gave me too. Thanks to those early elocution lessons, I have the voice you hear today – clear, melodious and *audible*. Many people listening to my wonderful shows think I am Oxford educated, and Americans think I'm from Boston.

About six months into my course, Miss Lambell asked me to a cocktail party in her South Yarra flat. I had only been to South Yarra once before when I had been taken prisoner by Nazis and now I was returning as a prematurely poised young woman and to a rather up-market apartment block, though the word 'up-market' had not yet been invented. I had asked Miss Lambell if I could bring a friend, meaning Norm, and she hadn't exactly said no, so he stood at my side as we rang the doorbell outside her flat overlooking the Botanical Gardens. The door opened just as I was brushing down Norm's shoulders but Miss Lambell didn't seem to notice, though she greeted Norm with a little smile of surprise. We were shown into a lovely room with a view of the city over tousled green tree-tops. It was full of stunning looking graduates from the Lambell Academy as well as men wearing navy blue blazers with gold buttons, paisley cravats and suede shoes. One man had very long hair which he kept flicking back and was smoking coloured cigarettes with gold tips.

On a big leopardskin couch (Pixie's trademark) sat a chubby man in a beret, red shirt and velvet trousers. He had a pointed black beard and a gold tooth which gave him a slightly wicked but not unappealing look and his arm was around the shoulders of a Malaysian type of woman with a slit up her aqua frock, who was laughing at something he had told her. There was a gramophone in the corner with an automatic changer on it, playing something a bit avant-garde and jerky that I didn't recognise. Later I peeped at the label which said 'Be-Bop Boogie'. Everyone was talking very loudly and when the drinks tray came round I think Norman was a little disappointed to find that there was no beer, only wine and nibbles of salami. Looking back it's funny to think how awestruck I was by that first glimpse of sophisticated life, considering what I now take in my stride. A few years ago in New York I popped in at a party where Gore Vidal and Norman Mailer had to be restrained from tearing each other's eyes out and Jackie Onassis, Gloria Vanderbilt and Tom Wolfe were flitting about. I didn't stay more than ten minutes before going on to the *real* party.

'You two are going to mingle,' said a stern voice and leaving Norm standing there looking for somewhere to put his olive stone – *and olive* – Pixie swept me across the room to meet that jolly little gnome on the sofa.

'Here's your new model, Charlie,' she said, 'isn't she everything I promised you and more? But no funny business, darling. She's bespoke.' At which Miss Lambell nodded across the room where Norm stood awkwardly, trying to make his wrists look shorter. Something Miss Lambell had said seemed to amuse the bearded man, for he burst out laughing, mopping his eyes with a big red hankie. The ethnic minority laughed as well. Holding out a paint-spattered hand, he grabbed mine and pressed it to his whiskery lips, like they do in the pictures.

'I'm Charlie Eltham,' he introduced himself, 'and you're everything and more than Pix led me to believe. Sit for me and I will make you the Mona Lisa of Moonee Ponds.' My heart missed a beat, rather like the music on the gramophone. How did he know where I came from?

'Your fame has travelled ahead of you, *chérie*. Our divine hostess has given you quite a build-up and for once she has not exaggerated.'

Although he was a bit of an acquired taste, Mr Eltham and I got on like a house on fire. He told some wonderful jokes with no point to them called Shaggy Dog Stories, which were fashionable at the time and you laughed just because they were so silly. I had a little more than my usual one glass of wine too I'm afraid, and when the time came to go I was walking on air.

Norman was pretty silent on the way home and I suspect a little jealous of my social poise so that I felt a teeny bit sorry for him and then, typical of me, annoyed with him for making me feel that way in the first place.

Charlie's studio was another world again. A big room with a window in the ceiling, smelling of turpentine. It was in a terrible mess with squashed-up tubes of paint and old rags on every surface and canvases stacked against the wall, on some of which were faces I knew: the Lord Mayor of Melbourne, Pixie Lambell and even a sketch of the Queen! He was wearing exactly the same clothes as he had been wearing at the party and he immediately grabbed me by the shoulders, gave me a scratchy kiss on both cheeks and sat me on a chair next to a black stove with a chimney that went right up to the ceiling. Retreating behind a big blank canvas, he peeped around it and said to my astonishment, 'Have you ever done nude modelling before, Edna?'

Oddly enough I wasn't as offended as you would think, thanks to my growing sophistication, but I quickly let him know that though I was happy to be the *face* of the future I had no intention of letting any other parts of my anatomy in on the act. I had brought a few frocks from my limited wardrobe but he pooh-poohed them all rather rudely and ended up draping me in a length of Miss Lambell's leopardskin crêpe-de-chine, which I had to stop from slipping for hours on end, giving me a slightly startled look. It is of course, the famous portrait of me known to the world as 'The Moonee Madonna' and now a firm favourite with Japanese tourists to the Dame Edna Museum in Melbourne.

Charlie was taking ages to paint me but I didn't really mind. It was fun visiting his studio in the Bohemian part of town. Interesting people would pop in for a drink: actors, journalists and turf identities.

'I'll get that smile of yours, if it kills me,' said Charlie one Friday evening. 'Can you give me another couple of hours tonight?'

Norm and I had a date at the pictures that evening. We hadn't seen much of each other lately, what with my duties at home, my sessions at the Pixie Lambell Academy and now the portrait. But it was so much fun to be with Charlie. He knew so many jokes and even used swear words which somehow didn't sound yukky coming from him. By comparison Norman seemed a bit, well, a bit too *nice*, I'm sorry but he did. I phoned him to say I couldn't make the pictures and to my surprise he didn't seem to mind much. It occurred to me that I hadn't seen him for at least a fortnight. As I put down the telephone I was aware of someone standing behind me. It was Charlie holding out a glass of wine.

'This should put a smile on that pretty mouth of yours, Edna,' he said and before I knew it his lips were on mine and I felt a funny flickering thing trying to get between my teeth. His hand was pressed against the small of my back and sliding south. My nostrils were filled with the smell of wine as I tried to extricate myself but in the effort to do so I tripped, and we both tumbled on to his old paint-strewn divan. He was rubbing his bearded face around my neck and at the same time trying to do something awkward with his belt when I finally struggled free.

'What's the matter?' he spluttered, staring at me crossly.

'I'm not the woman you take me for,' I said breathlessly, buttoning up my blouse.

'I don't think you are either,' he replied, with the look of a wounded animal. 'You're the first girl who's ever given me a knock-back. How come?'

'It's nothing to do with you, Charlie. I like you a lot and we've had fun but I am very involved with someone else – a former army officer and lifesaver, and we . . .' I bit my lip but went on, 'we are going to be married quite soon.'

Charles Eltham collapsed into uncontrollable laughter.

'Not that droob I saw at the party,' he said. 'You'll eat him alive, Edna. He'll never keep up the pace!'

'We'll see about that, Charlie,' I replied. 'Goodnight.' And with that I picked up my handbag, gave him a peck on his astonished cheek and swept out of the studio.

I lashed out on a taxi that night, my mind filled with confusion, shock and a strange exhilaration. I asked the driver to take me past the house where Norman lived with his aged parents. But he wasn't home.

'He's gone off to see Ingrid Bergman,' said old Mrs Everage, through a chink in the front door, 'with Madge McWhirter. I think they're going to the Chinese after that.'

It was a mild night so I dismissed the taxi and sat down beside Norman's front gate. I would wait all night if necessary. It wasn't until about one in the morning that Norm's Vauxhall pulled into the driveway and he got out, rubbing his mouth with a hankie. As I rose up out of the darkness in front of him, he nearly jumped out of his skin with fright and my next words made him feel no better.

'Go out with that New Zealand trollop once more and I'll never speak to you again!' and I gave him a terrific clout across the head with my handbag.

The next day, Norman Stoddart Everage and I announced our engagement.

CHAPTER XV

Tying the Knot

Pixie Lambell looked up from *The Cruel Sea*. She had been reading the latest best-seller quietly to herself, curled up on the leopardskin couch in her office. The door was ajar, so I had just tapped softly and walked in.

'You wanted to see me, Miss Lambell!'

My guide and mentor ground a black cigarette with a gold tip into a venetian glass ashtray and expelled a long trumpet of camphor-coloured smoke.

'Sit down, Edna,' she said, pointing to a yellow hammock-style chair on a black frame that would be hard to get out of. I noticed that beside it there was a small coffee table shaped a bit like an artist's palette with a book lying on it, about someone called Paul Klee.

'What's that thing on your finger?'

I glanced down at my lovely engagement ring, an unusual marcasite solitaire which glinted on my finger.

'Oh,' I replied, blushing, 'do you like it? It's something Norman bought me at Dunkling's Jewellers yesterday in his lunchbreak. It came in a lovely velvet box. Would you like to look at it?'

'I can see it from here,' said Pixie in a harsh, worldly kind of voice. *'Just!'*

What did she mean? I wondered. Surely *all* women got excited over an engagement ring? I'm afraid I had told her a little white fib due to nerves. Actually Norm and I had chosen my lovely solitaire at Adorna on the Corner – 'Pick your ring in our private cubicles.' Pixie snapped shut her book and lit another black Sobranie.

'Don't tell me Dunkling's charged him for that!' she said. 'It looks more like a free sample.'

I went pale inside and felt the tears rush up. Miss Lambell pushed her fingers through her Titian hair and shook her head.

'I'm sorry, Edna. My tongue ran away with me. Forgive me. But what in God's name is a beautiful, talented, intelligent kid like you doing with that chip of glass on your finger?' She stood up and started pacing the room. 'You could have a big career – modelling, acting, you name it. I know Charlie overstepped the mark the other night by the way.'

I shrugged my shoulders, tears rolling down my cheeks.

'Sure he's a lecherous old bugger,' Pixie continued, 'but he can pick the winners. You could take him down the street and he'd point to the women who are going to be beautiful *next year*. That's Charlie's principal talent; and you want to know something?'

I blew my nose and nodded, pretending I did.

'Everyone who has met you reckons you are "star material". It oozes out of your pores.'

She had crossed the room to me now and, taking both my hands, wet hankie and all, in hers, she said with quiet intensity, 'Mark my words, Edna. One day people will be prepared to pay big money for what you've got. You'll be able to write your own cheque, not just in Australia, but overseas, England, on the Continent, and in the States.* You will have men eating out of your hand. Why throw it all away on the boy next door?'

Something glistened in Miss Lambell's eyes now and it wasn't Visine. I was confused. I wanted all the things she said to happen, but I was afraid too. You see I needed tenderness and companionship as well and kiddies of my own. And normalcy. Yes, deep down I wanted to be a normal wife and mother with natural drives and juices. I feared that in becoming a career woman I might forfeit my femininity.

As if reading my thoughts, Pixie Lambell turned away and I

* The publishers of this bestseller (Simon & Schuster) would heartily endorse this prophetic statement.

could see she too was having problems with her lachrymal duct.

'Don't think you'll lose your femininity, Edna. You're the most feminine creature on the planet. A successful career couldn't change that. Look at me. I'm successful in my own way and vulnerable as hell. All I ask,' she adjured me, borrowing my hankie, 'is that you think hard before you give yourself a life sentence in some man's kitchen.' Then she looked at me in such a strange and crooked way that I found myself putting my arms around her and giving her a great big hug.

That night Norm took me out for a celebration meal at the Hey-Diddle Griddle, a sophisticated café which the restaurant guide in the *Melbourne Herald* had described as world-class. 'Continental and Australian meals a speciality,' it said on the window and there was a lovely waiter called Mario who wore a fawn and maroon cardigan under his dinner jacket. I think he enjoyed the odd ciggie too and would have a quick puff once he was behind the swinging door leading to the kitchen. Sometimes when he put the minestrone soup on the table I would notice two little jets of smoke coming out of his nostrils.

I had ordered soup, chicken-in-a-basket and Black Forest gâteau followed by a cuppa chino (as I thought it was spelt). The Griddle was one of the first restaurants in Melbourne with one of the new coffee-making machines. I was sprinkling some cheese on my minestrone soup, as you were supposed to do, when Norm broke the ice.

'You've been pretty quiet, Edna, but I think I know what's on your mind.'

'Bet you don't,' I snapped, meaning it to sound nicer.

'You're worried I'm going to stand in the way of your career.'

I tried to say something, but he put his hand over my mouth.

'Shut up and listen, Ed,' he continued with a brutality that was not unacceptable. 'Plenty of sheilas, er . . . I mean, girls, have combined their career with their marriage and it works if you let it. I want you to know that I'll never stand in your way. Even if I ever get sick or something, I want you to do what you have to do.'

What prophetic words. You may be sure they came back to me on that fateful day years later when I was about to step on to a stage in London and Norm had one of his first prostatological explosions.

However, as we sat there talking so seriously over the check tablecloth lit romantically by a wax-encrusted Chianti bottle, I could never have foreseen the day when the earnest young man holding my hand would be hooked up to some of the most advanced urological hardware on the planet.

'But, Norm,' I said, sipping my sparkling Sauternes, 'Miss Lambell feels—'

'Don't listen to that lezzo,' exclaimed Norman, flushing with anger, attractively. 'She's only interested in one thing and I'm bloody surprised you haven't spotted it!'

Frankly, Readers, I didn't quite understand what Norm was driving at and just as well I didn't or I might have broken off the engagement then and there.

'She's a wonderful person and she only wants me to be happy,' I declared. 'I am going to ask her to be godmother to our first baby.'

It was Norm's turn to look a bit worried.

'Hold your horses, Ed,' he said with a hollow laugh. 'I hope we're going to have a bit of fun first before the nippers come along!'

'Call me Edna prithee,' I said, slipping into my mother's hoity-toity Shakespeak. 'It's when we've *had* our little family that I intend to have fun, not before, kind sir!' And I meant it too. But we quickly changed the subject because Mario had arrived in a little cloud of ciggie smoke with our chickens-in-a-basket.

I hadn't spoken to Madge for about a week and I didn't care particularly if I ever spoke to her again. There was no doubt in my mind that she had led Norman on, that dark night. Let's face it, it would have had to have been very dark or a normal man with eyes in his head would have run a mile. I didn't want to know what had happened the evening they had gone to see Ingrid Bergman and yet somehow I did. Madge had certainly been giving herself airs since she started doing ballet, plastering her mouth with the new 'Forbidden Fruit' lipstick, wearing tight black jumpers and scraped-back hair in a pony-tail. I heard she used to flounce around the Didgeridoo Coffee Shop, a popular rendezvous decorated with Aboriginal motifs and boomer-angs hanging on the walls. Her cronies were mostly ballet types, long-haired sissies from broken homes who wore leg warmers and too much Tweed aftershave. So what else is new?

My old schoolfriend Phyllis Balderstone told me she had seen Madge holding court to a tableful of ballet boys, all falling about laughing at everything she said. It made me feel sick to think of it.

Mummy was passing through a period of apparent lucidity and even cutting Roy's and Athol's lunches from time to time. She had changed her tune a bit about Norman, even giving us her blessing. 'You could do a lot worse, Edna,' she once declared, looking at a snap of Daddy in uniform on the mantelpiece and sighing deeply. I never quite understood what she had against my father except that he had let her down by not dying when she wanted him to.

'Just one little question,' she said one night over one of her famous grey minces. 'Where, prithee, are you two planning to live?' Frankly I hadn't thought about it, though Norm had muttered something about applying for a war service home, even though, technically, he had never been to the war. Before I could answer with a speechless silence, she added astonishingly, 'You could always stay here for the first few months. The boys are growing up fast and an old woman like me won't get in your way.'

'Oh, Mummy!' I exclaimed, overcome. 'We couldn't—'

'What's wrong with this house?' she retorted angrily. 'It was good enough for us. But I suppose your ladyship wants to live on the other side of the river since she's been hobnobbing with her Ladyship at the charm school!'

I felt awful because in one way I did have dreams of a mansion in Melbourne's most up-market suburb, Toorak (an old Aboriginal word meaning 'up-market suburb' – it's not a very difficult language). On the other hand, we couldn't stay with Norm's parents. Their home was tiny – though spotless – and without accommodation we would have to postpone the wedding indefinitely.

'Look,' I assented, 'we'd love to. But promise to say something, Mummy, if we get in the way.'

The weeks that followed were joyous ones for me. I skipped my lessons at Pixie's Academy, not just because I was so busy having fittings with Miss Wilmot for my organza bridal gown, but also because my decision to tie the knot with Norman was such a bone of contention.

Old Mr Everage was in his late seventies and had for many years been a senior quality controller at the IXL jam factory. He had sweetly offered to help Mummy meet the costs of our reception at the Moonee Ponds Town Hall and she had grudgingly accepted. Mummy's brother Uncle Vic was going to give me away in lieu of Daddy and I wanted Pixie for Matron of Honour, so I wrote her a very nice little note and kept my fingers crossed.

By then I had wedding fever and the idea of getting married to my shy, strong, sensible bridegroom seemed the most natural thing in the world. I must have been in a particularly good mood because one morning after Norm and I had spent a very romantic evening at His Majesty's Theatre seeing a flesh-and-blood performance of *Annie Get Your Gun*, I found myself ringing up Madge McWhirter.

'I'd like you to be one of my bridesmaids on the fifteenth,' I heard myself saying. 'Phyllis, Val and Ann are the other three and Miss Wilmot will need a few fittings.' There was a long pause on the other end of the phone. She was probably still a bit keen on Norman – *after one night at the pictures, for heaven's sake!* – so having to walk down the aisle with me would really rub salt into the wound. Not that I had meant it that way, *or had I?*

'Listen, I'd love to, darling,' she said in that stupid showbizzy way she'd only just picked up lately. 'Have you organised a cabaret for the reception yet? I'd adore to dance my "Waste Land" for you.'

I had heard from my spies that this pitiful creature had devised a sort of one-woman ballet based on a long futuristic poem by someone or other. One of the Tweed cologne and chunky sweater brigade would apparently lisp the words of this twaddle into a microphone while Madge writhed all over the stage in a laddered leotard, waving her grubby feet at the audience and swatting invisible flies with her pony-tail.

'Oh would you, Madge?' I said surprisingly. '*Promise* me you will. It would give everyone so much pleasure.' And as I anticipated it did. A guest told me later that he had never heard louder laughter in the Moonee Ponds Town Hall than during Madge's performance. She never danced again.

★   ★   ★

Madame Thelma herself no longer existed, but the beauty salon bearing her name was still very much the preferred rendezvous of appearance-conscious Moonee misses. I was having my hair tinted and permed in preparation for the Big Day as some of my mauve roots were beginning to show. I stayed a brownette for many years after that funnily enough, and it was only in the mid-seventies that I allowed my scalp to rejoice in Dame Nature's lilac legacy.

'What will you be wearing to the altar that's blue, Edna?' said my bridesmaid Ann Forbes looking like a funny bishop under the dryer next to me.

'Mummy's given me a blue satin garter,' I shouted back, 'and Nana's opal spider brooch is old, I'm wearing a new pair of lace mittens and I've borrowed Val's mother's silk hankie.' Actually I was going to reinforce my good luck by wearing *two* old items: Mummy's garter and also her bridal veil. It was a bit brittle but perfect, if I could stand the overpowering smell of mothballs.

That night we all had another fitting at Miss Wilmot's who was making all the frocks including my going-away outfit inspired by the designs in an Enid Gilchrist pattern book. Mummy was financing my beautiful ivory organza and guipure lace ballerina-length creation and luckily my friends were paying for their own dresses, including Madge. She always cried poor but I suspect that her auntie, old Mrs Findlay, was not short of the wherewithal. She was of Scottish origin, like a lot of Kiwis, and my father always used to say she had short arms and long pockets. The bridesmaids were also being fitted with ballerina-length frocks in lovely shades of apricot and oyster, lemon and apricot and apricot and lime. When I first saw Debbie Reynolds in *Bundle of Joy* –

one of my favourite films incidentally, next to *Citizen Kane* – it was spooky to see how familiar the frocks were to my own wedding ensemble. But Australia has always been a pioneer in the world of fashion.

On the Saturday before the biggest day of my life, we organised a Kitchen Tea at 36 Humouresque Street. All my friends popped in and the Hidden sisters had been working overtime to provide a scrumptious afternoon tea of butterfly cakes, passion-fruit sponges and date and banana logs. I think I have mentioned that Mummy no longer baked after her last nervous breakdown, but she did make 'hedgehog' out of broken biscuits, chocolate and coconut butter (copha). Of course no afternoon tea spread would be complete without Lamingtons, a cake indigenous to Australia and invented by Lord Lamington who was once governor of Queensland. They are simply cubes of sponge, coated with thick chocolate and rolled in coconut. Little did we know that only a few short years later Lamingtons could kill. I can't remember all the details but some of the ships carrying the desiccated coconut to Australia exclusively for the Lamington industry were found to have lepers on board whose bits were dropping off into the coconut, poor souls. As a result there was a serious dropping off in the sales of Lamingtons as well as that other Australian staple, coconut ice. A lot of women of my generation have told me that the Lamington scare of the fifties was the single most dramatic thing that had ever happened in their lives, and I can quite believe it.

It was lovely to see all my female friends sitting around at number 36, laughing and chatting and so obviously happy for me – even jealous. They had all brought gifts of course which were numbered and placed on the dining-room table. Then everyone was given a pencil and paper and they had to write down in order what they thought the gifts were. When the presents were opened, the one with the most correct answers would win a lovely box of Bronnley's French Fern toilet soap. To my slight annoyance Madge guessed my gifts most accurately though the prize, in her case particularly, was sorely needed. Mummy once said, somewhat wickedly, 'If you want to hide anything from Madge, put it under the soap.'

I got a lovely array of prezzies for my dream kitchen including two cheese graters, three spatulas, four cake testers, a cake-cooling rack, umpteen tea-towels and face flannels, a potato peeler, six egg cups, a Chinese back scratcher (!), measuring spoons, pickling jars, an egg beater, set of wooden spoons, a *Country Women's Association Cookbook*, a set of swizzle sticks, and from bridesmaid Phyllis, a beautiful matching cup, saucer and plate with a gold scalloped edge which you could almost see through, to go towards that crazy tea-set that we all collected in the fifties. Madge gave me a packet of steel wool (wouldn't you know), and my old teacher, Miss Godkin, gave me a 'jaffle' iron which was a pair of metal cups on long handles into which you squashed a sandwich and heated it until it turned into a scrummy jaffle – an early fifties' craze which might even be on the way back. My future mother-in-law, old Mrs Everage, gave me a lovely set of kitchen scales which I never used though the Church Opportunity Thrift Shop was very glad of them when I dropped them off there on my way home from her funeral.

I had given everyone an indication of colour, aqua actually, and I secretly hoped that I could persuade my mother to redecorate her rather drab cream and green kitchen to make it more up to date.

We had a lovely afternoon chatting and playing our silly games, Twenty Questions, Concentration and Pass the Orange Under the Chin, and my old biology teacher, Rosalee Tumbey, asked me to give her plenty of notice about when she should start knitting bootees, which Mummy thought was a bit uncalled for.

Every morning I had been peeping in our letter box, a damp cavity in the brickwork of our front gatepost. It was a favourite haunt of snails and often our morning post would be covered with their silver signatures. I was waiting for a reply from Pixie Lambell. Still no word however, and when I rang the office she was never there according to Cynthia. These days I suppose she would have been 'in a meeting' which as everyone knows means, 'Talk to her? *You've got to be joking!*' Was I getting a wee bit paranoid? I wondered. That was a word meaning 'twitchy' which Scrabble players were beginning to use pretty freely around this time. But I was very anxious for Pixie's approval and it peeved

me to think that she felt I was taking a step in the wrong direction
– and a big one a that.

Norm and I had taken to going to church pretty regularly to
see Canon George Lake after the service in the vestry for a few
quiet chats about Holy Matrimony. He was a bit 'prosy' as my
mother used to say and as he droned on about the Significance of
our wedding vows, I found myself looking at the tinned spaghetti
stain on his dog-collar and wondering if I shouldn't lick my
hankie and rub it off for him.

It's not that I was ever a Heathen; let's face it, in my time
I've been called an up-market Mother Teresa, but it's just that
whenever the Big Experiences of Life crop up my Renaissance
mind is usually off with the fairies. For instance, when I was
confirmed at church and the Bishop of Geelong put his hands on
my head to bless me, I tried like mad to have a Mystical Moment
but all I managed to do was to smell the Brylcreem he had slapped
on his scalp in the vestry seconds before sweeping on stage, as it
were.

I had chosen my hymn 'All Things Bright and Beautiful' and
since Norm was an ex-serviceman, Canon Lake suggested that
Mrs Tribe the organist could play the Marines Hymn which had
actually been on the hit parade. The tune came from a beautiful
opera called the *Gendarmes Duet* and everyone knew it.

> From the halls of Montezuma
> To the shores of Tripoli . . .

Norm hadn't been anywhere it said in the song but Canon
Lake brushed that aside.

On the eve of my wedding day, came a telegram:

DEAREST EDNA SORRY NOT SEEN YOU IN AGES STOP THANKS FOR
INVITATION BUT REGRET OFF TO PARIS FOR THE COLLECTIONS
STOP HOPE YOU KNOW WHAT YOU'RE DOING STOP REMEMBER
ME IF THINGS DON'T WORK OUT YOUR FRIEND PIXIE

How could she, how *could* she? I skreeked to myself, tearing
the telegram into confetti. She's wrong, she's wrong, I kept
repeating. It *will* work. I'll *make* it work! One day I'd show her,

then she'd be sorry! With a little ache in my heart which only anger seemed to dull I racked my brains to find another Matron of Honour. I hardly knew Auntie Rita, my father's sister, and she was dead too which ruled her out. Mummy's sister Ruby was out of the question as well, being a Salvo, so at the eleventh hour I finally approached my old teacher, Rosalee Tumbey, to step into the breach. She was, of course, thrilled and I wondered after I had asked her, if she would get the tweezers to her upper lip before the service, or even give herself a quick little scrape with her Gillette Ladyshave. It always amazed me that a biology teacher could be hormonally imbalanced without knowing it, just as world-famous artists always wear hideous ties.

Although Miss Lambell's pessimistic words kept ringing in my ears, I felt poised and confident of the future as I stood at last at the foot of the aisle that historic Saturday afternoon, my three lovely bridesmaids and Madge behind me, and sweet Uncle Victor nervously fingering his hired collar.

'Good luck, Edna,' whispered Miss Tumbey, giving my arm a little squeeze. I bent to give her a peck but feared the dear soul's untended bristles might ladder my fragile veil, I'm sorry but I did. The church smelt overpoweringly of furs and talcum powder and way down the aisle I saw my Norman waiting with his best man. Suddenly Mrs Tribe came down on the organ like a ton of bricks and the tune some girls would kill to hear thundered through the church. Miss Tumbey gave me a little shove and I was off down the aisle.

Holy Trinity, Moonee Ponds, was packed that day and I will never forget all those friends and acquaintances turning and beaming at me as I glided gracefully towards my groom with a deportment which I owed to an absent and estranged friend. Inside my veil the smell of moth repellent was making me feel giddy and I leant very heavily on Uncle Victor as we hit our spots at the chancel steps. The lovely simple service passed uneventfully except for the sound of Mummy snuffling and old Mrs Pollock's fifty-year-old retarded daughter making funny noises, bless her.

When Norm, his shoulders bedewed as usual from a hasty toilet, slipped the gold band over my finger I tried desperately to feel some transcendental emotion, but none was forthcoming. Was I expecting too much? I wondered. Or was Supreme Happiness a bit like one of those diseases that you don't necessarily know you've got – until someone catches it from you?

I must have been in a bit of a daze because Canon Lake had been saying, 'You may kiss the bride,' about five or six times before we gave each other an awkward little buss through Mummy's repellent tulle, prior to popping into the vestry to sign the register. Norm signed first and scribbled in his details and when I picked up the Parker to inscribe my name I did what we theatre-folk call 'a double take.'

'Norm, darling,' I said, 'you silly billy. You're so nervous you've got your year of birth wrong! Look,' I said, pointing to the wet ink on the register. 'You've made yourself an old man of thirty-three!'

Norm blushed. 'What of it, Edna?' he said. 'You're as old as you feel aren't you? And you need a mature bloke to look after you.'

'I certainly do,' I averred a bit loudly. 'But you said you were only twenty-three!'

'No I never, darling,' protested my husband. 'We never talked about it. Thirty-three isn't that old neither. Look at you, *you* look older than nineteen!'

'Don't darling *me*, prithee,' I exploded, feeling my lips go white. 'People are *amazed* when they hear I'm nineteen. How old do you think I look, Canon Lake?' I said, rounding on the troubled vicar.

'Please, please, young people,' expostulated the minister. 'This is neither the time nor place . . .'

Miss Tumbey, my Matron of Honour, was wringing her hands and the other witness, Graeme Batty, Norman's best man, looked anxious.

'Steady on, old man,' he said to Norm. Everyone seemed to think my husband was an old man, it was like a nightmare.

'You fibbed to me about your age, Norman, that's the truth of the matter,' I cried, my voice rising. 'You got me here on false pretences!'

'Sssh!' supplicated the harassed vicar. 'For Christ's – I mean heaven's, sake, keep your voice down please, Mrs Everage. The acoustics in this church are very sensitive.'

I looked over my shoulder for this 'Mrs Everage' the cleric was addressing, only to realise that he meant me! *I was someone else now* and I couldn't turn back. Norman was trying to put his arm around me.

'Give us a break, Edna,' he kept saying. 'Don't turn on the waterworks. Not today, kid. Just sign the book and let's get outta here.'

I scribbled on the register and as I did so an enormous tear burst on the page and turned most of my name into a runny Rorschach's blot. I narrowed my eyes and looked at Norman. His hair *was* very thin and there was some wrinkling under his chin, as well as all those crow's feet. I glanced at the backs of his hands for death spots, but they were yet to appear. Somewhere at the end of a long tunnel in my brain I heard Pixie's voice. 'Hope you know what you're doing what you're doing what you're doing . . .'

Canon Lake was peeping through the vestry door into the church. 'They're getting restless,' he said. 'Please settle this later. I've got another couple at five.'

I put my arm through Norm's. 'We're ready thank you, Canon Lake, we shouldn't quarrel now. After all,' I added, looking meaningfully at Norman, 'life's too short, *especially his.*'

Soon Mrs Tribe's version of the Mendelssohn Wedding March shuddered through the church and we walked down the aisle into a blizzard of confetti on the porch. The wedding photos are all at the University of South West Virginia and so are the local press cuttings which all say I looked radiant. A royal friend of mine incidentally says she gets the 'radiant' bit all the time, though mostly it's a million miles from the truth. Yet with all those happy people throwing things at us, the blue sky above and that lovely black Buick with its white ribbon, I was beginning to think again. After all there was a far bigger age difference between Charlie Chaplin and little Oona, and Norm *did* look young – in the right light. I mustn't let Pixie win, I thought, as we rumbled off to the Moonee Ponds Town Hall . . . and into the future.

CHAPTER XVI

Sandblasted Reindeer

NOT SELDOM IT happens, in the early togetherness of some couples, that a Trouble arises which they both desperately try to lock out of their lives for ever more. But it waits and thrives on their threshold and only at night when they are lying together in their marriage bed, does it creep back through the transom and settle down between them in the warm linen, never to go away.

That was my terrible fear about my tiff with Norm on the very steps of the altar; I wanted to pretend it hadn't happened and never speak of it again, but it cast its shadow all the same. What if I was married to a terminal fibber? The brighter the lights, the darker that little smudge of doubt and insecurity on my heart.

We had sat rather stiffly in the back of the bridal car; Norm was shaking the confetti from his cuffs and picking the multi-coloured polka-dots of paper out of his hair. He looked so solemn and forlorn, I had to giggle in spite of my mixed feelings.

'Oh, Norm!' I exclaimed, falling into his arms and shaking with laughter – and a few tears, 'I adore you just as you are, even if you're as old as Methuselah. I know we never discussed our ages, there's a lot of things we haven't discussed, but we both have a lifetime ahead to do it.' Norm's fingers dug into me a bit as he hugged me back.

'Ed,' he said, gently caressing my organza, 'my silly little Ed. You're the best kid in the world.'

My Reception didn't take up the whole of the Moonee Ponds

Town Hall but they partitioned part of it off and there were trestle tables covered with delicious things: cocktail frankfurters on toothpicks beside saucers of Rosella tomato ketchup, sausage rolls, asparagus rolls, corned beef, cold ham and chicken and lashings of salad garnished with sweetcorn and beetroot. Jugs of mildly alcoholic punch stood on all the tables as well as a modicum of ale for those who partook. On the stage Mrs Tribe, straight from the church, was arranging the sheet music of her profane repertoire on the upright Blüchner, whilst her husband set up his little drum kit.

'Oh, Mummy,' I said, as I took my place beside her at the door to greet the guests. 'It all looks lovely. It must have cost a fortune.' And then I added untruthfully, 'You shouldn't have!'

'Mr and Mrs Everage sweetly helped,' said my mother, nodding towards the almost senile couple who loitered nearby, looking as though they weren't quite sure why they were there or, indeed, what was happening.

'Although he's long since retired,' my mother whispered, 'Ern Everage got all the jam for the sponges and the tinned pears and peaches for the fruit salad from IXL for *nothing*.' Again that tiny shadow; I had always thought that that little old couple had had Norm late in life. Now I knew differently.

Roy and Athol grinned at me sheepishly in my bridal finery. They looked such big fellows in their nice suits that Norman had obtained for them at a staff discount from Ball and Welch, and they had their girlfriends with them too, Dawn and Jeanette. I know Mummy was worried about Dawn Purdie – sick with worry. She told me she was praying it was just puppy love because she had noticed a couple of deeply disturbing signs: the tiny gold crucifix around Dawn's neck for a start and the way the girl had once, during a Scrabble game, said 'haitch' instead of 'H'. Neither the mark of a good Protestant upbringing. Little did I know as I was being nice to her then, that this insipid fluff-ball would one day be simpering out of the cover of the Australian *Woman's Monthly* over the headline: EDNA'S NO DAME! BY HER SISTER-IN-LAW (EXCLUSIVE). Yuk!

The guests filed past, hugging and kissing me, pumping Norm's hand, and depositing their prezzies on a special table.

Some of the girls were still weeping a little from the beauty of the Service and only Phyllis Balderstone asked me in a whisper why we'd been so long in the vestry.

On stage the music had struck up. 'Charmaine' followed by Victor Sylvester's 'Exhibition Swing', played rather stiffly by the Tribe couple. Luckily the wrong notes were drowned by the laughter and growing hubbub of our happy guests and a few people were even dancing. Norm's best man, Graeme Batty, was blowing into a microphone and talking to a rather damp-looking youth with a Cornell Wilde★ haircut, who I realised was Madge's sissy sidekick for her cabaret later on. Frankly I couldn't wait.

I must have had a few too many punches that night for the lights and the speeches got blurrier and we were all laughing at anything. My three-tier cake was a triumph from the Hidden sisters, and as I took the big knife in my hands and guided it into the deep almond icing until I felt it penetrate the dark, cherry-studded fruitcake, I thought of my honeymoon night only a few hours off, and of what, if anything, might happen.

Old Mr Everage made a speech which no one could hear because the microphone kept piercing our eardrums with loud pinging noises and Norm said something short and sweet and very affectionate which made all the girls go, 'Aaah,' Mummy cry and me rather proud that my husband was a man of the world and not a silly acne-covered schoolboy.

By then, Norm's best man, Graeme, was definitely as full as a Catholic school, to use one of my late father's rather more uncalled-for expressions, and he read out some stupid and rather crude telegrams which caused most of us to look down with crooked smiles of embarrassment.

We had asked the Tribes to play our theme song, 'My Dreams Are Getting Better All the Time', and Norm and I danced, even though the tune they played was completely unrecognisable. Soon it was time for me to whiz home and get into my going-away outfit, this time a tailored burgundy suit freely adapted by Miss Wilmot from the *Enid Gilchrist Pattern Book*, so I missed Madge's 'Waste Land', though when I returned to the hall the guests were still weeping with laughter.

Norm's Vauxhall was ticking over outside the Town Hall and

★ An American movie star revered in Australia.

my brothers had tied old spaghetti and baked bean tins to the back bumper and scribbled 'Just Married' and other slogans all over the car with white tennis shoe cleaner. The guests swarmed out to see us off with rice and more confetti while Norm was getting our conveyance into gear. I stood on the running board with my slightly bruised bouquet and threw it high above the heads of my well-wishers. It landed with rather a loud smack and from the depths of the crowd came a little whimper of pain. 'Who caught it?' I called laughing as the car nudged off through the crowd.

'Madge did!' shouted Val Dunn. 'On the back of the neck!' I hoped it would bring her good luck, I did sincerely, though I later learnt that the impact of my wedding bouquet had wiped out an entire nerve centre.

We were to spend the night at the Windsor Hotel before honeymooning in Tasmania, that slightly spooky but lovely little island to the south of Australia, which is very often left off the map. We were going to bring the car over with us on the *Princess of Tasmania* and take two weeks pottering around before returning to Moonee Ponds and setting up house at 36 Humouresque Street. Mummy was going to lock her room and go back to Wagga-Wagga for a few months to stay with old friends. 'You won't want your silly old mother in your hair,' she had said, reading our thoughts. 'But now your father's gone I won't be around much longer anyway.' I've noticed that when people talk like that they usually go on living for ever.

The Windsor is a lovely old-fashioned hotel; the only one in Melbourne that didn't get pulled down during the next decade. The assistant manager showed us up to a big, slightly gloomy room with its own bathroom, so that we would not need to skulk up and down the passage to use the amenity as in other hotels. Hanging over the high double bed with its eau-de-nil quilt was an Original of waves breaking on a cheerless shore and the room also contained a big mahogany wardrobe, a locked cabinet full of knick-knacks and small china ornaments on glass shelves, an uncomfortable armchair and a small round wooden table with a glass top on which stood a half bottle of chilled Barossa Pearl with a card saying that it came with the Compliments of the

Management. Barossa Pearl was my favourite beverage in those days – in moderation. It was an Australian champagne-type drink from the Barossa Valley and people who had been Overseas always said it was of world standard. It had been served at our wedding for the toasts too and I'm afraid Norman and I had had an 'elegant sufficiency' of it already (to use one of my mother's favourite expressions).

Norm, still fully dressed, was spending rather a lot of time poring over the map of Tasmania, so I slipped into the bathroom to apply my night cream and prepare myself for whatever Dame Nature had in store for me.

I know that a certain element of my Readership – a small one I hope – is expecting to hear lurid and permissive details about my wedding night but this is not that kind of book, I'm sorry but it isn't. Call me old-fashioned, but I have never discussed my honeymoon horror stories with other women and I don't expect them to share theirs with me. In point of fact I know that men are more nervous about their nuptial night than women are, on the whole. Suffice it to say that *I* remember every detail of my wedding night.

Tasmania was lovely and I made sweet new friends there whom I still adore: June, Joan, Joyce, Reg and Judy and Ken and Berta to name but a few. In the Olden Days Tassie was a penal colony and because I am psychic I got quite a few very spooky vibes in some of the more remote nooks and crannies of that fascinating island. In fact I woke up on quite a few occasions screaming and kicking as I relived my own convict experiences in a Previous Life. I imagined that there were steel bands around my wrists and legs, pinning me down, and it was with relief that I woke up to discover that what I thought were handcuffs were only my husband's anxious fingers as he tried to soothe me back to sleep.

Once back in Moonee Ponds we commenced to redecorate and modernise the old house and I secretly worried whether Mummy would recognise the place when she at last came home from the Bush. Naturally we didn't touch her old room; it was locked anyway, though through the keyhole we could see she had started seriously to accumulate. Roy was off at military camp and there was some talk that he might even be sent to Korea, whilst little

Athol, already six feet tall, spent a lot of time staying with friends and studying accountancy at the Technical College.

Soon I had my aqua kitchen, well-stocked with wedding presents too, including five toasters (one pop-up), four waffle irons, a Sunbeam Mixmaster, a nest of salad bowls and a set of useful 'splayds' – a cross between a knife and a spoon, invented I think in Norway. At this stage in my life I had fallen in love with Scandinavian design as I would soon fall in love with teak and Thai silk. We had bought a brand new Frigidaire on layaway which hummed and occasionally shuddered quietly in the corner where the old ice chest had once stood. It's funny to revisit my old kitchen these days and see a little rope fence in front of my fridge and a sign on it in Japanese saying, 'Do Not Touch. Postcards Available at Desk'. We repainted the rather dark stained wood in the lounge a lovely off-white, took away the gloomy leadlite double doors leading to the dining room and replaced them with the sandblasted reindeer that I had always dreamt of. I also began to invest in art and soon over the fireplace hung Tretchekoff's hypnotic 'Chinese Girl with a Green Face'.

Life passed very happily; the boys were no trouble, Norman was an angel and Mummy wrote from Wagga to say she was staying an extra month with the Beauforts. As I hung out Norman's up-to-the-minute Y-fronts on our brand new rotary hoist which had replaced that dreadful old clothes line in the back yard, my cream Bakelite 'triple-throated' Kreisler radio sang cheerily through the duck-egg blue venetians:

'Shrimp boats are coming
Their sails are in sight
Shrimp boats are coming
There'll be dancing tonight!'

A few months later, I paid a visit to the Collins Street surgery of Mr Granville-Bantock, my gynaecologist. I had had a few giddy spells and queasy turns and our GP, Dr Joseph Holbrooke, had suggested that I see a specialist to be on the safe side. After a quick exploratory Mr Bantock looked up and said, 'May I be the first to congratulate you, Mrs Everage.'

About what I wondered? But I was not kept wondering for long.

Mummy came back from the country and didn't seem to notice all our home improvements. Norman had put louvred windows in the back veranda as a 'crash pad' for the increasingly absent boys and their old room had been turned into a gorgeous pink nursery. I must say my mother was wonderful when she had her wits about her and over the next few months made me put my feet up at every opportunity until the very last minute. Actually it was in the middle of *Singin' in the Rain*, when Gene Kelly was sloshing around in the gutter, that my own waters broke. I was rushed to Bethesda, Mummy's old hozzie, for the birth of little Lois.

I am now coming to a part of my story which has never been told. Not a word of what follows has ever been breathed to the press, whispered to the media or mentioned in books about my life. But this would not be the honest volume I promised I would write if I continued with the cover-up. It is a secret Norm and I kept for many years but now it must be told and I will be relieved when it is, as will my shrink, Dr Sidney Shardenfreude (whom I see for others).

Lois was a little sweetheart, more like Norm than me actually, and Mummy and I really spoilt her. I am not quite sure any more about the order of events that followed, but she was only a few months old when I decided to take her back to Wagga for a few days with Mummy to show her off to our old friends and rellies in the Bush. The Beaufort family were old farming folk from the district who lived on the wild outskirts of town in a pretty primitive dwelling with a tin roof and an outside toilet. Little Lois slept in her portable bassinette on the back veranda, well-protected by fly-proof netting from creepy crawlies, and Mummy and I shared a pretty lumpy mattress in the spare bedroom. My mother didn't seem to mind it but frankly I was used to city comforts and I felt strangely uneasy about the whole trip.

A couple of nights later, I woke up with a start and fumbled for my watch. Four o'clock! Lois should have had her bottle at one, I thought guiltily. What if she had been crying out there and I hadn't heard? Pulling on a pink chenille brunch coat, a present from Auntie Ruby, I rushed out to the back veranda. The fly-wire door was open and Lois's cot was empty. We never saw her again.

I must say after that I went a bit off my head and only Mummy and kind Dr Holbrooke helped pull me through. Norman was marvellous too, though he blamed himself for letting us stay in such a dump. Naturally the police and all kinds of people were involved and they eventually discovered an important clue on the back veranda: the unmistakable footprints of a rogue koala, previously thought of as a comparatively harmless Australian animal. Needless to say, word must have spread through Australia's marsupial community giving other creatures the idea because since then there has been a minor rash of copycat abductions, some even attracting media attention. If only animals could latch on to the idea of conservation, the world would be a much safer place. I have told this terrible story in a deliberately bland and detached way because I relive it every time I think about it and I know all women reading this book whose kiddies have gone off with marsupials will identify with me.

There was a kind of beatnik colony in the Bush, not far away from where little Lois disappeared and it is just possible that she may have been found and cared for by a nudist, vegetarian, 'Ban the Bomb' weirdo or else brought up to feel part of a caring koala family. When I saw that wonderful documentary *Greystoke*, I became more and more convinced that somewhere out there, up a tree perhaps, was my daughter. The Bush holds many secrets and little Lois is one of them. Whenever I go to the country I make a point of getting out of my limo, standing on the edge of the forest and calling out, 'Cooee, cooee!' – just in case. Perhaps somewhere in the world my lost daughter may be reading these words now.

At the time, delirious with worry, I babbled all these theories to Dr Holbrooke who smiled kindly and doubled the Bayer aspirin, but it took me a long time in limbo before my old zest for life – and the physical side of my marriage – came back to me. Frankly, Readers, every time Norm tried to commit intimacy, I would burst into tears. However, slowly the nightmare faded and I felt my old self. The day Dr Holbrooke looked up again and said, 'I think we had better book you into maternity next April,' my heart leapt for joy. 'But I trust you won't be treating the new arrival to an Outback holiday,' he added with a merry twinkle.

Mummy had pretty well become a recluse in her bedroom at this stage and even cooked her own meals on an electric frying-pan on her dressing table. My preparations for the new baby finally banished all thoughts of Lois from my mind and my special girlfriends whom I had taken into my confidence and sworn to secrecy were very 'supportive', before the word had even been invented!

I forgot to say that Madge McWhirter had gone back to New Zealand to stay with her mother's half-sister. I suspect that harbouring the Martha Graham of Moonee Ponds was too much of a handful for poor old Mrs Findlay. Very pregnant, I remember waddling down to Port Melbourne to see her off and I was naturally very sweet and affectionate to her, since I never expected to see Madge again. We'd lost touch a bit since my wedding and the tragedy, but she told me she was still having therapy on her neck where my bouquet dealt her a glancing blow. I tried to explain that it was lucky all the same, no matter what part of the body you caught it with, but poor old Madge looked none too hopeful as we parted. She gave me a little squash and whispered tearfully, 'You're my only true friend, Edna. Something tells me we'll be very close one day.' I sincerely hoped Madge wasn't psychic, though subsequent events have proved her horribly right. These days she is too close for comfort and even as I write these words, I can hear issuing from our bathroom the unmistakable buzz of her vibrator as she attempts to tone up those crêpy old throat muscles of hers.

Trevor (after Trevor Howard) Bruce (after my father) Everage was born at six thirty in the morning of a lovely spring day in September. When they told me he was a boy I quickly examined his damp little head with its pulsating fontanelle to see if he had inherited my wisteria hair colouring – a bit of a drawback for a boy. Fortunately he had his father's brownish fawn colouration.

Mr Granville-Bantock asked me if I wanted to have him 'done' or not, and I must confess that I asked him to be slightly more specific, since I had always thought that bubbas were 'done' when they were born, rather like cakes. More permissive readers will, of course, know what he meant and so did I in due course, but I had to ask the doctor's opinion.

'Well,' he enquired sapiently, polishing his glasses. 'Is your husband?'

I didn't know, but I promised to ask him later when the opportunity arose. In the end, I think Bruce (as we called him) did have a little op on his front bottie and I gather one is enough; it isn't an annual necessity like pruning, apparently.

Although I hadn't been able to nurse Lois, I managed with Bruce and he was quite a thirsty little man too, sometimes taking up to an hour on each. As I have said elsewhere, Dame Nature made me a bit on the flat-chested side but when Bruce, and then Valmai and finally Kenny came along, I filled out to meet the needs of their greedy little bubba-gums, and Mr Granville-Bantock told me quite recently that theoretically I was still capable of breast-feeding *at my age*! I related this story at a dinner party last Saturday night to my old friend Warren Beatty, and he looked quite interested. Needless to say, it's a handy thing for people to know especially if they ever get marooned with me on a desert island, or trapped in a lift, or both.

Brucie thrived and I was glad we were starting our family early. With Norm so much older I was keen to have youngsters whilst he was still comparatively mobile. Mummy came out of her shell, or rather cocoon, from time to time and babysat, though she was already clinically confused and starting to call people by the wrong names. If she addressed me, for example, she might sometimes say, 'Do you want me to defrost the fridge, Ruby . . . I mean, Nancy . . . I mean, Rita . . . I mean, Victor . . . I mean, Norm . . . I mean, Edna?' I never quite understood why my name always came at the end of the list and eventually I learnt to answer to the name of any relative, male or female, living or dead.

It was not long before toddler Brucie had a wee sister, Valmai Shirley, and we had a family photo taken by Melbourne's finest child photographer, Peter Fox. It was a black and white study, beautifully retouched and looking at it now I can see why we gave Valmai the second name of Shirley, because her little curly top-knot and adorable smile were spookily reminiscent of the famous child star. Later, Valmai's hair straightened out and I am sad to say a smile hasn't crossed her lips in years; certainly not in my presence. But that is another story of gross ingratitude which you will be dumbfounded to read, a few pages on.

Because of Lois, I spoilt Valmai and never smacked her, even when she once ate her own business. She won't thank me for mentioning that fact in this fearless best-seller I'll be bound, and I doubt if she will much enjoy her friends reading it either at the Trotskyist Women's Agit-Prop Guerrilla Puppet Workshop. 'Spare the rod and spoil the child' was another of my mother's more lucid sayings and perhaps if I had given Valmai the occasional pat when she was naughty I might still have a daughter I could be proud of.

There is a type of man who likes a big family and barely gives his poor wife a chance to get back on her feet. Norman was certainly not in that category. He was doing well at Ball and Welch holding a responsible position in the Accounts Department and always scrupulously bringing home his envelope on Friday nights. He was like a second father to my brothers too and very sweet to my mother considering that she mostly addressed him as 'Ruby'. I was always very houseproud and still am – that is to say I am now proud of all my houses. In those humbler days however, I got my chores over early, took Brucie to playschool and settled down in my brunch coat by the wireless with a cup of tea and a Bayers to listen to my favourite radio serials, just like any other normal young wife and mother on the planet. If I had ever had dreams of another life for myself, they were dreams only and very rarely did I feel a hankering to be doing something else, somewhere else, with someone else. Call me old-fashioned if you like. Like most women of my generation, I suppose I felt as though my biological cycle was complete and from now on I could put on weight, wear mules to the shops and neglect my depilatory. I shudder to say it but that was how I felt.

The papers were full of excitement because Melbourne had been chosen for the next Olympic Games and the bulldozers and jackhammers were working round the clock demolishing and pulverising the old-fashioned germ-prone Victorian buildings in case visitors flocking to the city from all over the world might think we were an old-fashioned backwater. Unfortunately they pulled down most of the hotels as well, and the probability of an accommodation crisis in 1956 threw the Powers That Be into a panic. Advertisements began to appear in the *Morning Murdoch* asking if ordinary housewives would care to billet foreign athletes in their spare bedrooms to ease the housing problem. Norman had made a couple of wonderful extensions to our house already: there was the back bedroom off the veranda of course, and he had managed to create two small, if low-ceilinged, children's bedrooms in the roof under the gables, accessible by a steep wooden staircase off the front hall. Our family was growing and so was I, for I was expecting my third and last infant – the world-famous couturier, Kenneth Montgomery Everage.

While I waited for Kenny's arrival during that Christmas heat-wave, my feet upon a hassock, a pair of bootees on five needles on my fluttering tummy, I watched little Valmai and Brucie romping in the lounge and peering at each other through those beautiful double doors, their chubby, sticky fingers tracing the outline of my sandblasted reindeer. I felt a very happy woman, complete, and at peace. Yet as always, when things seemed perfect, there was, deep in the core of me, that little niggling shadow I could not yet put a name to.

CHAPTER XVII

Mercury on
the Carpet

I T IS HARD for anyone knowing me today to believe that there was once a time in my life, long ago, when absolutely *nothing* happened to me. It was as though I had been snap-frozen, not by cryonics but by marriage. It was not a painful experience at the time; I was barely aware of it, but my hopes, ambitions and creative aspirations were 'on hold' as if my life were a colourful free-wheeling family-oriented video and Dame Nature had pressed the 'pause' button.

My tots were my life. Brucie was a solemn, conscientious little man, Valmai, the apple of her father's eye, and little Kenny – my favourite (between you and me) though I know we mothers shouldn't have them!

'He's just like you were, Victor,' my mother once said to me, during one of her periods of partial lucidity. I could not be sure whether Mummy meant Kenny was like Uncle Vic at that age or me, or someone else altogether, but mother adored my youngest as much as I did and I'm afraid we both spoilt him dreadfully.

Mummy was spending more and more time in her room either knitting, pottering or sifting through her old magazines and letters which were starting to form little piles on the grimy carpet. Considering that she regarded my poor father, who accumulated so few possessions, as a 'hoarder', she was a million times worse; though if anyone so much as set foot in her room with a box of moth balls or a duster she would have killed them. Mummy's room was strictly out of bounds to the whole family and sometimes a few days passed before we caught a glimpse of her. She must have got up in the middle of the night to fetch a few provisions from the kitchen and we only knew she was still alive by the smell of burnt baked beans wafting under her door at lunchtime and the burble of her wireless when she listened religiously to her daily serial, *Blue Hills*.

However, one day Mummy emerged triumphantly brandishing an old box of toys that I had played with as a kiddie.

'I found some toys for Kenny under my bed,' she crowed excitedly, proffering the cardboard box swarming with silverfish. 'You would have thrown this out if you'd had your way. But I knew it would come in handy one day,' she cackled. 'There's method in my madness.'

It was the first time I had heard my mother make a casual reference to her habitual frame of mind.

We opened the box and gave the mouldy contents a good squirt with Flit. There was my old teddy, chewed bald by eager bubba-gums, and a pink celluloid rattle which I certainly had no intention of letting Kenny suck, unless it was well soaked in Pine Sol. But at the bottom amongst a lot of kapok and dead moths lay a little toy that brought childhood memories leaping back to me. It was a small drum-shaped red box with a glass top containing a silver kidney of mercury. You rocked the box in your fingers so that the mercury broke up into beads and trickled into some little holes in the form of a star. I took it in my hand and looked at it in wonderment. Adult education types will know what I mean when I say that that tiny toy aroused in me the same gush of spooky memories that old Marcel Proust experienced when he munched that madeleine cake!★

'I thought we'd lost this years ago, Mummy,' I whispered huskily.

'It's made in Japan,' she snapped. 'You're lucky I didn't chuck it on the incinerator.' Then she added, more gently, 'Do you think Lois would like to play with it?'

She meant Ken but I felt a pang for my little lost Lo. And yet

---

★ See 'Transitional Objects and Transitional Phenomena', in *Playing and Reality* by D. W. Winnicott (1971).

I was thrilled that Mummy had found that magical toy again and Kenny, so like me, adored it too and quickly picked up the knack.

Kenny's hair was looking lovely by the way, with my natural wave, though I was relieved that he too, like Brucie, had inherited his father's brownish hair colouring. I somehow think that if I had bequeathed my own wisteria locks to my adorable little one, he would not have had all those big macho motorcycling friends he has today.

As the Melbourne Olympics drew nearer, I noticed that the newspaper advertisements requesting citizens to billet athletes became more insistent. Norm and I had a little confab. Somehow I felt it was part of our patriotic duty to offer a roof to one of these poor musclebound mites but the problem was *where*? The small home in Humouresque Street which, after all, my mother had only 'lent' us (if she could but remember), was already straining at the seams. Mummy holed up in her little room, Norm and I in the master bedroom, Valmai and Kenny in the nursery, Athol occasionally in the veranda room (Roy was still in Korea), whilst the new little attics housed Brucie and a small toy-strewn rumpus room.

'What about the old boxroom?' I said, suddenly looking up from the paper.

'It's no more than a cupboard, Ed,' retorted Norm who didn't much like the idea anyway. 'There's no windows and only a tiny ventilator, a bloke could go dippy in there in ten seconds flat.'

I remembered being locked in there by Mummy as a kiddie and the funny old convict outfit I found in a drawer. 'It might suit a pygmy,' I ventured optimistically. 'We could just about fit a camp bed in there and it *is* private!'

'You're the boss,' said Norm, as he usually did, going back to his paper.

To cut a long story short, after an initial interview, one of the Olympic Accommodation Officers paid us a house call and looked at our boxroom. I'd got rid of the cobwebs and even put a pretty little ballerina shade on the naked bulb, so that it looked quite cosy, if compact.

'I don't mind telling you, Mrs Everage, we're desperate,' said the official peeping into our boxroom.

'It's dark all right,' he observed, thinking aloud, 'but we got a shot-putter on the waiting list from a place called Lapland.' I must have looked blank for he continued informatively, 'I took a squizz at the atlas and it's way up near the North Pole. I'd reckon our bloke'd have to be a *bloody Eskimo*! This cupboard of yours will be a *palace* compared with the igloos those poor bastards call home.' He rubbed his hands together and shivered. 'Bloody freezing in here too, but I wouldn't be surprised if our Lapp didn't lap it up!' He laughed uproariously at his joke, gave me some forms to sign then and there, and drove away.

Frankly the Olympic Inspector had struck me as being a pretty crude type but then he *was* an Australian Government Official. However, Norm and I would receive quite a nice-sized reimbursement for our patriotic gesture, and in those days every little helped.

Throughout the early years of my marriage, I still kept in touch with some of my old girlfriends and imagine my pleasure and embarrassment when I learnt that Ann, Val and Phyllis had entered me in a competition without my knowing it! It was Australia's internationally acclaimed, award-winning 'Lovely Mother Quest'. All you had to be was a mother and not necessarily that lovely, judging by the photographs of other entrants in the *Morning Murdoch*. Under pressure from my girlfriends, I had sent in the latest Peter Fox family photo, and imagine our excitement when it appeared one morning on the front page with the headline: MOONEE MUM IN BID FOR TITLE. I knew I had only an outside chance, but it was fun all the same. The winner had to pass all kinds of tests for beauty, deportment and cookery. She not only had to be a caring mother with a beautiful speaking voice but she also had to be a regular subscriber to the *Morning Murdoch*. The lucky contestant would be chosen by a panel of judges and at the end of the year crowned Australia's Loveliest Mother by the Prime Minister's wife, Dame Pattie Menzies. The prize was a trip to London for two, all expenses paid, a wardrobe of frocks from the House of Delphine and 100 guineas spending money. I filled in the questionnaires and forgot all about it, I'm sorry but I did, though the yellowed cutting from the *Murdoch* is still glued to the back of the old kitchen door in the Dame Edna Museum (multilingual postcard available at desk).

In the midst of all this excitement the doorbell rang one Monday morning and the biggest man I have ever seen stood on the doormat. It was our athlete. You will not be surprised, I hope, to hear that I did not speak a word of his language, which I suppose is Lapp. So I did the next best thing and invited him across our threshold in loud broken English. He looked rather bewildered standing there with his suitcase but I made lots of beckoning gestures and he was soon sitting in Daddy's old Jason Recliner staring at the cup of tea and asparagus roll I had given him as though they were offerings from another planet. Frankly he didn't look like the Eskimo I was expecting, which is just as well because I had drawn a blank at three butchers asking for blubber, the Eskimos' most scrumptious dish. He actually looked comparatively normal though very tall and tanned, wearing a powder blue tracksuit with a jacket top and lace-up training shoes. He handed me his passport and pointed to his name: Uuno Klammi (pronounced: you-no clammy!), not the kind of name that would help an Australian youngster get on in the world I'm afraid. But then in those days, except for a few Aborigines and Balts*, Australia was a homogenous and monoglot society, and the phone book was mostly full of real names; nice names of English and Irish origin. The only weird ones we ever encountered were on American movie credits; like Jesus-Maria Fong, Barry K. Penderecki, Brigitte Stassinopoulos, and Yehudi Waldheim Jnr. Every time names like that came up on the screen, Australian audiences laughed uproariously. But now I'm sorry to say, with the offbeat elements who have flocked to my homeland over the last twenty years, we no longer lag behind in the spooky name department.

My main worry was how Mr Klammi was going to fit into the boxroom. At a rough guess he looked about two feet longer than the little bed I had squeezed in there. But by a system of waving, beckoning and smiling I got him to the door and after peeping in he said something in Lapp which didn't particularly sound like

---

* Fugitives from the Baltic States.

'Call this a bedroom? You'd have to be joking!', so I gathered he must have been used to a good deal worse.

That evening I gave a little welcoming tea for our athletic guest, and Brucie, Valmai and little Kenny stared at him with eyes like saucers. Norm and I tried chatting to him in Australian, very slowly and loudly, but he just smiled and nodded in a bewildered way so we gave up in the end. Only Mummy who had come out of her shell and actually put on a bit of face powder (mostly on her shoulders), wittered away and actually tried to feel his muscles which struck me as a bit OTT★ at the time. In bed that night, Norm summed it up. 'One thing's for sure, Ed,' he said in the darkness. 'Old Klammi's a bit of a dark horse if you ask me.'

I made a little 'mmmmn' of agreement.

'At this rate I reckon we'll be none the wiser about our guest when he pushes off after the Games.'

Days passed. Uuno sat down for meals, ate enormous amounts of steak, patted the children rather roughly on the head and went out to the backyard where, stripped to the waist, he did press-ups on the lawn and pull-ups on the rotary hoist all morning, not unobserved by the neighbours either. Mummy, who was making Kenny a romper suit at the time, sometimes used to sit in an old deck-chair under our pittosporum tree watching this performance and knitting. After lunch our guest would be picked up in a car by some other very tall men in tracksuits and taken off somewhere Olympic for the rest of the day. He never complained about his room, though I peeped in at an early opportunity and noticed that he had folded up the camp-bed and was sleeping on a blanket on the floor! On top of his suitcase was a little framed photograph of a woman with blonde plaits, smiling and showing a lot of gum. Nice-looking for a Lapp, I suppose, but I would have thought that a tall handsome Olympic athlete could have done a little better for himself.

It is hard to believe that a family in a crowded house like ours could have accommodated such a large if silent person without being constantly aware of him, but the fact is, we weren't. Apart from eating huge meals, he was no trouble at all and at night, at about half past eight, he gave us all a polite little nod and disappeared into his cupboard.

★ Polite Australian usage for 'over-the-top.'

One day Norm came home with a very big and very heavy parcel.

'I reckon if we've got an Olympic athalete [*sic*] under our roof, we might as well take a squizz at the Games,' he said enigmatically, pulling off the brown paper wrapping. It was our first television set, a beautiful teak-veneered Astor 21. What a wonderful husband I had! And how educational this would be for our little ones who settled around it like moths almost as soon as the first bluish-grey image quivered into focus.

Naturally after that our family evenings took on a new pattern as every night we all sat enthralled around the instrument. Our neighbours followed suit and soon, as dusk fell, every living-room window in our street flickered with that ghostly blue light, like a will o' the wisp. That's when Mummy became a bit of a TV addict too; but loyal to her favourite radio shows she would always retire early and we would hear the key turn in her bedroom door, followed soon after by the muttering of her Mickey Mouse Mantle model. I tried watching the Olympic Games in spare moments between children, but I'm afraid I never got so much as a glimpse of our Lapp shot-putting, or whatever he did. Besides, the Lovely Mother Quest was hotting up and I had started a refresher course in deportment in the evenings. It brought memories of Pixie Lambell flooding back. Where was she now, I wondered, six years down the track? What a help and support she would be, if only she hadn't 'dropped' me for wanting a normal life.

'Normal'? As I stood one morning at the kitchen sink, up to my wrists in the grey water on which peas floated, and gazed out through the already chipped duck-egg blue venetians at the back garden where Mr Klammi performed his umpteenth press-up, I wondered how 'normal' my life really was. Was there another 'normal'? I wondered, as I spied my mother casting off madly amongst the bushes, and a few feet from her, the limbering Lapp. Norman was rushing out, late for work again.

'Hooroo, Ed. See you later,' he said barging into the kitchen and grabbing his jacket off the back of a chair. There were a few little teardrops in my eyes so I didn't glance over my shoulder at my departing husband.

'Bye, darl,' I croaked. Suddenly from the lounge came a crunching noise accompanied by a sharp and very uncalled-for expression from Norm.

'What is it?' I exclaimed, squelching my tell-tale eyes with the back of a wet wrist.

'That bloody Kenny,' I heard Norman cry. 'Told him a dozen times not to leave that stupid doover in the middle of the lounge. Getting mercury up off a carpet is a real bugger.'

I rushed in to the scene of the disaster. Norm was looking down at my precious little crushed relic with a baffled expression.

'I'm late, Edna. I gotta go,' he said, 'but it was *right in the middle of the floor!*'

When he had gone to work I sat in an armchair for a long time feeling sad and empty as though my life were a toy, full of little holes which needed to be filled with bright silver beads. I then went and got the dustpan and brush. Norm was right about the mercury.

★   ★   ★

It was one of those rather hot, sultry nights we used to get in Melbourne before the hole in the ozone layer changed everything. I had the bedroom window open for a bit of air but the curtains didn't stir. As I lay there unable to sleep, Norm heaving and snuffling a few feet away, I heard, in the distance, the iron rumble of an all-night tram. Occasionally a fan of yellow light opened and closed on the bedroom ceiling as a car passed down Humouresque Street. I must have dozed off, for I was back at school showing the other girls my little mercury star box, when a tall boy in a powder blue tracksuit appeared out of nowhere, smiling at me. I tried to give him my box as a present but he didn't seem to understand and kept shaking his head.

'Please, please,' I said, 'take it.' But no words came, my mouth just opened and closed drily. Then the school bell rang.

Not long ago I told this dream to Dr Sidney Shardenfreude (whom I see for my children) and I asked him point blank what it meant. His reply was typical I'm afraid, and made me wonder, quite frankly, why I keep pumping money into his practice. He looked over at me on the couch and said, 'Vot do *you* sink it means, Dame Edna?'

Couldn't you punch a person like that in the nose?!!

I was still dreaming and the school bell was still ringing. I seemed to be swimming very slowly to the surface, trying to reach the bell to stop it, then I woke up. The phone was ringing in our lounge; ringing in the way phones do that have been ringing for quite a while and are about to stop. I jumped out of bed and stumbled across the hall and into our sitting room, without even turning on the light. Plucking up the black Vulcanite receiver of our 'Coronation Model' I sleepily challenged the transmitter. 'Yes, this is Edna Everage,' I yawned.

'Kevin Farelly of the *Morning Murdoch* here,' said the phone. 'Are you sittin' down?'

'What time is it?' I said, squinting in the direction of our dark mantelpiece at my lovely Drummond's art deco chiming eight-day in figured walnut with a chrome bezel.

'Sorry, Edna,' said the phone, 'it's two in the morning, but we got a big story breaking tomorrow, and we need your comments – and a photo.'

'I'm sorry, Mr Whatsername,' I said, trying to make my neck click, 'I'm half asleep. What do you want exactly?'

'You've won the Lovely Mother Quest,' came the voice. 'We've had a tip-off. Our photographer Trevor is on his way around to your place now so hop into your glad-rags so we can get a nice pickie for the front page.'

'I'm sorry?' I heard myself exclaim. *'I'm sorry?'*

'Oh, and congratulations!' he said and hung up.

For a minute or two I sat in the darkness making sure I wasn't dreaming. The rest of the house must have been sleeping like the dead not to have heard that phone, I thought.

Suddenly, I felt a great warm rush of excitement and pride, quickly followed by a little nagging doubt. Was it a hoax call perhaps? Some jealous person playing a sick joke on me? However, the wave of excitement soon returned and I *had to tell someone*. I rushed back to our bedroom. 'Norm, Norm,' I cried, shaking the damp Viyella bundle, 'I've won it, I've won the Quest!' But he was dead to the world and only grunted. I shinned up the little wooden stairs where Brucie lay sprawled in his bed, then down again to the nursery where the little figures of Kenny and Valmai slept, mouths open, in funny positions.

'I've won it,' I whispered. 'Darlings, *I'm a Lovely Mother!*'

The boxroom door was ajar. Why not? I thought. He won't know what I'm talking about but I'm *so* excited, I've got to hug someone! Athletes are always hugging each other. He'll know it's good news. This was long before I became a close friend of Desmond Morris, but I was already, even then, pretty fluent in terms of body language. A second later I realised the boxroom was empty! His little rug, neatly folded in a corner. Where was he? I gasped. Had he done a moonlight flit or was he perhaps jogging around the block? My conjectures were interrupted by the sound of muffled music:

> Love and marriage, love and marriage,
> Go together like a horse and carriage . . .

It was Mummy's wireless. She must have left it on, or else she was still awake. 'I must tell her my wonderful news, my wonderful, wonderful news.' I ran down the hall and turned the handle on her door. It was unlocked and I walked straight into her room, stumbling over a dusty pile of *Woman's Monthly*s and accidentally kicking an empty baked-bean tin. The pink-shaded lamp with a candlewick trim glowed beside her bed. On it lay a male in his birthday suit doing vigorous press-ups.

'Mummy!' I called, turning quickly away out of modesty. 'Where are you?'

'I'm here!' came my mother's muffled voice from amongst the bedclothes. 'Where do you *think* I am prithee?'

'But, but . . . who's that?'

'Uuno.'

'I *don't* know! But, I think I know . . .'

'My friend, Uuno Klammi, if you *must* know!' replied the woman who bore me, from somewhere under the Lapp.

The front doorbell chimed loudly. I froze.

Heaven help us, I thought. THE PRESS!!

Mr Klammi was carrying on regardless.

'Can't you hear the doorbell, Edna?' shouted my mother as I stood there, immobilised by panic and disgust. 'And close the door after you! I never thought a daughter of mine would enter a room without knocking. I hoped I'd taught you nice behaviour.'

The doorbell rang again and now someone was hammering at the door.

Nice behaviour, I thought, with a sick shudder. How long has *that behaviour* been going on? While I struggled to keep the home going, my mother had been locked in her room night after night, holding her own Olympic Games! On the evidence of a quick glance it seemed she was working up to the Decathlon.

'Coming!!' I bawled through the rippled glass of our front door. 'Coming!' And I dashed into the bedroom, threw on my brunch coat and stabbed at my mouth with Helena Rubinstein. As I opened the door there was a burst of flashlight.

'Kevin Farelly,' said an ambitious-looking young chap in a crumpled suit. 'Howsit feel?'

'Feel?' I retorted weakly.

Norm was coming to in the bedroom and I heard his voice. 'What is it? Who are they, Ed?'

Mr Farelly lit a cigarette while two other photographers and a television crew set up lights from a van parked outside.

'Yeah. Howsit feel to scoop up the big prize when you're just an ordinary Melbourne housewife living in a suburban house where nothing exciting has ever happened?' he interrogated.

I could have given him a big story then if I'd wanted to but, call me old-fashioned, I've saved it up for you.

The next morning I could have looked better on the front page, but I could have looked worse. They got an interview with Norm in his pajamas saying that all he wanted was the best for me and that he would hold the family fort while I went overseas. Mummy, thank heavens, lay low. Our guest didn't appear at breakfast and I was relieved to discover his room empty. Mummy of course sulked for several days and I confess I didn't tell Norm because I didn't know how to. But I boiled Mr Klammi's blanket – twice.

I was plucking a few dry underthings off the hoist for the official cocktail party in my honour that evening, when I noticed Mummy sitting under the lantana bush, knitting sullenly. I stared at her coldly, with narrow eyes, as she looked up at me over her needles. It was a lewd and shameless look which I hope no daughter reading this ever glimpses on a parent's countenance.

'He's gone,' I said, 'and I don't think we'll be seeing him again.'

'He's one of the world's best shot-putters,' said my mother foolishly.

'Well,' I replied, and I never mentioned the matter again, 'from now on he'll be putting it somewhere else.'

CHAPTER XVIII

Que Sera Sera

MY FRIEND MOTHER Teresa comes to London about once a year for the Harrods sale. It's not the merchandise; she just likes sleeping in the street. Last time we chewed the fat she told me, 'Edna, true happiness only comes through Renunciation,' or words to that effect. Tess was right. Let's face it, Possums, when isn't she? And I'm here to tell you that I began my Life of Renunciation years ago: I decided to renounce Obscurity.

Call me old-fashioned, but since then I've never shunned the limelight. Even in those far-off days when my career was just beginning I must have had a 'good self image' years before that phrase was invented. A hairdresser friend of my son's called Hazel once told me, 'If you've got it, flaunt it,' and his words hit the spot with me. Frankly, Possums, I never say no to a little media coverage, which is an incredible paradox when you think what an intensely Private Person I really am. Yes, Privacy and Vulnerability is my bottom line at the end of the day.

When the Australian press announced that I had won the Lovely Mother Quest I got my first tantalising taste of publicity. Suddenly there was a celebrity in Humouresque Street, Moonee Ponds and it was ME! The Mayor of Moonee gave me a little reception where I was able to wear one of the gorgeous frocks I had chosen at Delphine's as part of my prize. That nice reporter Kevin Farelly who had first broken the news (and the story) became a kind of unofficial press officer and arranged profiles and interviews for me in national newspapers and journals. Soon, almost unbelievably, my face was peeping out of the front cover of the Australian *Woman's Monthly*, surrounded by gladioli – my lucky flower. Norm took it all in his stride knowing that my feet were planted firmly on the ground and my little wisteria head was, and is, the last one in the world ever to get swollen. All that in spite of autograph hunters at our front gate, and an avalanche of fan mail from grateful women – some overseas – who were tickled pink by my victory.

I appeared on a couple of TV quiz and talk shows too, where I astonished the other panel members with my quick wit and clever answers, and the producers always wanted to sign me up for a series. On a popular talent show I even sang that beautiful anthem 'Advance Australia Fair' with orchestral accompaniment, and astonished even myself with my powerful yet lyrical interpretation. They used epithets like: 'Mrs Everage, you're a natural' and 'You're so fresh, so colourful' – and that was when TV was still black and white! I am not being conceited here by the way, Readers, just truthful, and if this book is not truthful *forget it*!

Throughout this time until my Crowning Ceremony and my departure for England on the *Himalaya*, I continued to lead the normal, day-to-day life of a housewife and mother. The children's sandwiches were cut, my mother, though disgraced, was still fed, and when Norm came home from Ball's at night there was always something grey and tasty in the oven.

One Saturday morning, the front door chimed (a lovely contemporary innovation that had replaced the funny old-fashioned bell on the front door which you used to have to tweak).

Such a pretty child stood on my 'welcome' mat; blonde ringlets, adorable smile and spotless sunfrock.

'Are you Mrs Everage?' she asked in a slightly cultured voice as I dried my housewife's hands on a 'Killer Toads of Tasmania' hand-crafted, Irish linen, Taiwanese tea-towel. She handed me an envelope.

'It's a letter from Mummy,' she said. 'May I come in while you read it?'

She sat demurely with a curious grace and poise on our Genoa velvet couch while I read the letter and read it again. Then I picked up the telephone and dialed her mother's number, smiling across at the radiant child.

'Mrs Newton-John?' I queried.

My interlocutor replied in the affirmative.

'I understand you would like little Olivia to pop in and see me on Saturday mornings for a chat and the occasional singing lesson.'

The girl's mother concurred.

'But I am not a trained singer,' I protested. 'And you say in your letter that you want Olivia to absorb some of my wonderful aura and star quality. I'm afraid you flatter me, Mrs Newton-John!' I concluded modestly.

The perspicacious parent then launched into a catalogue of compliments which I would blush to repeat. Suffice it to say that she had seen some of my TV appearances, read my frank and wholesome interviews and could think of no better guide and mentor for her daughter, who had already shown marked signs of artistic talent.

'A fee is out of the question, Mrs Newton-John,' I remonstrated. 'If you wish me to "nurture" your daughter – to use *your* expression, I will do my best. I am off to the old country in a few months' time after my Coronation. However when I return I will be happy to go on seeing her on Saturday mornings for a long as she wants to come.'

As we terminated this, as it happens, historic conversation, I swear I heard that charming woman on the other end getting a bit weepy with gratitude.

Although the next few months were very full ones for me, with more TV appearances, free beauty treatments and requests from cosmetic firms and garment manufacturers to endorse their products, I looked forward to my hour or so on Saturday morning with gorgeous Livvy. We would warble away together, some of the latest hits as well as classical arias like 'Home Sweet Home' and 'The Bonny Banks of Loch Lomond' and that child sang like a bird. My own young family often joined in, though Valmai I fear had great difficulty in holding a simple tune; a disadvantage which in later life has not prevented her from accepting major singing roles in some of the lesser known plays of Bert Brecht at the Trotskyist Women's Agit-Prop Guerrilla Puppet Workshop.

My 'fame' was obviously spreading, for Olivia was not the only talented child whom parents begged me to groom, and perhaps influence. Some delightful young brothers lived nearby with their English parents, Mr and Mrs Gibb, and soon Barry, Maurice and Robin joined my little Saturday group, singing and strumming on their plastic banjos, along with a tall rather sallow young lass. Her talents did not seem to lie in the musical sphere and I had to tell her poor mother the truth as nicely as I could. Poor Mrs Greer was heartbroken, for she was a devoted parent and struck me as being a very nice and genuine person.

'Couldn't she just pop in for a little chat?' she pleaded. 'She adores you and you stimulate her more than you know.'

What could I say but yes, and even today Germaine tells me she cannot find words to express her gratitude.

What a funny change had taken place in my life almost overnight. Norman and I saw perhaps less of each other than we should have, though generally we managed a little chin-wag late at night in the velvet darkness of our bedroom.

'Big day tomorrow eh, Ed?' came that dear voice.

'Yes, Norm. It's my Coronation at last, so please try not to wear that shirt with the bloodstain on the collar, there's a pet.'

'Reckon you'll be away in England for the best part of six months.'

'Don't make me feel guilty. It's the chance of a lifetime, Norman, and the children understand and want me to be happy. You could've come. I asked you . . . *didn't I?*'

'You'll have a lot more fun hitting the high spots with your mate Val Dunn and you know it, Ed. I'd only be a wet blanket,' mused my husband, fishing.

'Oh, Norm,' I replied, stroking his winceyette, 'I'll miss *all* of you, but think of the lovely slides I'll bring back. And I won't spend all my prize money, promise I won't,' I added rashly. 'We can buy you a new . . . well, a new hernia belt.' My husband had developed a little problem in his groin but it wasn't too serious according to those who'd seen it.

'You're one out of the box, Ed!' Norm declared. 'And it's a real treat to see you coaching those youngsters on a Saturday morning too. . . .' We talked for a while of my little 'pupils,' of my hopes for them, their quaint sayings and their growing dependence upon me. I would miss them while I was away.

Then I told Norm of the places in England I planned to visit, the flesh-and-blood shows I hoped to see. I talked of my aspirations, my longings and my fears until a gentle heaving of the damp-flannel hump beside me and the smacking of dry lips in the dark told me my husband had had an early visit from the Sandman.

★   ★   ★

I pulled up the warm collar of my new coat but the wind still seemed to go right through my bones. My gloved fingers tightened around the rail and I tasted salt on my lips. It was still hard for me to believe that I was on board the *Himalaya*, sailing for England, the last little bit of Australia still a grubby shadow on the horizon whilst all around me that heaving cabbage-green water marbled with foam.

'Better go back to our cabin and get ready for dinner I suppose. Don't know about you but I'm freezing.' It was Val Dunn, my old girlfriend, at my side, rugged up and red-nosed, shouting above the driving wind and squawking gulls.

'I hope my bubbas are all right,' I said out loud as we negotiated the steep stairs down to our second-class cabin, clinging to the banisters for dear life.

'Ann Forbes adores them, Edna,' Val reassured me, 'and Kenny and Valmai get on so well with little Ian and Jeanette.'

I was grateful Ann had volunteered to take my three youngsters while I was on my dream trip. They would have been too much of a handful for Norm even though he had offered, and Mummy was no longer a stable influence, I'm sorry but she wasn't. I felt that if my father had been alive to see her recent behaviour, he would have turned over in his grave.

Norman had assured me that he could 'hold the fort' though I was a teeny bit worried on the night of my Coronation as he was popping in and out of the little boys' room all night. He later confessed that he was having a few 'plumbing problems', and as I tottered around in the little cabin Val and I shared, selecting a nice frock for dinner (first sitting), I wondered how I would cope if my husband were ever seriously indisposed. 'No problem,' came a little voice inside me as I realised how lucky I was to have once been Florence Nightingale.

Over the next week at sea the weather got rougher and I could barely focus on my *Kon Tiki* Expedition. I was Queen Boadicea in a Previous Life but I doubt if she spent a lot of time feeling awful under a rug, playing housie-housie in the Indian Ocean. Frankly I couldn't concentrate on those organised games though Val really threw herself into them. I suspect she rather fancied the Purser, a rather dapper American from the USA called Chip. She was certainly pathetically grateful to me for choosing her as my companion on this all-expenses-paid holiday of a life-time.

I was really starting to get into the swing of shipboard life by the time we had reached the Suez Canal and we all went ashore for the day to buy *pouffes* and visit the Sphinx and the Pyramids. Naturally those old Egyptian relics brought back the odd Past Life Memory. I think it was my American friend Shirl who told me that she once *was* the Sphinx, but since I didn't know her in those days, I failed to spot the resemblance.

When it came to the last big fancy-dress Ball on board before we hit the English Channel, I'm afraid I opted out, though I might as well have gone, the din kept me awake half the night. I lay there alone in the little cabin imagining Val in the arms of her Purser and I could hear the band playing 'Love Letters in the Sand', 'Magic Moments' and the lovely song that seemed to haunt me in that pivotal year of my life:

> When I was just a little girl
> I asked my mother what would I be
> Will I be famous, will I be rich
> Here's what she said to me:
> Que sera sera . . .

Where was *my* life heading? I wondered, restlessly. This free trip, this sudden limelight. Was Dame Nature trying to tell me something? Would I too be famous? Rich even? I drifted off to sleep and dreamt again of that wonderful intoxicating night before we sailed from Port Melbourne when I was crowned Australia's Loveliest Mother. Gracious Dame Pattie Menzies, wife of Sir Robert, Australia's last refined Prime Minister, put the satin sash over my bosom and the beautiful coronet on my head. Around my shoulders was a sumptuous red cloak edged with white fur just like the Queen wore on the calendar. Although Delphine's and other élite Melbourne couturiers had given me tons of lovely new frocks, I wore one of Miss Wilmot's that night, freely adapted from the *Enid Gilchrist Pattern Book*. It was a halter-neck ballerina in cyclamen Thai silk with an aqua tulle stole and a smidgen of aqua underskirt showing. Thai silk was hardly known in Australia then, though it caught on like wildfire in the sixties. I think our womenfolk were a wee bit afraid to wear it at first because they didn't quite know where it had come from; or how spotless its weavers were.

Then the Chairman of the Quest, Sir Colin Herring, made a lovely speech and cameras flashed as the Editor of the *Morning Murdoch* presented me with a cheque for 100 guineas and an envelope containing my round trip tickets for two on the luxury liner *Himalaya*. After that there was a wonderful party in the ballroom of the Hotel Australia. Norm had bought a brand new dinner suit, utilising his Ball and Welch staff discount, and a stylish bow tie you actually had to clip on yourself.

Sick with excitement I was travelling up in a lift to the ballroom when I observed, too late, some Palmolive shaving cream on Norm's left lobe, another bloodstain on his collar and quite a few wisps of hair on his black barathea shoulders. I was trying to brush these off when the lift doors opened and for the first time in my life I smelt the Perfume of Success.

Entering that glittering ballroom, I did a double-take as we theatrical folk call it, when I realised that amongst the fashionable throng laughing and sipping champagne like ordinary people were some of Melbourne's internationally acclaimed TV personalities. There was 'Happy' Hammond chatting to lovely model Gretta

Myers and Norman von Nida the golf champion sharing a joke with Panda, one of Australia's most beautiful women. Dame Enid Lyons wearing a stunning inhumanely culled silver fox stole, caught my eye and smiled graciously. The distinguished man beside her looked very like Sir Bernard Heinz, conductor of the internationally acclaimed Melbourne Symphony Orchestra. My heart missed a beat but I sailed into the room with all the seeming confidence and poise of a fully paid-up, card-carrying glamour-puss. Famous faces were everywhere and Sir Colin Herring introduced me to a galaxy of celebrities. Some of them even kissed my hand and bowed as I was presented to them.

In a corner of the crowded room beside an enormous arrangement of flesh-pink glads, stood a well-dressed couple, their backs turned, whom I felt I knew.

'Mrs Everage,' said Sir Colin, 'I want you to meet two of our distinguished judges.'

The couple turned. 'Miss Pixie Lambell and Sir Charles Eltham!' My jaw dropped as Sir Colin continued, 'May I present your unanimous choice, Mrs Edna Everage.'

There was a long and rather funny pause as Pixie and I stared at each other.

'Don't tell me you've met already?' said Sir Colin.

'Heavens no!' cried Pixie quickly, giving me a little signal. 'But I wish we had, don't you, Charlie?'

'I certainly do!' averred the artist, winking broadly.

I realised that Norm was standing awkwardly a few paces behind me, combing his thinning hair and looking at his nails, and for the first time in my life I felt a wee bit embarrassed by him, I'm sorry but I did.

When Sir Colin had drifted off to talk to the famous actress Zoë Caldwell, Pixie took my hand.

'It wasn't because we knew you, Edna, please believe us. Your photos and credentials were light years ahead of the others.'

Still holding Pixie's hand I blushed, and thought I might even cry.

'I'm not one for idle compliments, Edna,' Pixie resumed, 'but you look wonderful tonight. You threw away your last chance. I beg you to seize this one with both hands - because you've got what it takes, and believe me, *the sky's the limit.*'

'I'll drink to that!' chuckled Charlie, immersing for a moment his moustache in a glass of champagne. I heard a cough over my shoulder.

'Oh,' I exclaimed awkwardly, reaching behind me for my spouse's clammy hand. 'I don't think you've met Norman, my er . . . husband.'

Norm pumped their hands so vigorously wine was spilt.

'Pleased to meetcha,' he said, when I had performed the introductions. Then looking at Charlie quizzically, 'Hang on, aren't you the joker who put the hard word on my Ed. . . ?'

I gave him a little kick, not hard, just enough to cause intense pain.

'Norm is always mixing people up,' I interposed quickly, but what could have been an 'incident' was providentially redeemed by an announcement from the compère, famous crooner Geoff Brooke, wearing a midnight blue tuxedo.

'Dame Pattie, my Lord Mayor, Archbishop Mannix, ladies and gentlemen. I call upon the winner of this year's Lovely Mother Quest Mrs Edna Everage and her husband to lead us in the first dance of the evening.' Everyone looked at us, clapping and smiling and Dennis Farrington's Augmented Dance Band struck up 'Que Sera Sera'. Norman looked at me blankly.

'Come on,' I hissed. 'Have you got two left feet? They want us to do a lap of honour.' And so we did, a little clumsily perhaps with me leading as hard as I could and trying not to look too much taller than Norman even though I was. Yet inside I was very relieved that a nasty moment had only just been averted.

. . . Whatever will be, will be
The future's not ours to see . . .

* * *

'Wake up, Edna, wake up! It's the lights of England!' It was Val still in her glad-rags but with suspiciously smudged lipstick and more than a hint of sherry on her breath, shaking my shoulders.

She was smoking too, and had a glass in her hand. It seemed to take me ages to decide where I was. I had just been dancing with Norm in the Hotel Australia ballroom, so what was all this twaddle about the lights of England?

I sat up, suddenly aware of the present.

'Come on, Edna. Throw something on and come upstairs. Everyone's on deck.' Val hiccupped excitedly and rushed off in a cloud of Rothman's.

By the time I had tottered to the rail with as many woollies on as I could find, the sky was grey and the twinkling lights of Southampton not far off. I strained my eyes for the first sight of the famous white cliffs of Dover or at least a few bluebirds, but it was too early and too misty to see them, I presumed.

As I watched England looming up I thought again of my great, great, great, great, great, great, great Grandmother, give or take a great. Rattling her manacles in the steerage section of Captain Cook's uncomfy craft, she must have stared tearfully at this same coastline wondering if she would ever see England again.

CHAPTER XIX

Hot Mud

V AL AND I had been booked into some prestige London accommodation by an official at the Australian Embassy. It was called 'The Blue Door – Private Hotel' in a suburb called Bayswater near Hyde Gardens and only one stop on the Underground from Oxford Street and Park Lane Street.

I was a little nervous the first morning as I rode on the Central Line but I needed to go to the Australian bank in Sackville Street to get some travellers' cheques and collect my mail, so I braved those steep escalators. London seemed a wee bit grubby and with a good deal more Aborigines about than you ever see in Australian cities, funnily enough. Transport must have been a bit of a headache in London too because there always seemed to be a lot of quite nicely dressed young women waiting about on the steps of our little hotel, presumably for taxis.

Our room was clean but a bit poky, though when Val complained I heard myself defending it.

'This is history, Valerie,' I chided her. 'People were much smaller in the Olden Days. This was probably a Medieval ball-room.'

Frankly, Readers, I said this off the top of my head and, though it was probably true, I wisely judged that Val Dunn would not have been sympathetic to the fact that I was once Mrs Samuel Pepys. In this enlightened day and age, there are still a few fuddy-duddies who have trouble taking reincarnation on board, even when it's staring them in the face.

Val glowered around the room a bit suspiciously, but said no more, wisely remembering no doubt that I held the purse strings.

'It's only a base anyway,' I mollified her, 'somewhere to leave our cases and put our heads down, but we'd better get our skates on if we want to do the old Tower of London, Buckminster Castle and St Paul's Abbey before lunch.'

There was some interesting mail at the bank: a lovely joint 'come back soon' card from little Livvy, the Gibb brothers, Germaine with kisses and hugs all over it, and a nice long aerogram from Norman saying he got my card from Aden, he missed me, and that Mummy was quiescent. Only the postscript irritated me slightly: ' . . . Bruce, Valmai and little Kenny are happy as sandboys round at Ann Forbes, Ed. You'll be pleased to hear they haven't mentioned you once since you left, so don't worry.'

I hope my bubbas don't forget me that quickly, I thought, fretfully opening a rather large envelope with a New Zealand stamp. It seemed to be an invitation printed in silver scrolly writing to someone's wedding in Auckland. Who did I know in that dump for heaven's sake? Some people I had never heard of called Hamish and Heather McDonald wanted me to attend the marriage of Douglas Hugh Allsop to their niece, Marjorie Kiri McWhirter. I was just about to throw this misdirected missive in the bin when I looked again: 'Marjorie McWhirter? . . . *Madge*!!'

A quick glance at the date told me that I could not possibly have attended the function even if I had wanted to since I would still be at sea on my way home when it happened. Only then did I notice the little flimsy blue letter tucked in with the card. My heart sank as I read it, for between the lines I could hear once again Madge's whining voice and almost smell that old-fashioned, soapy, but not necessarily clean odour she always gave off. What a fool I had been to think she was out of my life when she had just been 'waiting in the wings' to use a showbusiness expression. Her letter read:

Dearest Edna,
Listen, how are you? I have missed you a lot since I went home to Kiwiland and now the Auckland Star is full of your

pictures. Congratulations Edna. Who would have thought you would ever win a beauty contest . . .

At this point my fingers closed around the brittle blue tissue and I experienced a not unpleasant little rush of pure hatred. Uncrumpling the letter, I read on:

> Listen Edna, I hope you alright. You never wrote so I guessed you must be still peeved at me for something though I always loved you and never meant to get your back up. Listen Edna, I got some wonderful news . . .

Once more I looked up from the letter exasperated. Why did Madge – *all New Zealanders for that matter* – say 'listen' before every sentence they uttered? They must realise instinctively that while they are droning on everyone else is tuning out.

> . . . I met this marvellous man his name is Douglas Allsop and we really like each other. There's a bit of an age difference though not compared with you and Norm but he owns a tourist bus company in Palmerston North and is very comfortable not that I ask. Listen Edna, please come and be my matron of honour because I caught your bouquet and found Douglas. He say he will pay your fare. Be happy for me. Your friend always,
> Madge.

'Who would have believed it,' laughed Val when I blurted out the news later at the Blue Door. After our long day's sightseeing we were almost too fagged out to go to *Salad Days* that night but we forced ourselves.

Although Madge's letter had irritated me in the same way that the woman herself always did I was, I confess, intrigued to see what man would choose to walk down the aisle with my problem bridesmaid. Was he handicapped in some way? I wondered. These days I suppose I might have thought he had 'low self-esteem'. All of these thoughts passed through my mind in a caring way; if I had not been an old softie from way back I probably would not have minded who Madge tied the knot with.

For the next six weeks of our tour around the Old Country I must confess I kept thinking of that little Auckland ceremony. I had sent Madge a postcard of a lake from the Daffodil District saying how thrilled I was for her but that I didn't think I could sail home via New Zealand. However, a few days later, by coincidence, I met one of the Quest organisers at a reception at the Australian Embassy and we took a good look at my return itinerary. Out of the blue, with no prompting from me, he had suggested we go back to Melbourne on the *Rangitoto*, adding casually, 'It stops at Auckland for three days on 3 July. You could easily visit the mineral springs at Rotorua and rub noses with a Maori.' I remembered seeing the Queen doing that in a newsreel so I assumed it was comparatively safe.

The coincidence was too much. Madge's wedding was 3 July! Fate had *meant* me to be there, and I rearranged my plans accordingly. Poor Madge, I thought. Something is bound to go wrong at that wedding – terribly wrong – and someone supportive like me should be there to help her see the funny side of it, I reflected compassionately.

By now Val and I had snapped about 3,276 colour slides between us, and we worked out that it would take about three months to screen them for the neighbours back in Moonee Ponds, if you allowed four longish slide evenings per week without a break for sausage rolls.

I must confess that every now and then I had a little flutter of homesickness. I had sailed off before Christmas thereby missing that special family event with my fast-growing youngsters around me. The seasonal festivities on board ship weren't much to write home about either, though Val's friend Chip, the Purser, dressed up as Santa and they played 'Silent Night' and 'All I Want For Christmas Is My Two Front Teeth' non-stop on the loudspeakers, day and night. Whatever happens in the future, I thought, I will always make a point of being at home on 25 December to receive my presents – and to give some as well of course!

Most of our time in the Old Country was spent in the winter months but we were so flat out that the dismal weather didn't worry us. I particularly wanted to visit Stonehenge because I had an uncanny feeling there might have been a few old Druids tucked away in our family tree. Come to think of it, the Druids used to dye themselves all over with something called woad which turned them a mauvy-blue, spookily reminiscent of my natural hair colouring! I was also keen to pop over to the Continent and gay Paree between Stratford-upon-Avon and the Planetarium, but my itinerary was so tight I just couldn't squeeze it in. 'Next time,' I consoled myself, knowing deep down that somehow there *would* be a next time. I adored my visit to the Harrods Food Hall too, and Madame Tussaud's, little knowing that my own life-like statue would be there one day surrounded by awestruck visitors and Japanese tourists wanting to be photographed next to it.

Val and I split up from time to time, especially when Chip was in town for a few days. They seemed to be getting quite serious too, and what with Madge's dumbfounding news I think Val was beginning to feel she might be the only one in our little circle left on the spinster heap.

One night at the Blue Door when we couldn't sleep because of some funny thumping and groaning on the floor above, Val told me how all the girls envied my marriage to Norman, and then she concluded enigmatically, 'You've done absolute wonders with him, Edna.' I couldn't sleep at all that night what with Stonehenge and the Chamber of Horrors and those odd guests at our hotel who seemed to be traipsing up and down the stairs at all hours. Val's remark about Norm didn't exactly help me drop off either. What did she mean by 'done wonders with him'. What was wrong with Norm? I knew Mummy had felt I could have done better for myself; she actually said it. I knew too that he was always a bit awkward at social events, and I blushed to recall the meeting with Pixie and Charlie on my Coronation night when he had behaved like a hobbledehoy. I sighed as I realised that, adorable though he was in the home, my darling Norm was a bit of a liability anywhere else. Perhaps he was even from the *wrong side of the tracks*! But then, let's face it, what Australian isn't?

Certainly poor Norman had very few friends and although his letters didn't say so – they were bright and cheerful – I read his loneliness between the lines. A little ashamed of my disloyal thoughts, I now longed to be back at Humouresque Street to give that poor old duffer a big hug and a little TLC.

Our last night in London was the highlight of the trip. A

beautiful box at the Theatre Royal, Covent Garden, for the first night of *My Fair Lady*, a flesh-and-blood show starring Rex Harrison and Julie Andrews. Because we were sharing the box with some officials from Australia House and a couple of other dignitaries, I decided to wear my Lovely Mother coronet and fur-trimmed robe and as we took our places in the gorgeous plush-lined alcove overlooking that sumptuous auditorium, quite a few heads turned. A lot of people in the stalls and dress circle craned their necks, pointed at me and even fixed me with their binoculars as though they had mistaken me for someone else, equally important. What a marvellous show that was with a story that struck a deep and resonant chord within me: the humble flower seller (my ancestor sold flowers in the Olden Days!) is groomed by a handsome professor and finally turns into a famous high society glamourpuss. In the interval, as people bowed and kissed my hand and footmen offered me champagne I could not help but identify with little Julie. I'm sorry but I couldn't.

Sitting next to me in the box was a young man called Charles Osborne who had something to do with the Arts Council. He asked me if I'd ever done much stage work and was surprised when I told him very little. I mentioned *Macbeth* and Mary Magdalene and he said he was surprised that with my bone structure and beautiful speaking voice I hadn't played someone called Hedda Gabler and another person by the name of Phèdre which I know I have spelt correctly because I wrote it down on the back of my programme. He also gave me a little list of roles he felt I should attempt one day. Here they are (I quote): St Joan by Bernard Shaw, Marguerite in *La Dame aux Camélias*, Madame Ranevesky in *The Cherry Orchard*, Blanche Dubois in *A Streetcar Named Desire* and Brecht's Mother Courage.

Although I had never heard of any of these shows, I was very flattered to be cast in them by this sensitive young man. He was certainly very attentive and complimentary and said he hoped one day he might have the pleasure of seeing me on the stage at Drury Lane, and we had a good laugh about it. It gives me goosepimples now to recall that conversation because at the time I write these words, my name is up in lights in front of that *very same theatre*; probably the most beautiful and prestigious theatre in the world.

Mr Osborne told me he'd been a bit of an actor himself in his time (though he was no Rex Harrison I'm afraid) and he said he was often mistaken for Marlon Brando. I must say I pretended to agree with him, though he was as much like Marlon Brando as Madge Allsop resembles Marilyn Monroe. However, it's sometimes a good idea to humour the menfolk . . .

Val and I parted company when our dream trip came to an end. She was going to join the *Himalaya* and you-know-who for its return voyage, and I was booked on the *Rangitoto* to Melbourne via Rotterdam, Lisbon, Genoa, Columbo and Auckland. That first visit to England and those tantalising glimpses of the way ethnic minorities lived in Portugal, Italy and India only served to whet my appetite for world travel; an appetite which has never dimmed.

Although I was alone I was never bored by shipboard life. I catalogued my 5,712 slides, I read and re-read the sleeve notes on my *My Fair Lady* microgroove (the first ever to reach Australia) and I scribbled down a few ideas for a kind of stage show in which I just chatted to the audience as though they were in my own home; a revolutionary sort of show, though I didn't know it then, which had the feeling of a conversation between two people, one of whom was a lot more interesting than the other. That is my definition of the Theatre incidentally, Readers.

In London as I was buying lovely gifts for my family, I racked my brains for a suitable wedding present for Madge. I had told her, of course, that I would be there for her nuptials. Let's face it, wild horses wouldn't have dragged me away, but it was hard to think of a suitable gift. There are two kinds of people who are very hard to buy for: those with everything, and those with nothing. Madge fell into the latter category, but I decided in the end to go out on a limb and buy her a gorgeous twenty-four-piece English teaset at Harrods, all boxed up beautifully. It was surprisingly reasonable but the salesman pointed out that it was slightly imperfect. I told him that didn't matter in the least, since it would match the recipient.

I will not dwell on the journey to Auckland – my travel diaries will make another fascinating volume – except to say that on the

first of July, two days off the coast of New Zealand, the *Rangitoto*
hit a typhoon. It had been very blowy all day and we'd been
warned to batten everything down. Sea-sickness hadn't seemed
to worry me on the return trip, but I was feeling pretty queasy
now as the boat started rolling ominously, and I looked out the
porthole at a huge wave, the colour of old-sock water. In no time
we were in the thick of it; there were terrible crashes and groans
from the bowels of the ship and I had just decided that the safest
place for me was my little bunk, when my suitcase and all my
luggage came crashing down from the top of the wardrobe and
slithered down the sloping cabin floor.

The storm raged for a day and a half and I only managed to
totter down to the near-empty dining saloon once for a very slopy
snack. Naturally I was chums with the Captain who was about
the only other diner present that day, and I took the opportunity
of asking him what time we were due to arrive at Auckland. He
laughed grimly. 'Listen,' he replied, and I realised at once he too
was a Kiwi. 'We haven't a hope of arriving on schedule, I'm
afraid, Mrs Everage. We've gone way off course trying to dodge
the dirty weather and I don't reckon we'll make Auckland until
the fourth.'

'But Madge's wedding!' I expostulated. 'I'm Matron of
Honour!'

'I'm sorry, Mrs Everage,' explained the skipper ruefully. 'It's
out of my control, I'm afraid. But please feel free to use our
telegraphic services to get a message to your friend.'

So that, Readers, is how I missed Madge Allsop's wedding.

★   ★   ★

'Oh, Edna! Edna! Yoo-hoo!' came a familiar voice on Auckland
pier.

'It wasn't the same without you, really it wasn't, was it,
Douglas?' Beside Madge stood a slightly elderly looking man in
a fawn suit, shirt, tie and hat. Even his face was fawn, though
kind.

'Madge was really cut up that you couldn't be there, Edna,' he
said. 'She even wanted us to postpone the ceremony, but it was
too late to do a reshuffle.'

I had left most of my things in my cabin, but a porter had loaded one suitcase and Madge's wedding present on to a trolley as we ambled out to Douglas Allsop's vehicle. My legs felt very wobbly and peculiar to be on dry land again, but to my surprise I was pleased to see an old familiar face, even Madge's, and I wanted to hear all the wedding details. It seemed to have gone off so smoothly and yet . . . why the dickens did I have this constant feeling in my bones that something had gone wrong? I suppose the only misadventure that occurred was my own failure to turn up on time.

'Let me take a snap of you two together,' said Madge giggling in an irritatingly girlish way. Douglas put his fawn arm around my waist while Madge crouched beside the car with her box Brownie to get a shot of us. When Madge takes a snap it's such a performance you have to hold a smile longer than the Mona Lisa.

'Listen, Edna, when we get home Doug has got some exciting news for you, and she mustn't say no, must she, Doug?'

'No to what?' I snapped nicely.

'All right,' said Madge as we drove on through some rather steep and windy streets. 'We'll tell you our little plan now but if you don't agree I'll never speak to you again.'

Hark at her! I thought. I've gone out of my way to attend this waif's wedding. I've nearly been *shipwrecked*, for heaven's sake, and now, just because she's got a little gold band on her finger, she thinks she can lay down the law to me! But I bit my tongue. And I was curious.

'Doug and I feel,' Madge began, 'that you are the most important person in our lives and you have always been wonderful to me.'

I smiled nicely and gave a little self-deprecatory shrug.

'Yes, you have!' Madge insisted. 'And we want you to come on our honeymoon, don't we, Douglas?'

'*You what?*' I exclaimed.

Douglas came in quickly, touching my hand. 'We know your ship sails in three days, Edna, and you must get back to your bairns, but we would be honoured if you could join us at the Grand Hotel, Rotorua, for a day or so. I've taken the liberty of

booking you a nice room and the hot springs and mud baths there
do wonders for tired skin.'

I looked at the wizened camel-coloured man beside me in the
driver's seat and then over my shoulder at Madge who was
grinning excitedly.

'If this hotel specialises in treating tired skin,' I replied, 'you
and Madge have chosen the perfect place for a honeymoon.'

'Please say you will, Edna,' pleaded Madge in the back seat.
My remark had obviously gone straight right over her head.

★   ★   ★

Douglas's home was apparently in another city called Palmerston
North where his business was based, so he was just staying at an
Auckland hotel for the wedding. For convenience Madge was still
lodging with her auntie Heather until the couple commenced
their real honeymoon as husband and wife. It seemed a bit
old-fashioned to me but then, it was New Zealand.

When I had agreed, rather sweetly I think, to accept Doug's
invitation, Madge became almost hysterical with excitement
and insisted on stopping off at her aunt's home to unwrap the
gift I had brought them. Needless to say, when her eyes fell
upon the green and gold Harrods wrapping paper, she became
even more agitated, but disappointment soon prevailed when
we discovered that every single item in that twenty-four piece
teaset had been smashed to smithereens. It must have happened
during the storm, I suppose, and I confess that I felt a bit sorry for
Madge who just stared pitifully into the rattling box. Suddenly
with an 'Oh, how lovely!' she delved into the straw and
produced one tea-cup reasonably intact except for a missing
handle.

'Oh look, Douglas!' she exclaimed cuddling up to him. 'Look
what Edna's given us. It will be perfect for our toothy-peg
brushes.'

It's a funny fact of life that the second I ever feel genuinely
sorry for Madge, she says something to make me regret it.

We left Madge at her aunt's to pack a few things prior to our
departure for Rotorua at the crack of dawn, and Douglas Allsop
and I drove back to the Star Hotel alone. I wanted to congratulate

him on marrying Madge, but I felt a bit of a hypocrite. Instead he did most of the talking and he obviously adored her.

'Have you seen many of her shows, Edna?' he enquired.

'Shows?' I queried. 'What shows?'

'Her ballet shows. Madge never stops talking about her dancing days,' continued the deluded husband. 'I have a few quid put away, and when we come back from the honeymoon I've got a good mind to book the Auckland Town Hall so she can put on her "Waste Land" show in proper style. Madgie says it's a big crowd pleaser in Australia.'

'I missed it I'm afraid,' I retorted politely. 'But it certainly pleased some of my friends. In fact,' I added with truth and tact, 'they were so pleased the tears were rolling down their cheeks.'

As I said goodnight to Douglas at the hotel and prepared to book a long-distance phone call to Norm, I felt rather sorry for that sweet cicada of a man. Madge had obviously told him a lot of wicked fairy tales and I could see heartache looming not too far down the track. In point of fact it was closer than I realised.

I didn't trust myself to mention any of this to Dame Margot Allsop when we picked her up in the car next morning and set off for Rotorua. She had brought an enormous amount of luggage which filled most of the car, so it was an uncomfortable journey and I was very pleased when we at last reached New Zealand's famous volcanic zone. Even as we approached, the air started to smell of rotten eggs. Knowing Madge as well as I did, I instinctively wound down the window only to realise that that horrid sulphurous odour came from without.

The Grand Hotel was lovely and old-fashioned; so lovely and old-fashioned, in fact, that I believe that they have since pulled it down. But it was only a hop, step and a jump to the thermal baths where all kinds of wonderful treatments are available. We checked in and I was relieved to find my own room was not immediately adjacent to the honeymoon suite. My hearing is far too good I'm afraid.

We had a light lunch of pumpkin soup and brandy snaps (New Zealand's favourite dish) and Madge changed into a brand new and rather girlish floral frock.

'Listen, Edna,' she said.

'I'm *listening*, Madge,' I retorted through clenched teeth.

'We're booked on a tour of the hot springs this afternoon. Isn't that exciting?'

And so it proved to be.

We joined a party of tourists at a place just outside Rotorua from which great clouds of steam constantly issued. Our guide was a famous old Maori woman called Guide Rangi who claimed to have rubbed noses with every member of the Royal Family since Queen Victoria. She seemed to be a sweet old thing and Madge got a good slide of her doing it with me too, though I wasn't taking any chances and soon after slipped into the little girls' room to give my nose a quick pat of diluted Pinesol.

The volcanic pong was almost unbearable as we filed along little cinder-strewn pathways and over bridges and causeways a few feet from seething lava, boiling water and mud, popping and phutting like black porridge. It was far too steamy to take photos but Madge kept insisting. When we came to a little rustic bridge over a really fierce mud crater, she insisted on getting the umpteenth shot of Douglas and me leaning on the rail. I felt sure that Posterity, perusing all those snaps, would think *I* was the bride!

But my mind was frankly elsewhere. I had got through to Norm the night before on a bad line, but the conversation had been strangely unsatisfactory; let's face it, what telephone conversations aren't? *Had they missed me enough?* I pondered, as I replaced the receiver and had a little weep.

Guide Rangi was about fifty yards ahead in the mist.

'Hey! You two!' she was calling. 'Sir, lady! Can't you see the sign?'

'Smile,' called Madge. 'Smile again. I forgot to wind it on!'

What sign? I wondered, lifting my elbow off the rail and glancing behind me. Tacked on to the flimsy parapet was a notice, easily missed: DANGER – DON'T LEAN ON RAIL!

'Edna,' called Madge, 'over here. Smile!'

There was a loud crackle and I glanced to my left. The side of the bridge that had just been supporting me was gone and Douglas stood beside me, leaning back slightly and waving his arms in a funny windmill motion. He was looking at me with a puzzled expression and a faint little smile, as if to say, 'What the dickens is going on?'

There was a loud thwack and a kind of glug. Guide Rangi screamed and a lot of tourists ran back to the bridge and, clinging to each other, gaped at the black pock-marked surface and the floating fawn hat.

It eventuated that some of the people who witnessed the tragedy were trained swimmers too, but not, unfortunately, in boiling mud.

CHAPTER XX

A Stage
in My Life

'Ooo-HOO! Ooo-HOO! Is anybody home?'
It was a glorious Melbourne autumn day, the sky a
lavender blue and the plane trees in Humouresque Street
chafing their big yellow leaves in a soft breeze. I had run to the
front door while the Silvertop taxi driver unloaded the car and
tottered up the path with the baggage. They must be in the back
yard, I thought, as I ran down the familiar hallway, turning a
blind eye to my kitchen which looked as though a bomb had hit
it. The fly-wire door snapped shut behind me as I stood in our
little back veranda and gazed down the garden where my beloved
Norman and our three nippers were busy around the incinerator,
hurling on great armfuls of gold and russet leaves from which the
blue sweet-smelling smoke trickled upwards.
'Ooo-hoo! Ooo-hoo, Possums! Look who's here?' I trilled,
using our family's favourite term of endearment which I have
since extended to the rest of the human race.
'Hello, Mum!' cried Bruce, a little gangly figure busy with his
rake.
'Hello,' exclaimed Valmai rather off-handedly, as she approached the bonfire with a kebab of leaves on a dry stick. My
wild-eyed old mother, in a frayed army greatcoat and looking a
bit like Queen Lear, was wielding a garden fork. She gave me a
little wave without even looking up.
Norm, in an old khaki shirt and baggy trousers, squinted

through the smoke, 'G'day, Ed!' he shouted. 'I got the whole team working for me today. Wanna give us a hand?'

Although the smoke was at the far end of the garden, my eyes were smarting for another reason. Wasn't my husband at least going to interrupt whatever he was doing for a few seconds to cross the lawn and embrace the mother of his children, who had been away for the best part of six months? Only little Kenny, in a filthy pair of shorts, with scabby knees and a glacier of lettuce-green mucus uniting lip and nostril, came running towards me, arms outstretched. I tweaked his nose with my hankie and gazed into his eyes noticing his custard corners and the amber crystals of neglect in his eyelashes.

'Where's my prezzie?' he demanded. 'You promised you'd bring me lotsa prezzies.'

'Soon, Kenny, soon, darling. Just let Mummy unpack,' I said, turning away to hide my tears of hurt.

I went back to the front door to pay the driver. There seemed to be a dickens of a lot of suitcases on the porch.

'These aren't all mine!' I complained sharply, blowing my nose.

'A lot of them are mine, Edna,' came a voice from the front garden. It was Madge.

'But, Madge,' I protested, 'I thought you were taking the cab on to Mrs Findlay's – your aunt's. I mean, I assumed you were. Surely you don't expect to stay here?'

'Didn't I tell you, Edna?' replied my bridesmaid, wide-eyed and innocent. 'Oh gosh, I'm sorry. She went to her reward about three years ago. When you bought me my ticket to Australia and said you'd look after me, I just thought . . .' The woman had started to cry and the taxi driver was beating a fast retreat with my change.

'For heaven's sake, Madge,' I began crabbily, and then more like myself, 'Please understand. I couldn't see you destitute, not after the awful thing that happened, but I've a husband, a young family and a mad mother. This is just a small suburban house. How could you possibly think we had the room?'

From somewhere behind me in the home, came Valmai's whining voice. 'Where's our prezzies, Mum? You promised!'

'Listen, I understand, Edna,' whimpered the widow. 'I just got my wires crossed, that's all. I thought perhaps . . . just for a few days while I find myself a cheap boarding house. I'll get out of your hair now.' And with that Madge wrapped her bony fingers round the handles of a couple of huge suitcases and tried to tug them in the direction of the front gate. For a while I watched her receding figure. It receded very slowly since the cases were so heavy they never left the ground, and were actually ploughing up the lawn. Finally inside me, something snapped.

'Come back, Madge, you silly billy!' I yelled caringly. 'You can stay a few days. I'll reshuffle. All right? I'll put Kenny in with us, Brucie in with Valmai and you can borrow the attic. But for goodness' sake, stop dragging that luggage. You're wrecking a hand-weeded lawn.'

Madge gave me an early version of her grateful look, which I have since learnt to interpret as her 'gimme more' look.

'If you want to make yourself useful, make us all a cup of tea. I'm going into the back garden to reintroduce myself to my family.'

I was cross with Ann Forbes, very cross actually. She had promised to cherish my children and she had sent them home on the morning of my return like a bunch of neglected ragamuffins, but they were healthy enough, though a bit off-hand with me, to put it mildly. Was I imagining it, or was my husband a little distant as well? They were all happy enough however when I unpacked their presents; some lovely initialled hankies and Swiss Y-fronts for Norm, toys and books for the youngsters and, not before time, a new matinée jacket for my mother. Poor little Madge sat in a corner of our lounge watching the happy family scene, and Norm noticed her too, for he crossed the room and awkwardly handed her an envelope.

On that nightmare day in New Zealand when Douglas Allsop was there one minute and gone the next, I put another call through to Australia to tell Norm the dreadful news. Like most Australian men he is not terribly good at expressing condolences, or anything really, so when he saw Madge in the flesh he didn't so much as mention her bereavement. Instead he had popped down to our local newsagents and bought a nice appropriate card with a picture of a vase of violets and the words 'In deepest sympathy' scrolled across it. He didn't say a word when he gave her the envelope but I noticed Madge reading the card with an odd expression on her face. I found it later too, still on her armrest, and opening it I read: 'In Loving Memory of a Wonderful Mother'. Poor old Norm had bought the wrong card but it was the thought that counted, I suppose.

To my surprise on my first night home, Norman announced he was going to Lodge. It was a special night or something, one that he couldn't get out of. I was reading the children their stories when he dropped this bombshell and I didn't want to show my disappointment, not in front of them, but I thought to myself that he could go for a ride on a goat any blessed night of the year except this one. He really didn't seem to care, and I could hear him whistling away in the bedroom as he got ready. Come to think of it, he'd been whistling the same tune all afternoon, on and off. I went into the bathroom to wash my face, for I'd had another little weep tucking up the children. There beside the basin was a funny chunky glass bottle with a big round wooden stopper full of specimen-yellow fluid. It was called 'Man Aftershave Lotion'. Just as I stared at it, Norm barged in in his singlet, still whistling that stupid tune, unscrewed the lid and gave himself a bit of a splash under the arms.

'What's that prithee?' I heard myself cry, echoing my mother I'm afraid. Then, my voice quavering, I shouted at my warbling spouse, 'Those masonic mates of yours are luckier than your poor little wife tonight!'

'Edna,' came Madge's wheedling voice outside the door. (What a past mistress of mistiming that woman was.) 'Edna, is it all right if I have a shelf of my own in the bathroom cupboard?'

I don't know when Norm came home that night. I tried to lie there with my eyes open as long as possible, playing my resentment tapes over and over in my head. My first night home . . . how could he?

I decided that when Norman at last got in, put on his jamas in the dark, as usual, and tried to give me a cuddle, I would just lie there stiffly with my arms at my sides. He might even attempt to peck me on the cheek, in which case I would make sure it was wet with freshly manufactured tears. But in spite of all these churning irritations, and little Kenny's phlegmy breathing in the camp bed next to ours, I must have gone out like a light.

Next morning the winceyette bundle was there beside me, reeking of that yellow stuff in the bathroom. Ken was still asleep too, so I slid out of bed, threw on my brunch coat, and made for the kitchen. There, in a nimbus of toast smoke, sat Madge, having a little cry at the kitchen table. I put my arm around her bird-boned shoulders.

'There, there, Madgie, don't cry,' I cosseted her. 'After all, you've had a wonderful marriage, even if it only lasted a day and a half. Don't they say it's the quality and not the quantity?'

Madge, to her credit, seemed unconvinced, and produced a letter she had been reading. 'This came care of you this morning, Edna. It's from the solicitors.' I glanced at the tear-stained aerogramme.

'They say there's no money. Douglas had mortgaged his bus company. There's nothing.'

She was sobbing again and I made an irreversible suggestion. 'You can stay here as long as you like, dear.'

'No, Edna, I'll manage somehow, I'll get a job. I'll teach dancing.' She opened her handbag and rummaged inside it.

'I don't really mind that Douglas was penniless,' she declared, snuffling, 'not with wonderful hospitable friends like you. It's just that I have so little to remember him by – only this.' From the talcy depths of her bag she produced a curiously misshapen lump of metal.

'I'll have a strap made for it, and wear it always,' she said brightening.

'But what is it, Madge?'

'His watch, Edna. It's all they could find. It doesn't tell the time any more because it's melted.'

'You don't say' was the obvious remark I *didn't* make!

'It's my Salvador Dali watch,' the widow announced proudly. Then, as now, I only found Madge totally unbearable when she paraded her smattering of culture.

There were some letters for me under the charred debris of Madge's breakfast, all rather newsy and interesting. A welcome-back card from Pixie Lambell, an invitation to a ball, a cocktail party and an art exhibition. The invitations said either 'Mr and Mrs Everage' or 'Edna Everage and Guest'. I heaved a little inner sigh as I pictured Norm's clumsiness and casual manners on such occasions. Was I getting snobbish? I wondered. It was an awful thought.

There was a lovely warm letter from Mrs Newton-John saying that Livvy had been practising her singing and all the children longed to see me again. Another letter from some people called Gibson begging me to give acting lessons to their tot, Mel. There was a message from my brother Roy, back from Korea, to say that he was staying pretty well permanently in Frankston. That was a relief because it gave us a lot more room to play with. There was another postcard from Athol who was studying fertilisers or something in Mildura mentioning a sweetheart. I hoped it wasn't that Dawn Purdie, but I feared the worst.

The last letter was one of the most important in my life. On the top was the address of a semi-posh Melbourne suburb. I poured myself a cuppa and read:

Dear Mrs Everage,

I am a young actor in Melbourne and I am planning a kind of revue or variety show about Australian suburban life trying to point out its funny side. I will be playing all the parts myself and one of them is the role of a housewife who has just been on her first overseas trip, and is interested in cooking, interior decorating, family and flower arrangement. I have read a lot about you in the press over the last year or so and wondered if you could spare an hour or more of your valuable time to see me and perhaps help me in my research. I suppose I want to pick your brains. If you could meet me I would suggest lunch at a nice restaurant in the city called Russell Collins, say next Wednesday at half past twelve? If agreeable, kindly phone me on BX 5116.

Yours sincerely,

Barry Humphries

'What's a cheek, Edna?' said Madge overhearing me as I threw the letter on the kitchen table.

'Weird types are starting to write to me now,' I complained. 'This one sounds a bit of a cissy too. He's planning some kind of show where he dresses up as a woman and makes fun of our wonderful Australian way of life. What kind of homes do people like that come from? He's probably breaking his parents' hearts.'

Madge looked suitably impressed and picked up the letter.

'Oh, I don't know, Edna. Listen, he doesn't sound all that bad. It's a bit of a compliment to you in a way. You might call it the price of fame.'

'Hmmph!' was all I said. I could hear Norm whistling under the shower and Kenny was crying.

★   ★   ★

Russell Collins was in the basement of a twelve-storey skyscraper on the corner of Russell and Collins Streets. It was ultra-modern. You went down some terrazzo steps and between two metal posts with lights in them. As you crossed the lights a glass and chrome door whooshed open, as if by magic, and you were in an active, dimly lit restaurant full of nooks and cubicles in blond-wood veneer. There were vases of poppies on all the tables and nice ornaments and wall plaques giving it a homely feel. While I was waiting for my strange correspondent to greet me (I hadn't the faintest idea what he looked like), I read one of the pretty pottery plaques. It showed a little thatched cottage with smoke curling up to a ceramic sky. In funny twiggy writing was the motto: 'Life's a melody if you'll only hum the tune.' It stuck in my mind. It seemed so wise, so simple and yet almost impossible to grasp. It must be philosophy, I reflected.

'Mrs Everage?'

'Yes.'

A tall, rather stooped young man had accosted me and was pointing to a little table near a goldfish tank. We didn't actually introduce each other but I knew it had to be Mr Humphries. As he led the way, I noticed that although wearing quite a nice suit, he had suede shoes on (not a good sign) and his hair was so long it hung over one eye. A long time, I thought, since that's had a squirt of shampoo!

While I was carefully studying the menu, he lit up a Rothman's without even asking me and I gave a little cough, which seemed to pass unnoticed. When the waitress arrived in black with white starched collar and apron like they always used to wear before grubby jeans and T-shirts, he ordered whiting fillets and I plumped for the house specialities: cream of tomato soup with croutons and sweetcorn on toast.

To be perfectly honest, I enjoyed my lunch. If people ask me straightforward questions about my life ('lifestyle' hadn't been inflicted on us then), I'm happy to oblige. I'm an interesting person; let's face it, you wouldn't have got this far if I wasn't. I certainly interested this Barry Humphries person because he kept asking me to repeat things (when I described my home for instance) and scribbling them down excitedly in a notebook. His stage show was a couple of weeks off at the Assembly Hall, and he was obviously a bit nervous. He was also, like a lot of university types his age, more than a bit of a know-all. In former, more lucid days, my mother summed up the type very well; she used to say, 'Know-all, know nothing!' My Readers will be acquainted with plenty of people who fall into this category; no names, no pack drill.

We parted with a promise from me that I would come to a few rehearsals and help him with his 'female impersonation' though it made me a little uncomfortable, as it still does, to think of a man trolling around in women's attire, I'm sorry but it does. Perhaps it was his mention of a fee that twisted my arm.

After lunch I suppose I was on a bit of a 'high' to use that expression for the first and last time. I decided to have a little wander round the city centre, browsing in the arcades and graciously signing occasional autograph books, proffered by awestruck pedestrians who recognised me. I was in no hurry to go home since, very sensibly, I had delegated a few of my chores to Madge Allsop.

If she was going to move in with us for a while – she'd spotted Athol's postcard and decided to shift herself downstairs to the boys' larger room – my old bridesmaid was going to have to pull her weight and sing for her supper. I'd asked her to clean up the kitchen, defrost the fridge, make the beds and collect Kenny from

Kindie and Bruce and Valmai from school. I had also told her to put in the casserole early at medium to high and at five o'clock, to switch her bottom to low.

I suggested these tasks caringly, and as occupational therapy to stop her becoming morbid. I'm sure that grief counsellors reading this will back me to the hilt.

We had bought a new radiogram to play our *My Fair Lady* microgroove and, that afternoon I lashed out on two more discs: *Mantovani Magic* and Mario Lanza in *The Student Prince*. By the time I got home, still chirpy from my lunch and carefree afternoon, it was nearly six o'clock and, funnily enough, I wasn't in the least surprised to see dark smoke pouring out of the front door of my home. With a hankie pressed to my face, I battled my way through to the kitchen, retrieved the ruined casserole, switched off the appliance, opened all the windows and looked for Allsop. In the end I found her chattering away to my mother in the back garden. Although it was nearly dark, the children were running amok and there was no sign of Norm.

'Hello, Edna,' said Madge when I finally came across her. 'Have you burnt something? There's a funny smell.'

'It's nothing,' I said, sarcastically too I'm afraid, as I bundled my mother back to her room. 'Norm doesn't eat charcoal so I'll have to find him something else for his dinner.'

'Oh!' exclaimed my hopeless house guest. 'Norm isn't coming home for dinner. He phoned.'

'And where has he gone, prithee?' I enquired, slipping into mumspeak, my voice breaking. 'Not Lodge *again*?'

Madge shrugged, gave a silly grin and then flinched, as though I was going to hit her. Funnily enough, I almost did.

That evening I fed and bathed the children, scratched up some scrambled eggs and a salad for Mummy, me and Madge, read them more stories and hurled myself fretfully on to the couch in our lounge. I tried listening to a bit of Mantovani but I wasn't in the microgroove mood. Madge plonked herself in the chair opposite and turned on the TV to watch Graham Kennedy in *In Melbourne Tonight*. Gloomily, my eyes followed hers to that quivering grey rectangle. Kenny's cough could be heard from the bedroom.

'That Ann Forbes sent my children back to me with every germ in Moonee Ponds!' I railed.

'You're lucky to have kiddies at all, Edna,' quavered Madge. 'Poor Douglas and I never even . . .'

I hauled myself up off the couch and made myself stroke the back of her head.

'Perhaps we women can get far too dependent on our menfolk, Madge,' I consoled her, simultaneously glaring at the clock. It was *ten past eleven*! Where the dickens was he?

As if in answer to my anguished query came the sound of whistling on the front porch and the scratch of a key.

'Hello, girls, keeping out of trouble?'

Norm came over and gave me a quick kiss on the top of the head.

'And how's my Madge?' he said, running over, plucking her off her chair and swirling her around the room.

When they'd both stopped laughing and giggling, I enquired in my iciest tones, 'Where were you tonight, Norman?'

'Working back at Ball's, Ed. Didn't Madge tell you, we're stocktaking?' With that he picked up the paper and settled down to read the sporting page. I gave Madge a long hard look and went to bed.

★　★　★

'That's two nights this week, Madge, and he muttered something about a meeting next Wednesday.'

Madge warmed up the teapot.

'I don't like it,' I said. 'Something feels wrong. And that tune he's always whistling?'

' "Some Enchanted Evening".'

'What?'

'It's called "Some Enchanted Evening", from the new film, heard it on the wireless.'

'I should never have gone away. I should never have left him alone for four months,' I whimpered. 'He's an attractive man; or he was.' I remembered the young soldier on the beach, little rainbows dancing in his armpit tufts, the rust on his buckle, the view up his nostrils.

Madge dumped two cups of tea in front of us.

'What are you going to do about it, Edna?' she said in a dry and unexpectedly pragmatic voice.

'I can't be a bloodhound, Madge,' I said. 'Much as I'd like to follow him to the very doorstep of the woman he's seeing, I can't do it.'

'Well?'

'Well, perhaps someone else could keep an eye on him. Someone discreet. Someone nobody would notice. A colourless, insignificant person with no personality whatsoever. A creature who is almost invisible . . .'

'Me?'

'Oh, Madge!' I gushed, clutching her hands and nearly spilling the tea. 'Would you, Possum? Just put on that old brown coat of yours and wait outside the staff entrance at Ball's. You'd merge with the brickwork. See where he goes and tell me. It will kill me, Madge, but you *must* tell me!'

There was a long pause, and then Madge's expression grew ineffably sly.

'I have some furniture in store, Edna,' she said. 'Just a few sticks. Could I have it brought round in the next few days to my new room?'

Wouldn't you know? I thought, rolling my eyes heavenward and giving a little tight-lipped nod.

'Of course, Madge,' I said. 'Be my guest.'

While I was experiencing all these agonies of doubt and distrust – Australia's Loveliest Mother for heaven's sake! – I made sure Madge was the only person to share my secret shame. Norman seemed oblivious to my moody manner. No doubt the tune he was always chirruping reminded him of a cosy night at *South Pacific* while I was freezing to death in London, trying to be a good ambassador for Australia. That sickly scent must be *her* favourite, I thought as I threw it into the pedal bin one night a week later, when Norman was once again 'out on the town'. Madge, as arranged, had attempted to 'tail' him a couple of nights before but he must have given her the slip in the rush hour crowds in Regent's Place.

On this fateful morning, he had told me some cock-and-bull

yarn about having to visit an old army friend in hospital after work. I was so sickened I didn't even ask him which hospital or which friend. 'Have a *wonderful* time,' I called over my shoulder as he hurried out the door. Later that afternoon Madge put on her old brown coat and a headscarf and set off for another chilly vigil outside the staff entrance of Norman's office.

'Better luck this time, Madge,' I said bitterly. 'Ring me immediately you have an address. Don't spare me.'

That same evening I was putting those poor fatherless children to bed when the phone rang. I rushed to the instrument and barked out the word, 'YES?!'

'I just wondered, Mrs Everage, if you'd like to come to a rehearsal at the Assembly Hall tomorrow night. We could send a taxi,' said a rather 'light', scratchy voice.

'May I ring you back, Barry?' I blurted hastily. 'I'm expecting an urgent call.'

But an hour passed and nothing happened. Madge must have dropped another catch. Some Sherlock Holmes she is! I reflected with a heavy heart, as I leant forward to wrench on the TV – and oblivion.

Brrring, brrring! Brr . . . 'Yes! . . . Yes, I'm listening, woman! You're ringing from where? . . . Speak up, Madge . . . He what? . . . He where? . . . Are you sure? . . . Is he still there? . . . Well get a taxi home as quick as you can so I can go out!'

For a long time I just sat by the phone feeling as though something had died inside me. It was unbelievable, though it made some sort of mad sense. Yet if I wanted Norman, it looked as though I was going to have to fight for him.

When Madge came home I was dressed to the nines. All we exchanged was one long tragic look on the doorstep as I bolted out to take over her taxi.

'Good luck, Edna,' she called. '*But hurry!*'

A cold wind was blowing the black rain down Little Collins Street as I paid off the driver and stood trembling outside the Pixie Lambell Academy of Poise. The building was in darkness but high up where the offices were, a warm light glowed. I remembered the leopardskin sofa, soft rugs, the exotic smell of those black cigarettes and all that henna hair. Entering the dim vestibule I whimpered loudly with a mixture of self-pity and rage. So this is where he came night after night, I thought, as the small lift bore me upwards. And this was the woman I had believed to be my friend, who had used her influence on the Quest committee to get me the prize – *and out of the way*! Very convenient, Miss Lambell! Very clever. Game, set and match!

The lift door opened. Above Cynthia's empty desk the clock said ten forty-five and already I could smell those foreign ciggies. I moved towards the door of her sanctum but stopped in my tracks. I heard a woman's voice, Pixie's, saying something huskily, lewdly. I listened more intently.

'Put it in my hand again, Norman,' she was saying, almost breathing, 'but not quite so firm. Women don't like it as hard as that.'

'How's *that*?' I heard Norman say.

'Mmmm! That's a whole lot better. You're really getting the hang of it.'

'*I'm so glad he is!*' I said sailing in through the door, looking braver than I felt, but my voice tailed off.

Apart from Norm and Pixie, there were three other men in the room all looking at me in astonishment.

'Edna!' exclaimed Pixie. 'Where the hell did you spring from?'

'Gee, Edna, you weren't supposed to know about this,' said my seemingly fully dressed husband. 'Who tipped you off?'

'I'm sorry, gentlemen,' Miss Lambell apologised turning to the others who were looking very nonplussed. 'This is my friend Mrs Everage, winner of this year's Lovely Mother Quest and an old pupil of mine.'

For once in my life I was lost for words.

'Edna,' resumed the redhead. 'Welcome to my Gentlemen's night class. You'll be pleased to hear that these menfolk, your husband included, have enrolled in my special etiquette course and tonight we are concentrating on a refined, yet sincere handshake.'

'Indeed?' I croaked.

'Norman,' commanded Pixie. 'When I first met you at the Australia Hotel you nearly snapped me off at the wrist. Now I want you to shake Edna's hand the way I've taught you.'

Grinning sheepishly, Norm crossed the room, making a silly

little bow; he took my hand, and gave it a firm yet gentle squeeze. He then brought it up to his lips and kissed it, like a few people did to Julie Andrews that night at Drury Lane. The other men all clapped but I pulled my hand away.

'Why didn't you tell me you were coming here, Norman? Why all that pretence about meetings and masons and hospitals?'

'I'll come in on this one if I may,' said Miss Lambell, her arms around our shoulders. 'Your life is changing, Edna, changing fast. You are moving in different circles and meeting more stimulating people as the months go by. Norman here wants to be a part of your new life but he's afraid of letting the side down, so he turned to me. I hope he won't mind if I repeat his very words, "Please, Miss Lambell. Teach me a few airs and graces so Edna can be proud of me. She's a wonderful woman and I don't want to let her down."'

'Is that what you said, Norman? Is that how you feel?' I whispered, fighting the waterworks.

Norman, hands in pockets, was looking at the carpet but he shot me a shy little sideways grin.

'Reckon so, Ed,' was all he said.

In the taxi going home we sat in silence arm in arm and I never, thank heaven, breathed a word to him of my earlier suspicions. On our arrival of course, Madge gave us a most peculiar look and I decided, I don't quite know why, to keep her in the dark for a day or so.

That night, trying very hard not to wake up Kenny, Norm did something he had not done since our first few months of marriage. He brought me a large mug of hot cocoa.

★ ★ ★

The Assembly Hall is part of a big Presbyterian church in the heart of Melbourne. I arrived at about seven thirty and sat quietly towards the back. In spite of the solemn churchy feeling it had, there were a few long-haired types, male and female, smoking and yelling to each other as they arranged lights on stands near the little stage. A girl in pedal-pushers and sandals, also puffing away, was strumming at the piano. I seemed to be hanging about in the gloom for ages while nothing happened. I have since learnt this is normal in the theatre.

Round about nine o'clock when my patience was running very thin, someone brought me a cup of tea and a biscuit. The piano struck up a sort of rock and roll tune. A man and two girls appeared, dressed rather stupidly, and sang something very wordy and 'topical'. It was impossible to hear the lyrics in that echoey hall but I caught the name Khrushchev a few times. Every now and then they stopped and peered into the darkened auditorium, shading their eyes with their hands while the producer, a rude bearded man sitting near me, told them what they'd done wrong, and they all started again from the beginning (or the 'top' as I've learnt to call it now).

After that shambles Barry H sauntered on to the stage dressed up as an old man in a dressing-gown and mumbled on about nothing for at least half an hour. He'd put white stuff in his hair and lines on his face but you could see it was him a mile off. What was I doing here? I wondered. And I felt pretty sure that in a couple of days a paying audience would be feeling the same.

When Barry had at last ground to a halt and was going into his peering into the audience, eye-shading 'How was I?' routine, Dan the producer, to my astonishment, called back, 'Brilliant, Barry. It was funny and compassionate!' What twaddle, I thought. Were these people here to entertain the public, or to constantly pat each other on the back? The other trio came on again and sang some ditty sneering at our local TV personalities which I thought was in very bad taste. While that dragged on I felt a tap on my shoulder and turning, saw behind me in the darkness a mad-looking woman with a pointed yellow hat and a baggy twinset. Her cheeks were rouged like a doll, her lipstick looked as though it had been applied while riding on the Big Dipper, and she had very hairy legs. To my amazement she addressed me in a man's voice.

'How do you think it's going so far, Mrs Everage?'

'Barry! You gave me the fright of my life,' I exclaimed. 'Who are you supposed to be, a clown?'

'She' looked a bit put out.

'This is my new character, my housewife. I'd like you to watch the next bit and take a few notes if you would. I want you to help me make it as authentic as possible.'

When he minced on to the stage a few minutes later, I didn't know where to look. He'd written a sort of poem sniggering at suburban life which, if I was any judge, would have the average Melbourne audience walking out in droves and asking for their money back. He delivered this in a high-pitched squeak and, to make matters worse, he kept interrupting himself to giggle at his own stupid 'jokes'. I watched Wendy, the pianist, closely during this performance and she hardly cracked a smile, whilst a few seats from me, Dan, the grumpy producer, kept lighting cigarettes and scratching his beard. About forty minutes later, when the monologue petered out, Barry had the cheek to peer once more into the auditorium to solicit our praise.

'How was that, Dan? Pretty good, I felt.'

There was a long, dark silence, broken at last by a cultured woman's voice. 'Pretty good, I *don't think*! Pretty awful, more like it. I have never seen such twaddle and hoo-haa on the stage in my life and I have just been to the West End of London!'

The woman's voice was mine!

Barry, on stage, went white under his fruit salad make-up and his jaw dropped open. Dan swivelled round and saw me for the first time sitting in the empty stalls. Wendy the pianist laughed with relief at the voice of sanity. It was a bit like 'The Emperor's New Clothes' in Allsop's Fables when the kiddie is the only one with the nerve to say that the King is in his birthday suit. I was the kiddie, and Barry, I'm afraid, the silly self-deluded monarch.

'Who's this at our rehearsal?' demanded Dan pointing at me. Barry, sitting in a chair head in hands, muttered an introduction.

'My God, not *the* Edna Everage from Moonee Ponds who won the Quest?'

I nodded proudly, yet modestly.

'Barry asked me for his opinion and I would be a hypocrite if I didn't speak my mind,' I declared, in a voice which could be heard clearly in every corner of the Assembly Hall.

'He is correct in thinking that Australian womenfolk and their way of life have a right to be recognised, but it is an insult and an obscenity that our position within the social infra-structure as we know it *per se* should be cynically promoted by a man *en travestie* who mocks and denigrates all that we stand for and hold sacred.'

Between you and me, Readers, this is only *roughly* what I said, but it had an electrifying effect on those little amateur theatrical folk.

Dan took me by the elbow and quickly steered me out to the foyer, while the others slumped around the stage disconsolately.

'We've got a problem, Mrs Everage,' he announced furtively, 'and you've put your finger on it. Humphries is a clever young man; devilish clever, but that housewife skit of his is going to kill this show stone dead, and deep down he knows it.'

'Barry wanted me to help, he asked for my opinion and I gave it. Call me old-fashioned, but I did, I'm sorry.' The producer nodded a lot and kept saying, 'Yup, yup, yup.'

'There's absolutely nothing I can suggest to improve that segment,' I continued, 'short of *me* getting up on stage and doing something myself.'

Dan looked at me strangely and stopped yupping and scratching his beard.

'You?' he gasped. 'You mean to say, Mrs Everage, that, er . . . given certain financial inducements, *you* might be prepared to step in tomorrow night and save our show?'

'I hadn't thought of it,' I said, sounding confident but with butterflies inside. 'But I know I could do a darn sight better than poor little Barry.'

Dan grabbed me by the hand and gave me a theatrical kiss on both cheeks – the first of millions incidentally.

'Wait till I tell the others.'

★   ★   ★

Barry H took it rather well considering. After all he wasn't being cut from the entire show and the presence in the cast of a comparatively famous person who had been on the cover of the *Woman's Monthly* would only put money in his pocket at the end of the day. That night I lost a little sleep fretting about what the dickens I might do, or say, when I got on stage the following night, but as it happened, I needn't have worried.

Looking back that first night is a bit hazy. Let's face it, it's a part of theatre history now, and scholars can read about it on microfilm in the Everage Archives at the University of South

West Virginia (apply: Miriam K. Benkowitz). Enough to say that I wore a beautiful cerise and chartreuse Thai silk ballerina from the House of Delphine, and when I stepped on to the stage the audience stood up and, well, ovated. I'm sorry but they did. All I did was what I always do: chatted. I spoke a little of my young family, I described my home and I generally shared my experience, hope and strength with the audience. They had come expecting scathing satire, 'knocking' and cheap ridicule. Instead I gave them a gentle, blow-by-blow description of a housewife's life, and they lapped it up. They even laughed, not in mockery, but out of relief that they had not paid a babysitter and shelled out seven and six for nothing.

While I was wittering away I noticed a little woman in the front row staring at the gorgeous vase of gladdies on top of Wendy's piano. They were beautiful flesh-pink specimens, with lovely ruffled and crimped florets. As you know I adore the gladiolus (whose name means 'little spear' for my non-gardening readers), and as my talk drew to a close I yielded to a sudden impulse, and snatching the sheath of dripping stalks from its vase, hurled them with tremendous force at that mite in the front stalls who had so eagerly coveted them.

I'm afraid that it was a few seconds before she regained consciousness and became aware of my floral largesse, but she immediately and unselfishly began passing my blooms among the front row so that soon the stalls were a little garden of gaily wagging glads. I concluded with a verse and chorus of 'Home Sweet Home' in which the audience rousingly participated, and my 'spear carriers' of the front row instinctively oscillated their stalks in time to the music! One of the great finales in theatre history had been born, a finale which I still use at the end of my wonderful shows.

I was a hit, and Barry H had to admit it. At the backstage party after the show Dan begged me to stay on for the run, and since Madge was at home to babysit I thought, Why not? The party was a bit Bohemian with a lot of red wine in flagons and not much to eat, but I felt naturally elated and filled with a healthy self-esteem, which is quite OK according to Dr Sidney Shardenfreude whom I certainly don't see for myself.

In fact I even had a little celebratory dance with Dan to the gramophone.

> Vol–ah–ray . . . Oh Oh
> Vol–ah–ray . . . Oh Oh Oh Oh!

Next morning Kevin Farelly, my journalist pal, gave me a rave write-up in the *Morning Murdoch*. Without quite knowing it, I had set my slingback firmly on the bottom rung of the ladder to Megastardom.

CHAPTER XXI

Rude
Awakenings

S ENSIBLE PEOPLE, LIKE you I hope, get fed up to the teeth with theatrical chit-chat: 'I did this' and 'Then I did that' and 'Here's me with so and so'. Do me a favour, *leave it out*! Call me old-fashioned, but I don't need to blow my own trumpet on these pages, or anywhere for that matter. In a moment I am going to press the 'fast forward' button on my life but you can be sure I won't let you miss any of the juicy bits.

Soon after my sensational début at the Assembly Hall, standing in for BH at the last minute, I became quite a local star. A lot of people who win Quests like the Lovely Mother tend to fizzle out and sink into obscurity I'm afraid, but not me. Suddenly there was a new demand for me to appear on TV shows and at charity functions. I even made a couple of little microgrooves which are collector's items today. It wasn't long before Barry Humphries couldn't do a show without including me on the programme, and frankly, Readers, *I* was the one they flocked to see, not him I'm afraid.

Norman was proud of me too, and often used to sneak into the audience to watch me as I stood on stage, not insulting the audience's intelligence or spitting on all they held sacred, but chatting quietly and intelligently about real life and real issues. Norman always sat on the aisle so that he could slip out at any time to the Men's Powder Room. He still had a minor plumbing problem rumbling away and we didn't take it very seriously at the time. I little realised that one day the eyes of the world would be fixed on my husband's prostate, but a lot of water would have to be passed under the bridge before then.

Instead of being tired in the mornings after a night at the theatre, I got up bright and early and still took the children to school, and so it continued over the next few years. Madge had become a fixture in the veranda room and my mother spent more and more time in her own little world, though the television set in our lounge lured her out every evening. Madge and Mother had become as thick as thieves, *wouldn't you know*?! And I was amused to hear that when they went into town shopping one afternoon someone had mistaken them for sisters! My brother Roy, the Korean veteran, was living in the country, and the youngest Athol had, I'm afraid, married that insipid Dawn Purdie at Our Lady of Dolours, and about six months later they produced Wayne. So what else is new? It's a frightful thought but I suppose it's only a matter of time before they force my poor weak brother to 'turn'.

At a time when most women I knew, including Ann and Phyllis and Val (who had married Chip the Purser incidentally), were all taking up bowling and toddling off on Saturday afternoons in their matronly white uniforms, I had started a brand new career. Bruce and Valmai were shooting up fast though Kenny was always my darling little boy, and still is. I like to think that during the next ten years my children were proud of my growing fame and success. It never occurred to me that deep down my daughter Valmai resented me and felt that I was an overpowering role model who she could never hope to compete with. To be fair I suppose, children didn't use the words 'role model' in those days, thank goodness, but it hurts me to think that during all those years when I lavished costly prezzies on Valmai and pumped telephone numbers into her education, she was secretly seething.

I still conducted my little kiddies' class on Saturday morning though my pigeons were growing up fast and spreading their wings. One morning, we were all sitting around the kitchen table as I imparted some of my philosophies of life, while Norm, wearing one of my 'Deadly Snakes of Queensland' hand-crafted, Irish linen, Taiwanese aprons, peeled the potatoes and did the washing up. He was marvellous like that and never thought it was sissy to do household chores. Just as well!

I noticed little Germaine Greer watching him like a hawk and then gazing at me with unfeigned admiration. Afterwards, as we stepped over Norm who was by then scrubbing the kitchen floor, she whispered, 'They do it so much better than we do, don't they, Auntie Edna? It's as though Dame Nature had cut them out for the job!'

I laughed at her childish wisdom, and only years later when I read one of her clever books did my heart swell with pride to think that all her ideas sprang from that seminal moment in my kitchen.

Dan rang me with exciting news. Barry's show was wanted by a Sydney impresario but only on condition that I headed the cast. I leapt at the opportunity I'm afraid, since it was only for a month or so, and Norm said he could manage Bruce, Valmai and Mother. I decided to take Kenny with me, and Madge as a babysitter. Frankly, I was a bit worried that my Melbourne musings might be lost on a hard-bitten, more common Sydney audience, but I need not have worried. By the time they were waving their gladdies at the end of the show, I was the toast of that harbourside city and Barry Humphries was having to like it or lump it.

I loved peering into the audiences and chatting to women I liked the look of, usually shy types. But the faces were beginning to get a little blurry and I decided I needed new glasses. I had always worn them and even as a child I pioneered the slightly upswept frames that I have since made famous. However, when I next visited the optician, I lashed out on the more glittering butterfly face furniture which is still my trademark today. I also began, discreetly at first, to let my natural mauve hair-colouring grow back. Audiences loved it and I wondered why for so many years I had been ashamed of my lilac locks.

It was inevitable, I suppose, that I would get the travel bug again. My last trip to the Old Country had been a whirlwind affair though we still had about a thousand colour slides the neighbours hadn't seen yet. I loved giving slide evenings because they reminded me of the wonderful places I had been to and they also aroused a healthy jealousy in people who had never been outside Moonee Ponds. I suppose I naïvely hoped that the marvellous things that were happening to me were within every woman's grasp. I still didn't realise what an exceptional, 'one-off' talent I had. I'm sorry but I didn't.

But there was one horrendous slide night which almost led me to cancel them for ever. In the middle of a lot of unsorted and slightly blurry views of Auckland in the rain came some totally black pictures, then a black picture with a spooky brownish disc in the middle. It was very like the UFO in *The Day the Earth Stood Still* and my heart missed a beat to think we might have accidentally snapped a flying saucer.

'What the dickens is that, Madge?' I cried in the dark.

She was next door in the kitchen heating up the sausage rolls and squeezing passion-fruit on to the pavlova for supper, but she poked her head around the door into our darkened lounge to inspect the slide in question. Madge expelled a kind of choked-off shriek and dropped a whole tray of asparagus rolls on the wall-to-wall. That woman's been scoffing the savouries and helping herself to the Barossa Pearl again, I thought. Serves her right if a sausage roll goes down the wrong way. But Madge recovered herself enough to point at the ambiguous image which still flickered on our portable screen.

'It's his hat!' she wailed. 'It's Douglas's hat floating in the mud pool!' And with that she retreated, keening into the kitchen.

Everyone went a bit quiet after that except little Kenny, whose musical chuckle broke the stunned silence. He was exceptional too, I thought proudly, and he seemed to have inherited my philosophy of cheerful acceptance.

But I am an impatient woman I'm afraid. I want what I want when I want it. I'm one of those people who, standing on the kerbside with one arm raised, wonders why a taxi does not immediately scream to a halt. When I press a button to summon an elevator I always experience a pang of disappointment and surprise when the lift doors fail to open instantly. If there were anything whatsoever wrong with this, I am sure that Dr Sidney Shardenfreude would have mentioned it during our conferences about Valmai. Yet having embarked on a high-profile career and tasted the heady wine of popular acclaim, I was a very restless and frustrated *Hausfrau*.

Over the next few years as my family grew up I had bursts of success, it is true, which I need not describe in detail. 'Why not, Edna?' I hear you women ask. Because, Possums, quite frankly I'm not in the business of making my Readers jealous; that is not the purpose of this book, which is to educate, inform, and inspire. I'm terribly sorry but it is.

Then, if Norm and I ever went out to an important function, his manners were impeccable thanks to Pixie's grooming. When I used to see Mrs Thatcher's husband at lunches at number 10 his quiet attentiveness and gentle courtesy reminded me very much of Norm except that he didn't seem to have to leave the table quite so often.

Just when I was beginning to think I would not experience anything more than the warm glow of a short-lived success on my own home ground, a telegram arrived – from England. It said:

FAMOUS POET JOHN BETJEMAN HAS LENT ME ONE OF YOUR EARLY MICROGROOVES STOP YOU HAVE MANY FANS IN ENGLAND AND WILL BE A BIG STAR HERE OR I'M A DUTCHMAN STOP HAVE ASKED YOUR MANAGER BARRY HUMPHRIES TO BRING SHOW TO MY NEW LONDON CLUB THE ESTABLISHMENT WHERE WE TAKE THE MICKEY OUT OF THINGS WITH ZANY WACKY AND IRREVERENT HUMOUR AND SATIRE STOP GODSPEED STOP PETER COOK.

My excitement at reading this was mixed with irritation to think that people overseas believed Barry Humphries was my manager. Bitter that my fame had eclipsed his by a mile, he was probably trying to save face by taking the credit for mine. Norm read the telegram, half thrilled for me, half sweetly crestfallen at its implications. If I became a star in England the pattern of our family life would change radically and Norman would have to take on even more household duties than he at present performed. My dear husband snapped off a rubber glove, mopped his brow with his apron, and pointed to Barry's name on the telegram.

'Not such a bad idea, Ed,' he pronounced. 'You need a manager right now if you're going to hit the big time overseas, and although Barry's a bit of a drongo, better the devil you know!' I thought it over and a few weeks later Barry and I met my solicitors Fennimore and Gerda and I signed on the dotted.

★   ★   ★

When you're alone and life is making you lonely,
You can always go – Downtown.
When you've got worries all the noise and the hurry,
Seems to help, I know – Downtown . . .

Soho in the sixties was a far cry from my spotlessly clean stamping ground in the neighbourhood of Moonee Ponds. As I made my way up Greek Street to the Establishment Club I clutched my handbag very tightly and tried not to look to left or right. In narrow doorways flanked by lurid pin-ups lurked unsavoury looking fellows who occasionally buttonholed passing men and muttered things to them. Young girls with painted faces from broken homes darted in and out of other doorways on which notices advertised 'French lessons' and 'Cane-bottomed chairs, a speciality'. On some corners grubby beatniks huddled in their navy duffel coats and Ban-the-Bomb badges. Everywhere there was a whiff of Wimpys and the blare of rock music.

Actually, it's amazing how much I did notice without looking to left or right, *and* having to steer a goggle-eyed New Zealand bridesmaid down that grisly gauntlet. The club itself was yet another hole in the wall and the little so-called theatre in which Barry and I had to perform was more like a dimly lit corridor than a room. You approached it through a, well, a bar. Lounging around in this slightly sordid area were a few girls with short skirts, pale pearlised lips, fringes and too much mascara. In fact their eyes looked like black darns in their unhealthy white faces. They seemed to have names like Suki and Vanessa and they were saying things like 'fab' and 'yuh', for 'yes' and everything, according to them, was 'sooper'. They seemed to take a great interest in Madge and me as we entered but I suppose they had probably never seen nice people before in their lives, poor mites.

I can hear my Readers saying, 'Why the dickens has Edna got Madge Allsop in tow? Surely she would be nothing but a total liability in a sophisticated set-up like this?' My Readers, as usual, have hit the nail on the head, but to leave Madge behind would have been even more disastrous. Before we flew off out of Melbourne (yes, Mr Cook had sent us air tickets!) Norman had lovingly reassured me that he could manage the family on his own. Brucie and Valmai were quite grown up now and certainly capable of caring for Kenny and keeping an eye on Mummy, so I departed with a clear conscience. However, if Madge Allsop had stayed behind, *as she wanted to*, she would have 'moved in' with a vengeance. I could see her making a pathetic play for Norm, wheedling herself even further into my mother's good books and poisoning my children's minds with silly twaddle. Because I was so busy with my shows, she had spent far too much time with them already and when Kenny once called her 'Mummy' by accident and hugged her, she looked like the cat that had got the cream. Anyway, she would be quite useful to me in London when my show at the Establishment was a smash hit. She could help me handle the sacks of fan mail, arrange my floral tributes, and answer the telephone. Besides, with all her drawbacks, old Madge was company, I'm sorry but she was.

We were greeted by a tall willowy young man in casual clothes and 'sneakers'. He had a boyish habit of inclining his head to one side, looking down his long nose and flicking back a light brown forelock, and he had a little upside-down smile, like a thin, kind shark. Peter Cook, for it was he, led us into the club where Barry Humphries was already ensconced. On the stage some university students were doing impersonations of Harold Macmillan and stopping a lot to laugh and light smelly cigarettes called Disque Bleu. When their rehearsal was over Barry started going through his endless chatter and then Peter asked me if I'd like to do my material.

'I don't do material, Mr Cook,' I replied. 'I just talk quietly about my life and my family and make it up as I go along, like real people do when they're chatting to each other.'

Peter seemed taken aback, but not unimpressed by this simple description of my 'act', and Madge and I went home to our little hotel to freshen up before the first night. Funnily enough I wasn't nervous though I was a bit worried as to how poor Barry's so-called funny material would go down with a London audience since he didn't mention Harold Macmillan once.

That evening the little tables in the club were packed with celebrities, and kind, supportive Peter pointed some of them out to me as we nibbled our steaks in the corner. That jolly little balding man with the wavy upper lip was John Betjeman the famous poet who apparently adored me. Over there in a grubby pink suit was a droopy man whose arms were too long for his body, chain smoking cigarettes with the wrong fingers. His name was Tynan, a critic apparently, and I blushed to think he had the same Christian name as my own manly little son. Jean Shrimpton, the famous glamourpuss, was looking bewildered. Holding forth at her table was a carrot-headed, camel-faced man in a crumpled corduroy suit called Dr Miller, who seemed to be trying to knot his arms together with some degree of success. I even noticed a few journalists with notebooks at the ready.

In no time, it seemed, I was in the cramped dressing room with Madge helping me into the lovely frock old Miss Wilmot had made for my London début. It was a glorious peacock and cyclamen Thai silk sheath with fly-away panels and I had teamed my accessories, shoes, handbag and spectacle frames with the ensemble. Madge was quite sweet really. 'I've got everything crossed for you tonight, Edna,' she said giving me a squeeze.

Peter Cook put his head around the door. 'You're on in a few minutes now, Mrs Everage,' he announced with a rather worried look. 'That's if Barry ever winds up.'

I listened at the door which separated my dressing room from the small stage. Barry's voice was certainly audible, droning on and on, but where were the bursts of laughter which used to sometimes interrupt his shows in Australia? Instead of laughter and the splatter of applause, I could hear an odd shuffling and clattering noise and even the sound of people chatting quite loudly amongst themselves.

Suddenly the door burst open nearly knocking me to the floor. It was Barry and he was covered with perspiration. As he threw himself into a chair he waved in the direction of the audience. 'Your turn now, Mrs Everage,' he barked rudely. 'See if you can do better with that load of pommy poofters. They wouldn't know a good comedy routine from a hole in the ground. They're just out there to be seen!'

I took all this with a grain of salt. Barry has always been a bad loser and I knew when I stepped into the spotlight the audience would be eating out of my hand. In fact, *when the time came*, the spotlight was so bright I was dazzled and could not see that crowd of eager, expectant faces peering up at me from their liquor laden tables but I started chatting all the same.

'Excuse I! My name is Mrs Everage, Mrs Norm Everage of Moonee Ponds, Melbourne . . .' My voice faltered. Why was everyone so quiet? I ducked my head and squinted through the light so that I could see what reaction I was getting but the three tables next to the stage on which I managed to focus appeared to be empty. '. . . It's lovely to be in the Old Country, so full of pomp and pageantry . . .' I looked into the audience again, this time shading my eyes. What I saw is not a sight I would wish on any other young actress, or old actress for that matter. The room was empty. It was like the *Marie Celeste*. Well, it was almost empty. At a couple of remote tables, slumped in embarrassed postures, sat the critics scribbling in their notebooks, but even they had left by the time my monologue wound feebly to its conclusion. I had brought all the way from Australia, by Qantas, several dozen magnificent gladdies which Madge dutifully passed to me through a crack in the door even though there was no one to catch them. But throw them I did, hearing the occasional gratifying tinkle of a champagne bottle or wine glass, as I shied those lovely blooms, symbols of my own invincible talent, across that deserted restaurant.

I had a bit of a weep afterwards. Barry had gone home in a huff, the worse for a few sherries I'm afraid, but Peter was very sweet and told me on the quiet that the audience had all been drifting out to the bar throughout the Humphries section and he thought my material would catch on eventually with discerning people. Talking of which, gorgeous John Betjeman popped in to say he'd watched it all from a shadowy corner of the room and he had thought it was all 'marvellous' and 'sheer genius'. Were they just being nice? I wondered. Or should I get on the next plane back to Australia?

Hours and hours later I was aroused from a tearful sleep by the telephone jangling in our little hotel room. Disentangling myself from the vice-like half-Nelson in which Madge held me captive, I drowsily raised the receiver.

'Edna? It's Kev Farelly callin' from Sinny.'

'Who? Who's calling from Sydney?'

'It's Kevin on the *Morning Murdoch*, Edna,' came the chirpy little fox-terrier voice down the wire from Australia.

'Sorry to getcha outta bye-byes but I wanna arse yiz a few questions about the show last night. They reckon yiz bombed.'

'WHAT?' I ejaculated.

'Who is it, Edna?' said Madge, lifting her slumber shades.

'Shut up, sticky-beak! No, *not you, Kevin*. Is it in the Australian papers already? Read it to me for heaven's sake!'

Kevin Farelly sounded almost cheerful as he rustled the newspaper down the phone and intoned, '"POMMY CRITICS SLAM OUR EDNA!" . . . Wanna hear any more?'

I groaned. 'No, Kevin, but go on.'

'Last night at London's swish Establishment Club before an audience of silvertails and assorted literati, Barrie Humphrey had a profound effect on his audience. They walked out. The Melbourne comic, famous for taking the mickey, didn't cut much ice with the Brit press who said what a few discerning Australian critics have been whispering for years: "Barrie's a bore!"'

'We all know that!' I snapped impatiently, pulling my nightie roughly around my shoulders and kicking Madge out of the way as she tried to pin her ear to the receiver.

'What about me, Kevin? What does it say about *me*?'

'That's the point, Ed, that's what I'm comin' to,' replied the journalist. 'They all reckoned you was Barry!'

'They *what*?' I exclaimed incredulously.

'You'll read it all in the pommy papers today, Edna,' he went on, relentlessly, 'but we got it all on the wire last night and so we've run the story real big. Fact is, they all think you're Bazza dressed up! Listen to this from the *Daily Mail*: ". . . after the mass exodus from Humphries' first monologue, those brave few who remained were treated to a second bizarre offering, in female attire! The antipodean wag can only be congratulated on the speed of his transformation into an attractive Melbourne housewife, but where was the comedy? Where was the satire? Where the social relevance? His 'Mrs Everage' might just as well have been a real woman. This is not the biting and iconoclastic material we have come to expect from Peter Cook's new club. Mr Humphries should pack up his frocks and go back Down Under."'

There was a silence on the other end, then Kevin Farelly's voice said, 'Well. . . ?'

'Well what?'

'Got any comments for the readers, Ed?'

'CERTAINLY NOT!' I barked, slamming down the instrument so hard that I splashed water on my watch.

'What is it, Edna? What's the matter?' beseeched Allsop as I moaned loudly and pulverised the pillow with my fists.

'You've got last night's programme haven't you, Madge? Let me see it. Quick sticks!'

The bridesmaid hopped out of bed and yanked a brochure from the pocket of her frayed fawn overcoat. I riffled through it frenziedly and, finding the place, thrust it under Madge's nose as I jabbed at the page with a minatory finger.

'Look, woman, look! I might have known! Where's my name? Nowhere! Who gets the billing? He does!! Who's there in big letters with a photo and a biog? HIM! You wouldn't think I was even in the show. *And neither did they!*'

I flung the programme across the bedroom and fell sobbing into Mrs Allsop's cadaverous embrace.

'Oh, Madge!' I choked, still fuming with rage and hurt pride, 'he hogged all the limelight and now I'm a laughing stock. The humiliation! The shame!'

Madge didn't know what to say, so what else is new?

'How will I ever shake off this stigma?' I resumed tearfully. 'Wherever I go and for years to come, people will remember this story. My femininity, my very *essence* has been impugned.'

Actually, I didn't say 'impugned' at the time, for the simple reason that I only took up Scrabble ten years later.

Since then, on and off, a particular type of gutter journalist has occasionally suggested that I am not a beautiful and talented woman, but a sick and twisted man dressed up as one. It is not a rumour which gets reprinted very often because every time it appears it generally costs the newspaper in question about a

million pounds in punitive and exemplary damages. But supposing for argument's sake I *was* Barry Humphries dressed up, how
do they explain the fact that he has managed to give birth to three
children, prithee? Do me a favour, leave it out!! Other female
achievers, it seems, have had to put up with a similar slur. I've
even heard vile innuendos that Mrs Thatcher is really a man.
Yuk!!

Next morning, the London papers all panned the show and
those few that mentioned me had all grabbed the same wrong
end of the stick. Luckily, Kevin had forewarned me. After only
a few performances, one of the managers of the club came to see
me. He wore a char-grey suit (in the early sixties everything was
char-this or -that), a pink shirt and a black knitted tie. His name
was Johnny something, and he'd been in some sort of Guards.
There are a lot of middle-class Englishmen called John who
cultivate the schoolboy appellation of 'Johnny' because they hope
it might make them seem a bit more dashing and interesting,
moreover it nudges them a few necessary rungs up the social
ladder. Show me a Johnny and I'll show you a bore. He was
perfectly nice, but he more or less said he was paying me off at
the end of the week. The show was over. Peter Cook rang up
and apologised, but not a peep from Barry who was wisely
keeping his head down. Our Establishment contract was regret-
fully terminated and we all went home to Australia with our tails
between our legs.

This was the lowest ebb in my career, but I have described it
honestly and courageously. I was hurt at the time and my confidence was badly shaken, but I decided to have a few tough new
clauses written into my contract with Mr H. I also vowed that if
I ever found success outside my native land, I would remember
this incident.

And so I did. It flashed into my mind one night in 1976 standing
on the stage of London's beautiful Apollo Theatre in Shaftesbury
Avenue, as the entire audience clutching its gladdies rose to its
feet in a tumultuous standing ovation. This was the brilliant
sunshine of success which I appreciated all the more keenly
because I had known the shadow of rejection.

'Hang on!' I can hear my Readers expostulating. 'Is Dame Edna skipping more than a decade of her riveting life story? Are we being short-changed? What's happened to Norm, Bruce, Valmai and Kenny? Is Madge still on the scene?'

To you I reply quite simply. A lot of other famous people string out their memoirs into umpteen volumes for crass financial gain. I could easily stop my story now and leave you all drooling for the next instalment, but I'm not like that. I'm sorry but I'm not. Senior citizens reading this book might not, to put it brutally, be alive for Volume Two. I also have to cater for people with reading disabilities or fans of mine who have never read a book in their lives; and research had determined that I have an enormous illiterate following. I wouldn't be doing them a favour by producing another volume that's going to take them a year to read with one finger. These are just a few reasons why I am skipping towards the Present, but to keep you in the picture, here's a quick résumé.

Gladys Beazley. My mother is a marvel really. She never changes, though I wish she'd change some of her underthings. She fluctuates a lot I'm afraid.

Norm. Continues to 'hold fort' whenever I am off on tour. Ongoing problems with his waterworks, but a marvellous husband and father.

Barry Humphries. Still my manager but under solicitor's thumb. His contributions to our show getting smaller by the year.

Bruce. Married! Too young of course, but while I was overseas, grabbed by a cradle-snatcher called Joylene Wacker who gives herself airs. She had the cheek to tell me at the wedding that she had rescued him from a domineering mother. Only realised on the way home she meant me. Minx! A kiddie already – Troy, I'm afraid.

Valmai. A real worry. Rebellious, moody, ungrateful. Married also to a very nice boy called Mervyn Gittis who I feel sorry for. One kiddie – little Wayne – and another on the way! I dread to think how this will end.

Kenny. Normal, thank goodness. Devoted, talented, affectionate. Wish he got on a bit better with Norm who calls him a cissy
sometimes, just because Ken hasn't rushed up the aisle with the
first little gold-digger who comes along. Kenny designed Ball
and Welch's Christmas window display this year using a thousand
yards of terylene tulle. He is also studying choreography at night.
Sometimes quite late at night. I've always taught him to believe
that when girls said 'yes' they meant 'no'.

Madge Allsop. I am now totally supporting her for which I
deserve to be canonised. Wherever I am, she's there. 'No show
without punch,' as my mother used to say. Getting rather vain
too, and big for her boots.

★   ★   ★

After the first triumphant night of *Housewife Superstar*, our little
producer Michael White phoned me. 'Do you think it's going to
be a hit?' I asked Mr White anxiously.

   'Absolutely!' he averred. (In 1976 'Absolutely' meant Yes.) He
went on to read me the rave reviews, and this time hardly a
mention of Barry. If you let her, it's amazing how, given time,
dear old Dame Nature sorts things out.

CHAPTER XXII

Water Under the Bridge

I WAS THE toast of London town. Some of the critics who had given me the 'thumbs down' at the Establishment Club or had even questioned my sexuality were eating their words, and Mr Osborne, who shared my box at *My Fair Lady* on my first visit to London years before, reappeared. He was now quite high up on the Arts Council, dishing out the taxpayers' money to disabled lesbian guerrilla basket-weavers.

'I prophesied your theatrical career,' he said rather smugly one night in my flower-filled dressing room, 'but you still haven't played the Theatre Royal, Drury Lane.' There's no pleasing some people, I reflected philosophically. Mr Osborne invited me to do a poetry reading with two poets called Allen Ginsberg and W. H. Auden. I read some of my own works and some other lovely verses by Australian women, holding everyone spellbound; whilst the other two – wouldn't you know – gave the audience a really hard time, mumbling their own murky verses. Mr Ginsberg's poems being more than a little on the uncalled-for side too! Mr Auden and I hit it off quite well backstage however, though his suit looked as though it had been slept in (by someone else) and the poor old thing wasn't exactly, as Norm would say, 'in showroom condition'.

As Wystan and I nattered on about art and life, I gazed sadly

at his creased old countenance. He didn't get a face like *that* from
eating strawberries!

Somewhere along the way, I received my Damehood. Please
forgive me, Readers, for not being more precise, but you ought
to know by now that honours mean very little to me. A queue
at the box office, a microgroove in the charts or record ratings
for a TV spectacular are the *real* honours in my life, not forgetting
of course the love of my family. I must confess however, that at
this stage I sometimes went whole days without those little mites
in Melbourne crossing my mind; it's awful I know, but that's
how it was.

At least I knew 36 Humouresque Street was running like
clockwork, and Norm deserved a medal for the way he coped.
My sister-in-law Audrey née Foote was a big help too, and darling
old Mummy muddled along somehow. It was Kenny who always
kept me posted, with wonderful long letters. He wrote in green
ink, and instead of dotting his i's he always put little circles over
them – a sure sign of artistic talent, I read once in the *Woman's
Monthly*. Kenny loved films, particularly the older type of movie
that I had enjoyed in my youth, and his favourite actresses were
June Allyson, Susan Hayward, Barbara Stanwyck, Joan Crawford
and Marlene Dietrich, though he adored Judy Garland too and
used to mime to her microgrooves. I wrote back telling him of
the wonderful people I was meeting, especially at parties given
by my little producer Michael White. Ken was over the moon
when I told him that the night before I'd been in the same room
as Ava Gardner, Gloria Grahame and Andy Warhol. I can't say
Andy bowled me over; he always looked like a ghost or, at his
best, a convalescent; always standing against the wall or by a
doorway in case someone important came in. If they didn't, then
at least he was near the exit. He wanted to make some silkscreens
of me, he said, but we never got round to it and I have no regrets.
Frankly I never quite saw the point of him.

I began to mention my Damehood, and I won't dwell on it
now, except to say that it was conferred on me by the late
Australian Prime Minister Gough Whitlam, and there is actual
archival footage showing him 'Dame-ing' me. It was for my
services to World Culture and since then, needless to say, jealous

types have made the odd snide remark to the effect that I'm not *really* a Dame. To them I sweetly say, 'All right, if I'm not a Dame, how come it took me all those years to get the Queen to drop my title and call me Edna?'

Another element also gave me a hard time for accepting a Damehood when I am fundamentally a left-wing radical. I guess I'm a bit of a paradox as a lot of famous women tend to be. For instance, I happen to be the reincarnation of Joan of Arc (probably one of the reasons why I can't stand barbecues). Joan was to the far left of Vanessa Redgrave – *and a Saint*! Let the cynics mull over that one.

Next door to my Shaftesbury Avenue theatre, Lady Olivier (lovely Joan Plowright) was doing her show which I think had something to do with seagulls. Needless to say, it didn't exactly have the audience in stitches and poor Joan was constantly thumping on the wall whenever my patrons laughed too loudly which was about every ten seconds. Success, I'm afraid, always carries a high level of noise pollution. I'm sorry, but it does. Yet I suppose it must be a bit irritating to be in a show adjacent to one of my theatres, gazing out across the footlights at a sparse and sombre little audience and at the same time hearing shrieks and roars of delight coming through the party wall. These days, I always request my patrons to keep their laughter and applause down, out of consideration to shows less fortunate than my own.

On the last rapturous night of *Housewife Superstar*, impeccably timed by dear old Dame Nature, came a bombshell. A phone call from my sister-in-law Audrey in Melbourne.

'What do you mean don't worry, don't worry? Of course I'm worried, Audrey,' I cried anxiously. 'I'm even worried before I know what it is. Is it Mummy? Is it little Kenny? Don't tell me Valmai's been playing up again!'

Audrey's voice faltered. 'They're fine, they're all fine, Edna. We're thrilled by your success. It's just Norman . . .'

'Norm? What's wrong with Norm?'

'Just a little check-up, Edna,' said Audrey calmly. 'Nothing serious. He was rushed to hospital last night with a police escort and is in intensive care doing as well as can be expected. Isn't it a lovely day today?'

'It's freezing and pouring with rain, woman!' I exploded. 'London is on the other side of the world. Do you seriously think when it's a nice day in Melbourne, it's the same all over the planet?!!' I took a grip on myself and added, more softly, 'What's the matter with him?'

'It's the prostate, Edna, if you'll excuse the expression. He's had a flutter there for quite a while and last night it just blew up. Luckily he wasn't wearing his new suit at the time.'

'Thank heaven for small mercies!' I replied. 'I'll get on the next plane.'

'Oh, Edna,' Audrey whined (she was beginning to irritate me, poor soul), 'we can manage and they say Australian doctors lead the world in prostate research. Don't interrupt your wonderful career.'

'Stop talking twaddle, Audrey,' I retorted crossly. 'This is a family crisis and Norm's prostate is as much a part of the family as you are.' I made a mental note to look up a decent medical publication and find out where the prostate was. It's a pretty elusive organ, a bit like the appendix I gathered; something we've all got but don't need any more. I certainly didn't need Norm's and it was on the cards that he would be learning to live without it too pretty soon, bless him.

Soon Madge and I were winging out way back to Australia, and a new era in my life if I only knew it.

Dr. Gerald Finzi took me to one side. 'Please don't worry unduly about Mr Everage,' he said.

'*Lord* Everage,' I corrected him, putting away my hankie and looking brave. 'But I can't help worrying about my husband, Doctor. He looks so pale there in that thingummy. What's it called?

It's an iron prostate,' replied the medico coughing and lighting a cigarette.

I sat in the chair he indicated while he paced around the small office.

'Mr er . . . I mean Lord Everage is hooked up to a unique piece of technological hardware which does for that litle rogue organ of his what the iron lung does for other parts of the human anatomy.' He stopped to cough.

You may not know it, Dame Edna, but Australia is at the sharp end of prostate research and we want to stay there. But we need funds.' He looked out of the window as though a lot of money was about to fall from the sky. 'I have a dream, Dame Edna,' he said, suddenly plonking himself behind his desk and lighting another ciggie from the butt of the last one. 'The world's first prostate bank and prostate transplant unit. It *can* be done! My team . . .'

I waited expectantly till he had reached the end of another bronchial paroxysm.

'My team here have been working with wombats and we have had an incredibly high success rate in transplanting wombat prostates. With your permission, Madam, I want to try the same thing with your husband.'

'I don't know whether I'd particularly like Norm with a wombat's organ,' I remonstrated with the doctor. 'Don't they do a lot of unnecessary burrowing?'

Dr Finzi laughed wheezily. 'You misunderstand me, dear lady. We would use a human donor of course, but you must realise that at this stage there is still a risk that your husband's organ could be rejected.'

'He ought to be pretty used to that by now,' I replied pragmatically, 'but you must do whatever you think is best.' I added bravely, 'I'm sure Norm would be happy to think that he was pushing back the frontiers of prostatology.'

Madge and I tiptoed in to have a last peep at Norm, his little head poking out of the end of an enormous chrome box covered with dials and flashing lights. He was pretty groggy but he recognised me and managed a wan smile. I was pleased to see that he was being looked after by a charming nurse who introduced herself to me as Sister Thelma Younghusband. Perhaps *too* charming. She was to supervise Norm's treatment on and off, for many years to come as it happened, and although at first she seemed a nice person to my innocent eyes, I little realised that even then that minx had my husband's prostate in the palm of her hand.

Having done all I could that day, and experiencing jet-lag after

my long flight, I was wearily climbing into my car in the hospital
car park, when a hacking cough behind me announced the presence of Dr Finzi.

'Just before you go, Dame Edna, I thought I should mention
that if your husband responds to treatment, he can come home.
But I suggest that he will need all that equipment pretty close at
hand. Do you have a spare room available?'

I was pleased, a bit shocked, goodness knows what. I said I'd
think about it. Then the doctor added, 'If ever you're looking for
a good cause to support, Dame Edna, we here at the clinic
would be very proud if you considered pumping money into the
prostate.'

As we drove out of the car park, Madge suddenly turned and
glanced back at the hospital. 'Look, Edna,' she said. 'Isn't that
Norm's nurse?' I followed her fawn finger. There in a window
on the first floor, staring out at us with a very odd expression on
her face, was Thelma Younghusband.

★   ★   ★

Humouresque Street was a pig-sty. I wandered in a daze from
one shabby little room to the next, observing the piles of old
newspapers, the empty cups with their sticky dregs and, in front
of our television set, piles of unwashed plates smeared with the
dried-up traces of baked-bean suppers, long since devoured.

Darling Kenny had greeted me at the front door wearing a
gorgeous purple tie-dyed T-shirt with drawstring sleeves and a
lovely pair of burgundy crushed velvet bell bottoms over his
clogs. He was as upset as I was at the state of the house. Apparently every time he cleaned or tidied it up, my mother would
emerge from her room and within minutes turn the home into
a rubbish dump. Since Norm had been rushed to hospital,
Mummy had gone from bad to worse and was behaving more
strangely than ever. Kenny had been studying dressmaking at
night school, and he kept his little Singer in a corner of our
lounge. However one night, when he was out with his friend
Clifford Smail at the Moonee Theatre watching *Beyond the Valley
of the Dolls,* Mummy had run amok with the machine and somehow managed to hemstitch her nightie to the curtains. I glanced

balefully at my mother's bedroom door, ominously closed. Funny, I thought. Her famous daughter back home after months in the Old Country, and she doesn't dare show her nose around the corner! Sure sign of a guilty conscience.

'Seen Valmai lately?' I asked aloud, noticing several ashtrays brimming with twisted butts. My delightful teenager, the most loyal brother Valmai is ever likely to have in her life, just sucked in his cheeks and raised his lovely brown eyes to the ceiling in an eloquent gesture which told all.

But I didn't have to pump Ken too hard to get at the truth. Apparently my difficult daughter had been putting her poor young husband Mervyn through hell ever since I had left for London. Most of the time he had to look after baby Wayne single-handed, while she went gallivanting off on trips she could ill afford with her off-beat friends. Reluctantly, Ken slowly painted a picture of my daughter which no mother in her right mind would particularly wish to frame and put on top of the piano. It seems she'd gone off to Bali for a couple of weeks, and not only come back with something called full-blown thrush, but smoking those ghastly Indonesian cigarettes. Probably why the whole house now had the yukky smell of cloves and stale smoke, I thought, sniffing disdainfully.

Ken said that whenever she had a row with Mervyn, which was every second day, she would come home here to sleep and always leave a trail of devastation and full ashtrays in her wake. Her latest fad was the Living Theatre, some rat-bag group of troubled young women who took their clothes off on stage and made little films of each other doing nothing, on huge government grants.

I was beginning to see that Valmai was jealous of me and was, in her pathetic way, trying to grab a bit of attention for herself, without the prerequisite of talent. Where would it end? I reflected with a shudder.

Gazing once more at the mess and chaos of my abused residence, I wished in a way that I could have blamed it all on Madge Allsop. But Madge had the perfect alibi; she had been with me in England.

'Look at my lovely lounge, Madge,' I shouted. 'Look at this mess! If you hadn't insisted on traipsing across to Europe, hanging on to my coat tails, you could have stayed here and kept the house as it should be!'

Madge tensed her shoulders slightly and looked a bit hunted.

'Kenny is still a student, Norm is a cot-case, and Mummy is a lunatic, so I hold you fully responsible for wrecking my beautiful home!' and with that I flung myself on the couch and sobbed uncontrollably in the arms of my son.

'Where was Norm when I needed him?' I fretted tearfully, as Ken cradled me in his Brut-scented embrace. I had taken that darling for granted all these years and now he belonged to Science – a human guinea-pig in a cold, impersonal hospital with strange hands hovering at blanket-bath time.

Suddenly, I had made up my mind. I remembered with a spooky shudder the face of that Sister Younghusband at the window. Norm *was* coming home – and soon! Hadn't Dr Finzi said it was all quite feasible so long as we had plenty of room for the technology? Well we didn't have room, but we *would*! In a trice my knuckles were rapping on Mummy's door. I could hear the radio jabbering loudly, one of those popular phone-in programmes where silly women pour their hearts out to feather-brained disc jockeys. I tried the door. It was locked and there was a distinct smell of burning beans oozing through the architrave. A brainwave struck me and I darted for the telephone. There was the number in the yellow pages under 'wireless stations'. Soon the operator, a bit overwhelmed after I had dropped my famous name, switched me through to Neville in the studio, and while he played a disc I explained my predicament.

Seconds later, I was on the air.

'Can you hear me, Mummy? It's your daughter Edna here, home from England. Turn off the wireless and unlock the door at once. And your beans are burning! Do you hear me?'

I looked across at her door, but nothing seemed to be happening.

'Come out peacefully, Mummy,' I resumed, remembering those thrillers on TV where policemen with loudhailers and guns hide behind cars at night, waiting for psychopaths to come out of front doors.

'No one's going to hurt you, Mummy,' I continued, warming

to my task. 'You are completely surrounded, so just come out quietly with your hands above your head.'

From my mother's bedroom I could hear the spooky echo of my own voice coming through the radio. Goodness knows what Neville's listeners thought of this bizarre broadcast, but it did the trick, for as I put down the phone, her door opened a crack, then a little wider, and my mother, in a stained nightie and threadbare matinée jacket, her arms raised high, tottered into the hall. If you've ever seen that wonderful old video of *Jane Eyre*, you'll know what I mean if I tell you Mummy looked like Grace Poole on a bad day.

Kenny did his rather elegant version of a rugby tackle, bringing the old darling crashing to the carpet, while I held my breath and took a quick peek into her room. It was no longer a room. Old papers, back numbers of the *Woman's Monthly*, bygones and junk were densely piled from floor to ceiling. A narrow tunnel or fissure ran between them, through which I just managed to squeeze; and proceeding along this rank-smelling maze, I at last found my way to the grey tangle of nylon and candlewick which my mother called a bed. There were things in that room amongst the rusty Heinz tins and stiff rosettes of Kleenex which no Reader of this book, particularly one who has enjoyed, or hopes to enjoy, a nice meal need closely examine. I felt a bit like Lord Caernarvon entering Tutankhamen's whiffy tomb and it was spooky to think that most of the time it contained a real mummy. Enough to say that I emerged gagging, my eyes weeping from barely suppressed nausea. I only hoped *my* mummy's inner chamber didn't have a curse on it!

Seizing once more a telephone directory and riffling purposefully through the yellow pages, I caringly addressed my mother as she lay almost languidly on the carpet beneath Kenny's restraining clogs.

'Darling,' I began, finding the number I sought under 'geriatric contractors' and dialling it. 'How would you like a luxury holiday in a beautiful hotel?' My mother glared and shook her head violently.

'You could take your lovely things with you, Mummy,' I said in my most beguiling tones. 'Well, some of them.'

The supine granny narrowed her eyes suspiciously. 'Can I watch TV and eat my beans there?' she enquired rationally.

'Of course, darling. It's a home away from home,' I declared with considerable truth.

A firm woman's voice came through the receiver.

'Dunraven Sunset Facility. Sister Choate speaking.'

'Oh,' I exclaimed nicely. 'This is Dame Edna Everage, housewife superstar. I wonder, do you have a vacancy for a refined lady; my mother actually?'

Sister Choate said she did and asked how soon and whether I needed the door-to-door collection service.

'Oh, it sounds such a pretty room. My mother will love a short vacation there I'm sure, and you say baked beans is your chef's speciality?' My mother's eyes lit up and a gleaming stalactite of saliva inched from the corner of her mouth towards the carpet.

'What was that? I beg your pardon?' came the Sister's voice down the phone.

'How lovely!' I persisted, in spite of exclamations of surprise and confusion on the other end.

'Mrs Beazley is excited about it already. Perhaps you could send the courtesy bus as soon as possible.' I gave our address and hung up.

'Oh, Mummy darling,' I enthused, helping her up as Madge arrived with some tea. 'You lucky old thing, having a holiday at Dunraven. We're all so jealous, aren't we, Madge?'

Allsop looked at us blankly.

'Kenny and Madge will pack a few of your little personals and we'll send some of your other things round later.'

My son and bridesmaid exchanged a despondent glance. But my mother, I am pleased to say, already excited by the prospect of a five-star vacation, shuffled back into her room for a moment only to emerge wearing a soiled white tennis shade and brandishing a tennis racquet from which the strings hung like spaghetti.

'This place is bound to have plenty of sports facilities, Edna,' said Mummy with worrying normalcy. 'I only hope they can find me a decent partner.'

Night had fallen suddenly, and my mother's expectations of her future accommodation were becoming, by the hour, almost rhapsodic, without any encouragement from me. She sat on the edge of her bed supervising the packing, while Kenny and Madge, wearing improvised surgical masks, rummaged in fetid drawers and closets which were little more than aviaries for moths. They managed, without Mummy noticing, to shift a large number of her so-called effects out the back door to the incinerator. It might otherwise have taken the Dunraven staff hours to dig her out if she had decided, at the last minute, to resist incarceration.

At last however, a van pulled into our driveway and four nice lads in white boilersuits filed into her room and with the minimum of unnecessary violence extracted my perverse parent and bundled her caringly into their Dettol-scented geri-mobile.

Once the doors had been slammed, I offered the helpful young orderlies a nice cup of tea while Ken and Madge continued to make a sizeable dent in Mummy's debris. Soon, the incinerator was roaring yet again, sending up huge and rather beautiful orange flames. Funnily enough, as those charming young men thanked me for the refreshments and climbed back into their van, I noticed my mother peering through the small barred glass window in the back, her adorable little face illuminated by the warm, flickering light of her combusting bygones.

CHAPTER XXIII

The Psychedelic
Christmas Pudding

I WILL NEVER forget the day Norm came home. Humouresque Street was agog. After my big success Overseas, I had become what we call in Australia an 'Identity', and the people of Moonee Ponds were naturally very proud of me. As a kind of tribute and celebration, the old street was decked with bunting and even the Mayor, Councillor Tom Puckle (a descendant of the explorer who discovered Moonee Ponds), turned up in all his furry finery outside our home to officially greet the ambulance and its celebrated occupant. Naturally the media were there in full force to capture the poignancy and warm human interest of Lord Norm's festive homecoming, and let's face it, there was a good deal of world interest in the event as well. We were, after all, making medical history since it was the first time one of these miracle machines had been installed in a private home.

'Will you be giving up your career to nurse your husband?' was the question on everybody's lips, and I even had a young whipper-snapper from the *Morning Murdoch* on my doorstep at the crack of dawn asking me if my retirement was imminent.

'Fiddlesticks!' I exclaimed, using an expression you don't hear much these days (and does anyone play that wonderful old game any more?). I thought of Dame Margot Fonteyn and her disabled hubby. *There* was a brave superstar who managed to pirouette about the stage *and* push a wheelchair at the same time!

As I was explaining to this boyish reporter that I fully intended to combine my work with my responsibilities as a wife and mother, I reflected, a little wistfully, how much time had already flown since Kevin Farelly stood on that very same porch in the small hours of the morning, and broke the news of my victory in the Lovely Mother Quest. What had happened to him? I wondered. Things had certainly changed a lot since those far-off days, and now the world press was beating a path to my door.

I put on a lovely new frock for the occasion. It was a beautiful 'ocelot' printed crêpe number from the famous Le Louvre in Collins Street. Poor Miss Wilmot, who used to make all my dresses, had finally been gathered; or in rag-trade parlance, gone to that big wardrobe in the sky.

As the Mayor and I stood nervously on the porch waiting for Norm's motorcade to turn the corner out of Puckle Street, I had my fingers firmly crossed that Valmai, my dissatisfied daughter, would not suddenly turn up in inappropriate clothing and draw attention to herself. Madge was no less of a worry, because she had developed an awful tendency to lunge. Even if there was only a minor celebrity present, she would lunge at him all the same, usually with her autograph book. Nice chums of mine like Barry Manilow, Larry Hagman and Roger Moore have taken pity on her and scribbled something in it, and my Readers will not be surprised to hear that now, at the time of writing, Madge's autograph book is a television series in New Zealand. They just put it on a little easel, point a camera at it, and a gloved hand (meant to be Madge's) turns a page every week. It has even won awards! – in New Zealand.

More recently, Madge has tended to lunge at Royalty, in the hope of being manhandled by bodyguards. The other day she even lunged at the Dagenham Girl Pipers in the hope of·being manhandled by a woman, poor wretch. But on the occasion of Norm's homecoming, I gave her plenty to do in my kitchen to keep her out of mischief. She was assigned the task of preparing some savoury dips for a few VIPs and hospital dignitaries. 'Dips' were the latest thing in Australia, and had rather elbowed out sausage rolls and Lamingtons, which most of us had to furtively scoff behind closed doors once the guests had gone home.

When the ambulance at last appeared, the local residents lining the streets cheered excitedly and pelted the white vehicle with streamers and the occasional glad. A little awestruck hush followed however, when they saw the enormous pantechnicon which crept along behind it. That was the conveyance which housed my husband's costly and cumbersome prostate support system, and which would soon be established in what had formerly been my darling old mother's bedroom.

For weeks previously, fumigators, builders, plumbers and urological engineers had been swarming through my home, installing a cement floor in what was now the 'Engine Room', and punching holes in the wall to accommodate the elaborate conduits and ducting which would soon link the iron prostate to my husband's adjacent bedroom. I had resigned myself, by then, to sleeping in a separate room to that of my beloved invalid. Since Brucie, and to some extent Valmai, no longer lived at home, I had redecorated the old nursery and moved in there. At Dr Finzi's suggestion my new bedroom had been soundproofed, since Norm's device was far from silent, and I had expressed my concern that the shuddering roar which it emitted day and night could well disturb our more sensitive neighbours. The doctor pointed out that Norm could, if he so wished, switch off the power and operate his support system manually, or rather by pedalling. Ultimately this proved impractical, since by about four o'clock in the morning he had generally ripped the sheets to shreds. A few years later we might have described this alternative power source as 'counter-productive'.

The local police almost had to fight off the media and the morbidly curious, as Norm, smiling bravely and in a new pair of fawn-striped pajamas and a beautiful new maroon check dressing-gown with corded revers and a tasselled belt, was lifted caringly out of the ambulance and carried through the front door, trailing his exciting tangle of technology. In a trice a small army of white-coated men and women wearing masks had tucked him into bed, plugged him in, and flicked the system into its 'go' mode.

Soon, outside in the street, the hushed crowds heard a piercing electronic whine followed by a loud and rhythmical vibration which almost seemed to shake the fabric of the house itself. Norm's prostate was throbbing back to life. A great cheer went up, and Councillor Puckle opened, after some difficulty, a magnum of champagne which shot a great arc of white froth into the assembled throng.

Once we got used to living in a house which quivered slightly, and in which you had to shout a bit to be heard, life returned to normal. I would pop into Norm's room at least once a day to fill his drip with something scrummy, tell him of my doings and sometimes even read him a few pages of *The Thornbirds*. Later, as I became busier, I invested in a wonderful page-turning machine with a mirror above it so that he could read for himself or watch TV in the mirror. If I ever asked him if he'd seen anything interesting on the box he always gave a pretty garbled and even worrying report, and it was only years later that I realised he had been viewing it all back-to-front!

Sometimes the poor old love had an attack of Plom's Disease (Poor Little Old Me) and he once held my hand and said sweetly, 'I want you to get on with your life, Ed. Don't worry about me, I've had a good innings.' When he said that, I looked away quickly and put on a cross voice to cover my emotion. 'Any more silly twaddle like that from you, young fellow m'lad, and I'll give you a smack on the bottie!' It's funny isn't it, Readers, the way we talk to our sickies as though they're kiddies.

Naturally Madge didn't object to the vibrations since they reminded her of New Zealand where the earth's crust is ridiculously thin, although Kenny used to get a wee bit impatient with our invalid, I fear. I have mentioned elsewhere how sad I was that Ken and Norm never really hit it off as father and son should. I suppose, in a way, they were as different as chalk and cheese. Kenny the sensitive, artistic, indoor type; whereas Norman was more sport-oriented, physical and even athletic despite being a basket-case. Ken more or less told me that he couldn't discuss his interests with Norm and it's true that my darling husband wasn't all that up on the early films of Barbara Stanwyck, art nouveau, the poems of someone called Cavafy and deleted show albums.

My son had become acquainted with an internationally acclaimed, award-winning Australian novelist called Dominic Gray. He lived with a lot of cats in a big rambling period-style home on the outskirts of Melbourne and loved to have young people around him. I have never actually read his famous books though I've tried a few times and can't get past the first few pages, but let's face it, doesn't that apply to most famous books?

I hadn't met old Dominic, but I was pleased that my son was starting to move in intellectual circles. Ken used to put on his glad-rags and go up there for little dinner parties with talented young theatre producers. choreographers, and airline stewards, and I loved to imagine them all sitting around into the wee small hours discussing the finer things of life. A far cry from my own culture-starved girlhood.

Not long after Norm's installation, Ken introduced me to a lovely young chap he had met at one of Mr Gray's soirées. I liked him at once and soon Clifford Smail, and quite often his mother, were our guests at 36 Humouresque Street. Clifford was a multi-talented lad like Kenny and seemed to know a lot about everything. As soon as he set eyes on my lovely old sandblasted reindeer dining-room doors, he almost danced with delight. 'Look, Elspeth,' he cried excitedly (Cliff called his mother by her Christian name which struck me as a bit uncalled for). 'What a FABULOUS piece of art deco!' He raved over Norm's old chrome and Bakelite standard lamp and smoker's companion too, and I explained that no one had told us they were art deco when we had bought them in the early fifties. If they had, I reflected, we probably wouldn't have. Apparently Cliff collected something called Lalique which I believe is French for dead people's wedding presents.

Cliff was a bit older than my son and wore a beard, although underneath I could tell he was rather handsome and would certainly be breaking a few hearts in a year or two, if he hadn't done so already. He came from Sydney and had recently won the Mr Leather Contest which I think had something to do with fashion. In Melbourne he owned a little restaurant called Smail's Place. It was long, narrow and rather dark, and they had the novel idea of writing the menu on a blackboard which polite young men in white polo-necked shirts used to bring to your table. They served unusual, rather continental cuisine including curried parsnip soup, rack of lamb still slightly raw, herb bread and *crême brulée* that you had to bash with a spoon to get at. The music was loud but quite nice, and Ken said it was called Vivaldi.

The night Kenny and Cliff took me there as a treat was also the night I met Dominic Gray for the first time; but only very briefly. He was actually storming out of the restaurant with a few of his young friends scampering after, because he had accidentally spied an artist at another table having dinner with a woman who was *not his wife*!

Poor old Mr Gray's eyes were almost popping out of his head with rage as he called to his entourage, 'Come on, Ian, Mario, Larry, Billy, Stavros, Timmy, let's get out of here! We're not sitting in the same restaurant as *a slut*!' He said this so vehemently, his denture shot out of his mouth and shattered on the tiled floor, and I last glimpsed him being bundled into a car outside, a hankie pressed to his mouth, as a nice thoughtful lad stayed behind to sweep up the author's teeth. How grateful I felt that my son had befriended that great rarity in this day and age: a man who still had a few moral values.

Call me old-fashioned, but I sincerely hope I've got some principles as well and one of them is honesty, I'm sorry but it is. I have tried to always keep my relationship with my children, and their attachments, as honest as possible though in some cases they haven't wanted to hear the truth.

You may wonder why this marvellous autobiography, so choc-a-bloc with self-honesty and fearless accuracy, does not chronicle my children's early lives in much detail. The reason for this is that I am telling *my* story not theirs, and they are too close to me, I'm afraid, for me to write about them without the conflicting emotions which all parents know. I'm aware that Bruce, Valmai and Kenny seem to have sprung into this chapter fully grown but isn't that always the way in Real Life? They're grown up before you know it, and their precious childhood has passed like a dream. You can point your children in the right direction, but you can't force their footsteps more's the pity, or choose the person with whom they walk life's path.

Joylene Wacker was, for better or worse, my daughter-in-law. Throughout her marriage to my son Brucie, I have been incredibly nice, patient, and helpful and when they had their first child Troy, I personally called at the hospital, straight from the airport, and had a real heart-to-heart with her. It wasn't the time or the place to tell her what I thought of the name Troy which, don't correct me if I'm wrong, is the name of a wooden horse in the Olden Days. But I did say something to Joylene which not many other women would have had the courage to say to a daughter-in-law who had just emerged from a seventeen-hour labour and a Caesarian Section. I said, and I held her hand as I said it, 'Joylene, if ever you and Bruce feel you can't make a go of it, please don't spare my feelings.' The poor thing looked a bit dazed as I continued, 'Divorce used to be a stigma, but it isn't now and it would be a terrible pity for you and Brucie to go on living together just for the sake of little Troy's security. If you and Bruce parted now I would understand perfectly. I will even thank you for your honesty.'

'But, Mum,' she exclaimed tearfully. 'What's this about divorce? Bruce and I love each other.'

'Love!' I ejaculated, with a musical laugh, and how I hated her calling me Mum. 'You youngsters don't know what love is.' Then I must have sounded rather early seventies when I philosophised, 'Love is never having to say "I've got a headache tonight."'

'But I *never* have a headache, Mum!' protested that argumentative little madam.

'Of course you do – we all do. And if the menfolk loved us, they'd know we did, without even asking. The point is this, Joylene,' I persisted patiently, even though the nursing sister was pointing to her watch behind Joylene's back. 'Little Troy will be fine if and when you and Brucie come to the parting of the ways. I can assure you that since Norm's illness I have cared for my family pretty well single-handed and they're none the worse for that.'

'But, Mum. Your family's grown up and look at Valmai. She's not exactly, well, *normal*, is she?'

'We're long past visiting hours, Dame Edna, and I think the patient is rather tired,' interposed Sister.

'How dare you attack my daughter when she's not here to defend herself, Joylene Wacker!' I exploded, drawing myself up to my full height and stalking out. *'And don't call me Mum!'*

Those were certainly not the words any woman would want to hear herself saying in a labour ward at the top of her voice, but

I couldn't help myself and Joylene had herself to blame. Was she deliberately irritating? I wondered. And how brave – or foolish – of my son to continue to put up with it. I was so agitated that when I got back into my car I still had the bunch of carnations in my hand I had meant to give my daughter-in-law. Yet some people don't want to hear the truth; one day I would have to accept that.

But Joylene had touched a nerve, as highly insensitive people sometimes can. Valmai was a handful. Her poor husband Mervyn Gittis used to sometimes come round at night sobbing about my daughter's attention-seeking antics. Valmai wanted for nothing and I often blamed myself for spoiling her. They had a lovely home which Mervyn had really battled for in the dress circle suburb of Highett, where most of the dwellings were cream brick with silver birches on their front lawns, and fishponds with chicken wire over them to stop the fish getting out. He was a one-parent family before the phrase was even invented since Val was either off on tour with the Living Theatre or making macramé, or mandalas out of scrap iron at the local women's craft co-op.

Norm had been home about a year when one day, out of the blue, the phone rang.

'It's a Mr Farelly, Edna,' called Madge from the lounge. 'Says he's an old friend.'

'Hi, Edna,' came the journalist's jaunty voice. 'Long time no see. How you doin'?'

Why did he sound slightly American these days? I pondered. What was this 'how you doin'' business?

'Well, thanks, Kevin,' I replied. 'Actually I've just had an invitation from the BBC to do a series in London and I think I might accept. Would you like to interview me?'

'Hopefully,' said Kevin, using that word which nobody in the seventies could live without.

'Well when?' I said looking for my diary.

'Hopefully now, Edna. We're breakin' a big story in the December *Woman's Monthly* and we'd hopefully like yiz comments hopefully.'

'What story, Kevin?' I enquired innocently.

'Yiz dorder Valmai has done a long frank interview with our ace features editor Trish Chipp, and she gives you a real serve.'

'Yes,' I said, going cold. 'Yes?'

'Jiz thought yiz might have a few comments hopefully. For old times' sake eh, Edna? After all,' continued the worm, 'I'm Chief of Staff now and I could swing you a nice bundle of the readies for your side of the story. We certainly kicked the tin★ for Valmai.'

'What is your headline?' I enquired, my voice shaking.

'It's a beauty,' laughed the rodent. 'THE DAME WHO DOESN'T GIVE A DAMN – Daughter Divulges Superstar's Secrets! Wanna hear more?'

Trembling, I quietly replaced the receiver until the little yapping noise of Kevin Farelly's voice stopped with a click.

'What is it, Edna?' said Madge. 'You've gone white.'

'Pack your bags, Madge,' I commanded in a funny far-away voice, 'we're flying back to London. I may be strong but I'm not going to be here when that magazine hits the streets. I'm sorry but I'm not.'

Madge, with little difficulty, looked blank.

I never confronted Valmai. What was the point? It would have been a red rag to a bull but I had a few words with clever Chris Bland at Fennimore and Gerda who shrugged and made the usual speech about the 'price of fame'. Going overseas and leaving Norm on 'automatic' worried me however, and I hoped no one popped the Christmas issue of the *Woman's Monthly* on his page-turning machine or the poor darling might short-circuit his facility and black out Greater Moonee Ponds.

Christmas was coming and I had made thoughtful plans to bring the whole family together at Humouresque Street. I had already asked my brother Roy and his wife Audrey who had never managed to have kiddies, and I was even thinking of inviting Athol and Dawn if I could dream up a polite way of excluding all those children. But now the whole thing had gone sour. Everyone would have read Valmai's wicked twaddle in the *Woman's Monthly* and the whole street would be whispering and sniggering at my humiliation. It was sickening to think that I

★ Australian slang for gratuity.

was being exiled from my home and family by that sneaky little journalist Trish Chipp who was probably very jealous of my success and had worked on my troubled daughter to line her own pockets. I also heard that treacherous Kevin Farelly, once nice and even a wee bit idealistic, had become a sort of lickspittle to Sir Mark Bartok, the Sydney toothpaste tycoon who had bought huge shares in the *Woman's Monthly*.

But even if Madge and I were far away I was determined that Norm and Kenny would have a lovely Christmas all the same and I began to bake feverishly.

Poor Norman was on a pretty strict diet and it must have been hard for him lying there smelling the aroma of mince pies and turkey wafting in from the kitchen. Madge did the stuffing, since that was something I could never bring myself to do, ever since a traumatic day years before when I had come into the kitchen unexpectedly one Christmas to find my mother wrist-deep in a dickie-bird's sit-upon. It stuck in my mind I'm afraid though when I asked Dr Sidney Shardenfreude (whom I see for Valmai's sake) what it meant, he said, 'Vot do you sink it means?' To think I pay that man!

I intended to leave them all a scrummy cold turkey, masses of mince pies and a nice pudding that Ken could reheat. As for Norm, bless him, all I could do was to sit on his bed after I'd been cooking and let him sniff my fingers. It was the closest the poor lamb could ever get to a lovely Chrissie dinner. Brucie had promised to pop out and see Mummy at Dunraven and bring her a plate of leftovers, and I left all the presents under the tree. The main thing was for Madge and me to get on that plane before the Christmas issue of that putrid magazine hit the newsstands. Since Kenny and Cliff were tied up at Smail's Place, Brucie drove me to the airport.

I felt sorry for my elder son being married to that restless woman Joylene Wacker. He never complained either; even pretended to be blissfully happy, but we mothers know, don't we? Bruce wouldn't say a word against Joylene which was loyal of him, though you'd think he could have been a bit more 'up front' (to use an eighties expression) with his own flesh and blood. He told me he'd applied for a government job which might take him

to London and I pretended to look pleased, as I imagined Joylene
trying to muscle in to first nights, Royal Galas, and fashionable
parties on my ticket. She is such a pushy little madam, I'm afraid.
But I was glad Bruce was settling to something. He has inherited
the Beazleys' versatility and can really make a success of anything
he turns his hand to, although Norm, not always as sympathetic
to his clever sons as he should be, used to say, 'Jack of all trades,
master of none.' In the seventies, Bruce had got in on the ground
floor of macadamia nuts (an Australian invention, incidentally)
and then macadamia nut furniture which was small, but lovely.

'I know you two don't get on, Brucie, and it breaks my heart,'
I said hugging him at the International terminal, 'but please be
nice to your brother Ken and keep an eye on your father. There's
some tinsel and plastic holly in the kitchen drawer to decorate his
ducting and you'll find some brandy butter in the fridge to put
in his drip on Christmas Eve.'

Madge had received a cheque from Douglas Allsop's solicitors
that Christmas. Apparently when everything had been sold up
there were a few shillings left in the kitty and Madge insisted on
paying our air fares if we went overseas via Los Angeles. She had
something up her sleeve, but it was Christmas so I let her have
her own way, old softie that I am. We were no sooner airborne
and the 'no smoking' light had gone out, than I heard a terrible
coughing in the seat behind me. Glancing around I saw, in the
blue haze of a recently kindled Benson & Hedges, the prune-like
visage of Dr Gerald Finzi.

'I'm off to Palm Springs for the International Prostate
Symposium,' he announced. 'It's being held by the Friends of
the Prostate, a wonderful organisation which you should support,
Dame Edna. Have you seen their Christmas card?' He handed me
such a pretty card with what looked like a psychedelic Christmas
pudding on it.

'What a delightful pudding,' I said, admiring it. Dr Finzi
laughed himself into a coughing fit.

'Mistaken identity, I'm afraid, dear lady,' he chuckled. 'That's
not a pudding, it's a prostate in full spate, doing its thing!'

Making a mental note, I told him how well Norm was progress-
ing.

'We know, we know,' replied the doctor, 'but I'm still hoping with this new chip technology, we can miniaturise your husband's hardware. In a few years it might be possible for him to be up and about leading a normal life with his prostate in his top pocket. Then there's cryonics.'

'What are they prithee?' I enquired, accepting a complimentary cocktail.

'Simple,' vouchsafed the medico. 'We snap-freeze your husband's organ in the hope that one day a doctor will be born who can successfully perform an operation on it. But I expect that would be cold comfort for Lord Everage.' When he laughed at his none too amusing jest, I was pleased to see that the consequent tracheal spasms kept him busy for at least fifteen minutes.

Madge was a dark horse. We were no sooner ensconced in one of those Elizabeth Arden pink bungalows at the Beverly Hills Hotel, when she was off on a mysterious excursion.

'It's my money, Edna,' she said, rather crudely, 'and I'll spend it as I wish.'

Had she been drinking, I wondered, to make a speech like that? However, there were meetings lined up for me with a couple of producers who were toying with the idea of giving me American exposure and I had chums to see, David Hockney, lovely Michael and Pat York, the Vincent Prices and darling Joan Rivers. Frankly I was a bit relieved that Madge wasn't tagging along for a week or so, since on social occasions people always felt a bit subdued by the sight of her sitting there glumly in her moth-coloured garments. How conceited of Madge, come to think of it, to imagine I'd miss her!

Joan Rivers had invited me to a scrumptious pre-Christmas lunch at her beautiful Bel Air home and she told me of the lovely Christmas present she had given her faithful old housekeeper. A free face-lift!

'My cosmetic surgeon is *to die for*, Edna!' enthused Joan, and then she added puzzlingly, 'How smart of you to send your maid to the same clinic. After all, we have to look at these women every day, don't we?'

'My maid?' I exclaimed looking across the table at Roddy

McDowall and Coral Browne in bewilderment. 'I don't have a maid and I don't know anyone who's having a facelift.'

Joan laughed and then put a hand over her pretty mouth. 'Ooops!' she said. 'Have I been telling tales out of school? It's just that my Bella is in the next bed at the Marmont Clinic to a woman called Allsop who says she works for you.'

I was so taken aback that I laughed it off not wanting to spoil the atmosphere of that lovely lunch by betraying my perturbation, or making my hostess feel she'd put her foot in it. That's me, I'm sorry.

But before I departed Joan was raving on further about this wonder clinic. Apparently, when you booked in there, they gave you an album of famous movie stars to leaf through in the waiting room, and you could actually tell your cosmetic surgeon who you wished to resemble. I shuddered apprehensively.

No prizes for guessing who was on the doorstep of the plushy Marmont Clinic that evening as the sun gloriously set behind the tall Hawaiian palms of Hollywood. It was more like the reception area of an advertising agency than a hospital, with big green shrubs in pots, black leather furniture and someone's scribble in a big gold frame on the African slate wall. Sure enough, they had a patient called Allsop all right, and she was doing well after radical 'rhino-labial reconstructive therapy'.

Soon I could hear the click of my Madonna-style mules down a corridor as a white-coated 'hostess' showed me into the presence of my post-operative bridesmaid. It was quite a shock. There propped up in bed appeared to be a large cotton wool bud. I picked up a limp fawn arm from the bed cover and scrutinised its plastic identity bracelet. Sure enough, the bandaged mummy in the bed was Mrs Douglas Allsop, and she was awake.

'All right, Madge,' I said in a controlled voice as I flung myself down in a modernistic chair beside the bed. 'What's all this about?'

A small aperture opened in the bandages. And closed. As the hostess left us together she said, 'Don't expect her to talk much for a few days until her face settles down. Doctor should be here directly to take off the bandages so you've arrived at an exciting moment.'

I shook my head wearily. 'Who did you choose, Madge?' I

asked, quite nicely. Madge tried to speak but her voice was muffled, so I moved closer, genuinely curious I'm afraid. 'Which film star did you pick, darling?' I enquired, more forcefully.

She squeezed my hand with a clammy claw. 'Joan Crawford!' mumbled the mummy. 'I opened the book and pointed to Joan Crawford.' Madge sank back into her pillow, the effort of speaking must have taxed that sore old face. But my attention was distracted by the sound of muttering behind me. An elegant young doctor stood there rubbing his forehead with his hand and whispering urgently to a nurse who stared anxiously at a clipboard.

'Excuse me, Ma'am,' said the doctor, addressing me. 'I gather you're a friend of the patient. Did I just overhear her make reference to Joan Crawford . . . *Joan* Crawford?'

As we spoke the nurse administered a little injection to Madge and began slowly spooling off her bandages.

'Why do you ask, Doctor?' I enquired, fascinated as my old bridesmaid slowly emerged from her lint chrysalis.

'Well,' he continued, biting his lip and shaking his head from side to side. 'It's just that we handle about fifty patients a day and the routine is, I walk into the operating theatre, look at the reference photo, and do the job.' He lowered his voice to a whisper, 'I guess some jerk must have accidentally turned the page or there was a goddamn gust of wind or something . . .'

'What are you trying to say, Doctor?' I exclaimed. The nurse had wound down to the last layer of bandages now.

'I guess we'll just have to start again from scratch and hope for the best, that's all,' he declared, running worried fingers through his hair.

A loud gasp from the nurse froze our conversation and we both swivelled in the direction of the bed. There, lying back in the pillows amongst a tangle of bandages, and smiling excitedly at us all was – *Broderick* Crawford!

The doctor sank into a chair, head in hands, groaning slightly as the nurse fled sobbing from the room. I ran to the bedside of my friend, now uncannily transformed into the craggy star of *All the King's Men* and *Highway Patrol*. I seized his hand in mine.

'Why, Madge, why?' I implored. *'In heaven's name why?'*

Broderick Crawford looked at me with a lovely smile. 'I did it for you, Edna,' she said. 'You deserve a beautiful companion, so I did it for you. Can you bring me a mirror now?'

CHAPTER XXIV

Kenny's Confession

MADGE WAS POLISHING my awards when I got home. Although my luxurious penthouse high over Mayfair had its own housekeeper, an adorable Spanish woman called Purificación Lorca, I never gave her the heavy duties. What was the point when there was a perfectly good old New Zealand bridesmaid on tap quite capable of Hoovering and wielding a duster? Besides, it was occupational therapy for Madge, and the harder she worked, the less guilty she probably felt about living the life of Riley at my expense.

I sank wearily into the big orange Eileen Gray sofa under Gilbert and George's portrait of me and kicked off my Maud Frizons. There was Madge, happy as a sandboy, buffing away at one of those spiky, futuristic bronze sculptures on marble bases that I had been collecting with embarrassing regularity for the past ten years. The onyx shelf above our fireplace was lined with them, in all shapes and sizes, and all inscribed to Dame Edna Everage for Outstanding Achievement in pretty well everything. It had been a charmed decade in many ways and those gleaming chunks of stone and metal were not just symbols of my meteoric success but milestones along the steep but rewarding road of Megastardom.

Madge had begun to rub some Brasso on a considerably larger lump.

'For heaven's sake, Madge, you don't have to polish that! That's Dame Elizabeth Frink's bust of me, it's *meant* to be that colour.'

Madge looked relieved, since the seven-foot-high solid bronze monolith might have taken her all night. I noticed that the polishing rags employed by my companion were long strips of white lint; undoubtedly some of her old cosmetic bandages. Since that dreadful episode in Los Angeles and the emergency surgery which followed, she had been under wraps, off and on, for the past ten years. It was a miracle really that she now looked more or less like herself; whatever that looked like. Frankly I couldn't remember, but poor Madge's vanity had led her a merry dance and guess who paid the piper?

Once you start having plastic surgery there is generally no end to it and Madge has been 'landscaped' so many times, and had so many nips and tucks, that by now the small of her back looked like a Brussels sprout. Far from having a rejuvenating effect on her, it only made her look more than ever like the Bog Woman.

'I've had a nightmare of a day, Madge,' I announced testily, snapping on a big wisteria Gallé table lamp. 'That's the last time I traipse off to the English Outback to see my grandchildren. Why people would want to live in a deconsecrated Methodist chapel on the Isle of Dogs beats me.' (Actually, it was deconsecrated by the Luftwaffe.) 'Brucie needs his head read, letting that Joylene run his life for him.'

Madge looked across at me trying to make up her mind if I expected her 'input', decided I didn't, and went on polishing.

'When they came to London – it must be at least nine years ago –' I continued, 'I tried to help that couple as best I could, but I had my new show, my TV series, and Norm back in Melbourne to worry about. Joylene insisted on living in Ruislip, which is practically in Scotland, and when she moved to Clapham it wasn't much better. Now it's the Isle of Dogs for heaven's sake! Yuk!'

'But isn't it supposed to be fashionable down there in the Docklands, Edna?' ventured Allsop.

'If it *is*,' I declared, 'the rats haven't heard about it. She's done the place up in what she calls "post high-tech", the affected minx. She gets around those rubber floors on roller skates in a silver lurex jumpsuit. She looks like garlic bread on wheels.'

'Poor little Troy and Lisa,' commiserated Madge.

'You can say that again. Still Brucie's doing well in the City with his new yuppies' lunch delivery service called the Serious Sandwich Company. It's no mean feat, Madge, persuading all those commodity brokers called Giles and Piers to enjoy smoked skate and walnut on rye with a bottle of Badoit out of a French tap, when they'd rather have a stale Scotch egg. I'm glad I've got a few shillings in Bruce's business actually,' I added prudently. 'After all it was me who suggested he give his service an up-market old-fashioned "feel" by getting those out-of-work Parsons Green chalet girls with jeans under their crinolines to drive around in little vintage vans delivering tasteful corporate snacks. It's a licence to print money.' Brucie's old-world vans were left over from a film about the First World War – I think it was the one where Jane Seymour played the Kaiser. He had them done up in a browny-red livery – actually a sort of livery livery, with gold writing on the side: 'Purveyors of Fine Sandwiches to the Gentry since 1987'.

As I raved on about Brucie's business, Madge didn't seem to be listening. She wearily stripped off her Marigolds and mopped her scar tissue with a Kleenex tissue.

'Listen, while you've been out there's been flowers, a fax and a phone call, Edna.'

The roses were from little Warren Beatty. Why did these men pursue me? I wondered. It was a compliment of course, but I was happily married to a man who was by now the most high-profiled prostate sufferer in the world. There had even been a *Time* magazine cover devoted to the Dame Edna Prostate Foundations which I had endowed in Melbourne and London. Yes, I had taken the late Dr Finzi's advice, and when the serious money had started to roll in during the eighties I had, typically, thought of others.

Unfortunately Norman's sojourn at Humouresque Street had been comparatively brief, since as soon as my back was turned the neighbours had all signed a petition objecting to the noise pollution of Norm's support system and he had been reinstated at the hospital pending a transplant. Frankly, I was beginning to lose track of his complex medical history but I received regular print-outs and I naturally kept close tabs on my husband as I did on all my other Wholly Owned Subsidiaries.

The fax was from Barry Humphries, my Australian manager

and sometime support act. How that man loves breaking bad news. There are people like that, people with terribly low self-esteem, who like to catch you off-guard with some unpleasant titbit of information so that you then turn to them for help, advice and support, thereby boosting their puny egos. Yuk! What a syndrome. Barry's fax was to inform me, as quickly as possible, that Valmai had been arrested for shoplifting for the umpteenth time and she had also been sleeping on the steps of Parliament House with a group of Aborigines protesting about cuts in government grants to disabled lesbian Aboriginal puppet film-makers. The 'Aborigines' turned out to be Yugoslavian malcontents over whom someone might have once waved a boomerang, but Valmai, it seemed, had got all the publicity she wanted, poor child. There was a pathetic photo on the fax of her being hauled off by police. I later learned she was working as a Sexual Options Counsellor in North London helping confused ten-year-olds find out what their options are (whatever that means!). Ridiculously overweight (she'd been digging her grave with her teeth for some years now), bleached Mohawk hair, and a banner saying 'Castrate Rapists Slowly'. Would I go bail? Barry asked.

'Certainly not! Never, never, never!'

'Certainly not what, Edna?' said Madge glancing anxiously at the fax, a screwed-up ball of paper in my hand. Purificación popped in with a nice cup of tea and vanished discreetly.

I broke down then I'm afraid, a far cry from the hard-nosed, street-wise Megastar you might think I was if you didn't really know me.

'Oh, Madge,' I sobbed, 'Valmai's pushing me too far. I have tried to help her so many times but it only makes her more angry. What have I done but used the wonderful gifts Dame Nature has given me? How can that be wrong, Madge? And yet Valmai blames me and keeps writing those ghastly articles with her flat-mate, that snake in the grass Trish Chipp.'

Madge took the cup out of my hand, sat me in a chair and started to massage my shoulders rather badly with her bony fingers.

'There there, Edna,' she soothed. 'You'll have to let that one go her own way. You'll have to try to detach. Why don't you talk about it to the others when you go to your next meeting of Megastars Anonymous? There are probably people there who can identify with your problem and help you.'

With a hankie of Bruges lace I gave myself a rather satisfying emunctory blast. 'You're right, Madge,' I conceded grudgingly. 'I'll do as you say, although those MA meetings are usually rather small, sometimes I'm the only person there.' I was starting to feel better; in fact more positive by the minute as I thought of the advice my peer group with problem children would undoubtedly give me.

'Tough love, Madge, that's what Valmai needs,' I announced. 'Tough love.'

★ ★ ★

Sir Mark Bartok sat at an enormous desk. Behind him, out the window, I could see St Paul's Abbey. He was a sturdy but shortish man of about sixty-five with a completely bald head and very thick glasses, and as I entered his large office he rose slightly and bowed. It was disconcerting to notice that throughout the interview that followed he never really looked at me, straight on that is. Beside him on the desk, its back to me, was a sort of television set which he never really took his eyes off. I could see its flickering green light reflected in his glasses. He lit a large cigar and only after he had taken several puffs did he ask if I minded him smoking. What was the point? I thought, feeling a little tickle in my throat all the same. I was appearing that evening at the Royal Albert Hall with wonderful Carl Davis in my profane cantata 'The Song of Australia' and I had to guard my priceless voice.

Sir Mark spoke with foreign-sounding accent, as though he came from somewhere.

'I'm only in my London office for a couple of days, Dame Edna, before I am going back to Sydney, but I have wanted to have some confidential talk with you.'

'Yes, Sir Mark, my bridesmaid told me you telephoned last night while I was out seeing my son and daughter-in-law.'

Sir Mark leant forward across his desk, but still watching the screen. 'I am a businessman, Dame Edna. Australia has been very kind to me since I got there many years ago. Today, I think of myself as an Australian. Like you I invest in many things: property, mining, hotels, the media. The Prime Minister himself is a close personal friend of me.'

Why was he telling me all this? I wondered.

'Dame Edna, I am going to put the cards on my table.'

Why, I wondered again, did genuinely frank people never use this phrase?

'You have seen the papers, you have seen the TV, you have read with the rest of the world reports of greed, corruption, graft and crime amongst Australians in high political office.'

'Yes.' I asked simply, as we women do, 'Is it true?'

Sir Mark gave a guttural laugh, showing a worrying gold tooth. 'Of course not, dear lady Edna,' he shrugged. 'It's all filthy lies circulated by the Opposition, but some of the mud sticks.' He ashed his cigar and leant forward again, confidentially. 'The Prime Minister is very worried about Australia's international image. He wants our leaders and state premiers to look, how you say it, squeaky-clean?'

'I don't know many of our wonderful politicians personally,' I said truthfully, 'but occasionally I meet them by accident. Spookily enough, I've bumped into quite a few when I've been visiting my bank in Switzerland. They must go there for the skiing . . .'

Sir Mark obviously didn't like winter sports for he interjected, 'Dame Edna, we want to offer you a job as Australia's International Cultural Ambassador.'

My jaw must have dropped. Then, too, I noticed another person standing in a shadowy corner of the office. A thin youngish man in a suit. Sir Mark continued, 'For years you have shown the world the true picture of Australia. You have inspired migration, tourism and investment. It is our tarnished image we ask you now to cleanse. Don't answer now, but think about it please. We would be generous.'

The young man stepped forward and handed me a small piece of paper on which was written what looked like a telephone number with an international dialling code in front.

'That,' said Sir Mark, puffing contemplatively on his Havana Royale, 'is *not* your official diplomatic salary, but a little something we would like, with your permission, dear lady Edna, to place at your disposal in any bank you care to name.'

After I had looked at the piece of paper, the young man retrieved it, and passed it to Sir Mark who lit it with his Wedgwood desktop Ronson and dropped it, a curled-up blackened flake, into the ashtray.

I promised to think about it, and I must say it was a very nice compliment and a wonderful opportunity too to refute all that evil and widespread gossip about our leaders.

The thin young man escorted me down to my waiting limo and, as I climbed in, I could not help but ask him a question which had been on my mind throughout that momentous interview.

'Excuse I,' I said, 'but all the time I was there Sir Mark never took his eyes off that little TV screen on his desk. What, may I ask, was he watching?'

The subordinate smiled faintly. 'The dollar,' he replied. 'That monitor is a direct link with the Stock Exchange. Sir Mark likes to watch the dollar.'

*   *   *

My mother is a committed Christian. She's mad, but she's a Christian. Yet it was not a crisis of faith that brought me scurrying back to Melbourne on a whistle-stop visit only weeks before my big opening night at the Theatre Royal, Drury Lane.

I had heard Mummy had relapsed a bit after years of stable, contented bewilderment, and I suppose I panicked as any loving daughter would because my mother's lucid recollections were essential if I was to write my memoirs accurately.

It was not the most convenient time in my career to jump on a jumbo. However, I had practically promised Sir Charles Mackerras that I would do his Brecht/Weill concert in Melbourne, so I could slot Mummy in there as well, and kill two birds with one stone. Frankly, Readers, I didn't need to rehearse for my London show. It was a month off and I never rehearse anyway. My shows are like Life itself: off the cuff.

Kenny, Cliff and Elspeth had come to London for my opening night and they were just the teeniest bit put out that I was whizzing back to Australia for a fortnight. I had offered them all accommodation in my penthouse, and Cliff's slightly common mother Elspeth accepted, but the boys insisted on staying in some funny little place near the Cromwell Road which was so cramped they were forced to share the same room!

'Why do you boys insist on roughing it all the time?' I asked them, but I only raised a sheepish laugh.

It is very remiss of me indeed not to have mentioned that for the past few years my frocks have all been designed by my son Kenneth. On one of my return visits in the early eighties Ken showed me some wonderful creations he had made for a fancy-dress party he and Clifford had thrown at Smail's Upstairs, a sort of artistic club above the restaurant that stayed open very late. The dresses were 'stunning' to use a Sydney vogue word that seems to have died out everywhere else.

My mind had flashed back to the old dreamlike days when Norm and I still shared a double bed at Humouresque Street and Kenny used to creep home late at night after his gruelling dressmaking classes. When he stooped over my side of the bed to give me a nice goodnight peck, he would often be so tired that he would forget to take the pins out of his mouth. The memory of my talented little porcupine came back to me as he showed me the wonderful designs he had dreamt up for my new show.

One of my investments over the years had been a little property near Rodeo Drive Street in Los Angeles. I had offered it to Kenneth as a showroom and he had leapt at the idea and put in a manageress, actually a manageress called Brian. Suffice it to say that when gorgeous Jerry Hall walked on to the set of one of my talk shows last year, she was wearing a real crowd-stopper and so was I. We were dressed identically! I had a quick peep at the little hand-sewn *griffe* at the back above her zip and there it was: 'Kenneth Everage Modes. Moonee Ponds, Mustique and Malibu'. The Moonee Ponds outlet was true and the rest were in the pipeline.

I was due to fly back to Australia to see Mummy (and Norm, how ghastly to forget him!) via Geneva where I had a meeting with my publishers and my financial adviser, Dr Ottmar Schoek. On the eve of my departure, Ken came up to the penthouse for a fitting of my finale frock.

'Don't put on too much weight during the next two weeks will you, Mums?' he said as he pinned on some lovely hand-made silk Taiwanese gladdies. 'We can't have you strutting your stuff at Drury Lane looking like Shelley Winters.'

I was exhausted. I suppose at the back of my mind, well, at the front of it really, I'd been mulling over Sir Mark Bartok's offer. There was a catch in it somewhere but I was too tired to see what.

'Kenny,' I muttered, noticing that he was still there an hour later looking at my Erté and Icart collection. 'You'll have to go home now, Possum. I've taken half a Xanax already and I'm going to bed.'

'Mums,' he said petulantly. 'Can't we have a talk?'

'Darling!' I protested. 'It's late. I'm off to Switzerland tomorrow with Madge, heaven help me, then straight to a confused mother in Australia, not to mention your poor dear father. Then I have to fly straight back to London to do my show. Please let your mother have her beauty sleep, there's a lamb.'

Things were getting a little fuzzy. A woman should never take a Xannie before actually getting into her nightie. Ken looked a bit peeved.

'All right, Ken,' I said, my voice feeling thick and furry with Dr Granville-Bantock's prescribed sedation.

'What is it you want to ask me? Or tell me?'

I can't remember his exact words, Readers. Frankly it's a miracle I can remember much about this incident at all and my Erté and Icart collection on the wall had doubled.

'I'm hilarious.'

'I beg your pardon, Kenny?'

'I'm hilarious, Mums. I have been for years. Clifford Smail is hilarious as well and there's nothing wrong with it; some wonderful people in history have all been hilarious: Lawrence of Arabia, Oscar Wilde, General Gordon, James Dean, Michelangelo, Beethoven, Florence Nightingale . . .' I *think* he said 'hilarious', Readers. I'm almost positive, and if it wasn't that, it was a word that meant much the same thing.

'Please, Kenny,' I slurred, 'not so fast, darling. I am too.'

'WHAT!' exclaimed my son, 'you too, Mums? You mean with Madge?!'

'No, darling, she doesn't get the point of me at all, but my Public thinks I am, I'm afraid, and thank goodness they do or we wouldn't have a home in Melbourne, Montreux, Mustique and Malibu!'

'I don't understand,' said Kenny miserably. 'What are you trying to tell me?'

I managed to struggle into a négligé and flop on to the bed next to Madge who was snoring quite loudly. I felt slightly drunk.

'I'm trying to tell you, Kenny,' I said wagging a finger at the puzzled young figure in stone-washed denim with George Michael knee-splits who stood before me, 'that it's past our bedtime and there's nothing wrong with being hilarious. But if you are, darling, then for heaven's sake try looking a bit happier about it.'

Kenny looked as though he were about to cry but I remembered no more. The Xannie had taken over.

CHAPTER XXV

The Royal Me

'**P**USH DARLING, *push*! Push harder, *harder*!'
Princess Diana was expecting her first baby and I was
talking to her.

'Push as hard as you can!' I exhorted her at the top of my voice.
But it was no use. She was calling me from a public phone and
her coin had stuck in the slot. To an ordinary member of the
public she just looked like a heavily pregnant Princess Diana
lookalike, hammering furiously at a defective British Telecom
instrument on the fifth floor of Harrods from which she regularly
gave me an incognito tinkle. I knew she'd phone again, probably
from Buckingham Palace next time, since her confinement was
drawing very near and I had promised to give her my famous
stretch mark recipe (patent applied for).★

Royalty aren't the only people calling me for advice, marriage
counselling or just a friendly gossip. Winnie Mandela, Joan Collins, Mother Teresa, Fergie, Imelda Marcos, Raisa Gorbachev,
Princess Michael of Kent, Pia Zadora, Margaret Thatcher,
Madonna, Princess Susan of Albania, Fawn Hall, Dame Janet
Baker and Barry Manilow are just a few of my regular callers
who expect me to drop everything while they pour their hearts
out. A couple on this list even call me long distance *collect*: no
prizes for guessing who! But let's face it, Possums, it is a big
compliment to me that these folk feel there is someone on the

★ See Appendix, p. 283.

planet they can 'let it all hang out' with who won't go rushing
into print. They know that whatever they say to me, however
intimate, will never go any further; well, no further than the
pages of this book which is only going to be read by a few million
extremely discreet people.

Princess Diana had been shopping for her new bubba that day
and had just wanted a little help with her shopping list and, I
suspect, a little motherly advice as well. It only seems yesterday
when my own waters broke but in the days and weeks leading
up to that historic event I suffered the usual fears and anxieties
especially in crowded places like department stores where I would
have given *anything* for the phone number of a kind, caring and
supportive Megastar. That was a few years ago and my adorable
royal caller now has two lovely kiddies but at little private dinners
at Kensington Palace whenever the subject of stretch marks comes
up – as it does quite often – she always says proudly, 'I don't have
any, *thanks* to Dame Edna.'

I wish I could persuade all the members of the Royal Family to
drop my honorific when they are talking to me and just call me
Edna. To one of them I once said, 'For heaven's sake, Liz, *please*
try! I come from Australia where informality is the keynote.'

'I'll try, I promise I will!' exclaimed my gorgeous friend. 'But
you have such an aura about you, it would seem disrespectful.
To me you will always be a Dame.'

Compliments like that don't grow on trees, do they, Readers?
And the little lady whose anonymity I am protecting certainly
knows how to dish out the compliments. In fact she does so in a
big way every New Year's Day.

For some years I had been unofficial Australian royalty – a bit
of a paradox really considering I am as left-wing as they come. I
know for a fact, however, that everyone has to have someone to
look up to; it is a human need and folk get rather pinched, peaky
and run-down without a glittering role model to put on a pedestal.
The same goes for my fellow Australians, for no matter how
emancipated, Americanised or republican they may pretend to
be, statistics have proved that they still buy twice as many newspapers or magazines if there's a snap of me or the Queen on the
cover. I'm sorry but they do.

I first met my British opposite number at one of those star-studded back-stage line-ups after a big glittering charity Gala. We stood in line as the Royal party headed by the Queen moved slowly down, chatting to each star, whilst a carefully vetted group of paparazzi took flash photos of the encounters. No prizes for guessing whose pickie made page one world-wide the next day. A lot of the stars seemed nervous. Little Leo Sayer on my right was almost shaking until I leant down and patted him gently on the head. Even suave David Frost was discreetly puffing a minty aerosol between his famous lips and probably blowing another hole in the ozone layer if he'd only known it.

The glittering party at last drew level with me and the theatre manager performed the introduction. Our eyes met, then our fingers as I prepared to curtsy. Did I imagine it or had *her* legs given a little bob? I wasn't the only one to notice since a slight gasp ran down the line of superstars and only then did I make my own graceful obeisance to my Sovereign. Dr Sidney Shardenfreude (whom I see for my children) has told me that people who are really going to hit it off in a big way with each other know from the first instant of eye contact, and we knew it then. Eye contact wasn't coming easy by the way, since the royal orbs were pretty well fixed on my tiara which is studded with a few *serious* stones. I keep it in a Swiss bank most of the time incidentally, and the one I sometimes wear in the street is fake (muggers, please note!).

Her little gloved hand was still in mine and I suddenly became aware that she was trying to push something into my palm. It felt like a small piece of paper. At that instant our eyes met once more and hers wore a look of pained entreaty that I will never forget. 'Please, Edna,' they seemed to conjure me. '*Please* keep my secret. Act normally.' Luckily I am a highly sensitive, acutely tuned organism used to acting normally, and my fingers closed around that secret scrap. Meanwhile cameras flashed and TV lenses winked around us but no one could have noticed that covert exchange between two intensely private people caught in the full glare of publicity. We chatted of course about how marvellous my performance had been but they were empty words compared to the urgent messages our hearts were sending forth.

As soon as the ceremony was over and the Royal party had left the theatre I rushed to my dressing room and locked the door, standing for a moment with my back to it, breathing deeply. Only then did I open my right hand and, sure enough, nestling in my silver lurex palm was a scrunched-up piece of paper. I opened it quickly and spread it on my dressing table. What I read caused my heart to stop for a moment. I read the single word 'Help' in a trembling urgent handwriting and beneath it was a London telephone number which for obvious reasons I will not divulge. I have an uncanny memory as readers of this autobiography will be aware, so I stared at that phone number, zapped it into my brain, popped the paper into my mouth and tried to swallow it. No easy task either as spies reading this book will have found out long ago. I was still chewing as Madge let me into my luxury penthouse high above Mayfair half an hour later. I packed her off to bed, flung myself on a sofa and picked up the phone.

It did not ring for long. 'Hello?' a small famous voice challenged the transmitter.

'It's – it's Dame Edna here. You asked. . . ?'

'Yes, oh yes. Thank heaven you've called. I knew you wouldn't give me away and I knew somehow you'd understand. It's just . . .'

She broke off and I wondered if I could hear tears. What terrible trouble had this poor lass found herself in that she should turn to me in her agony?

'Please, dear,' I said, the way I can, warmly, caringly: 'Tell Edna what's the matter? I am here for you. I always will be.'

'You won't think I'm silly?' she said with the artlessness of a girl, tears still glistening in her voice. But on her lips, I like to think, a flickering smile of trust.

'*Silly*?' I almost shrieked. 'Why *all* of us are silly sometimes,' I declared. 'Even I have been silly sometimes in my life and if I ever write my autobiography I will send you a copy, silly bits and all.'*

'Well,' she began a little shyly, 'have you got a good pavlova recipe?'

* I have.

'*What?*' I ejaculated, almost forgetting who I was talking to.

'You know, a recipe for an Australian pavlova cake,' she continued, oblivious to my exclamation of surprise. 'The Australian Prime Minister and party are coming to supper next Saturday night and I want to give them one of your national specialities but our chefs have drawn a blank. I knew only you could help save the day.'

'Who's that, Edna?' came a voice from our bedroom door and I saw my old bridesmaid standing there in her faded Oxfam winceyette, a glass of NightNurse *frappé* in her right hand and the bedroom extension in the other.

'Put that *down*, you stupid woman!' I yelled. 'Aren't I entitled to a minute's privacy? And change your nightie. It makes you look like Orphan Annie.'

The small voice on the phone said, 'I'm sorry? My nightie? What's wrong with it?'

'Not you!' I bellowed back after Madge had reluctantly replaced her receiver, or so I thought. 'I was talking to my lady-in-waiting, Your Majesty,' I added in a much nicer tone as I tried to pull myself together. 'I'll copy it out of my recipe book in the morning,' I promised in a practical voice, 'and drop it by at your place on my way to Harrods on Saturday morning. Will there be anyone home?'

'Better still,' said my midnight supplicant, 'pop over in the afternoon. Run up a pavlova for me and join us for dinner! That's if you're free?'

I pretended to look in a diary.

'We are!' came a New Zealand voice from the next room and funnily enough, Readers, that was the only time in my life, before or since, when I have felt that I could commit murder.

The Queen said, 'Naturally bring any staff you may require.'

'That won't be necessary, Ma'am,' I said very audibly. 'I hope I can run up a passion-fruit pav★ on my ownsome.'

After a few other pleasantries, expressions of gratitude and mutual esteem we rang off. After that I had a nice bath, rubbed

★ See Appendix, p. 283.

a little precious 'under-the-counter' Wombat Spleen Jelly into my crow's feet ('the dried-up beds of old smiles', to use my mother's marvellous expression), slipped into my favourite Janet Reger and gave Madge Allsop the rough edge of my tongue.

I can't say I slept too well either after that, in fact I felt distinctly queasy and I think it was probably something I'd eaten, more than likely the Queen's telephone number.

★　　★　　★

The pav was a triumph but the dinner was awful. My countrymen all seemed well topped up and womenfolk looked as though they might have overdone the pre-Palace Valium. I blushed for my homeland quite frankly. Considering how many refined and acceptable Australian menfolk there are, it has always puzzled me why they never find their way into Parliament. The Australian Governor General was there as well, a man who is supposed to be the Queen's representative and as rough a diamond as you could ever meet. He looked a bit like a tram conductor in a hired suit. Spookily psychic that I am, I found out later that he had once had a job with the Tramways Union!

I had arrived earlier that afternoon with a motorcycle escort provided by the Palace and I was shown straight up to the Royal kitchen where the chief chef was at my beck and call, stiffening egg whites, squeezing passion-fruit, whipping cream and sifting castor sugar. It wasn't long before my new friend popped her pretty little head through the kitchen door to shyly thank me and ask me if there was anything I needed. Because I was wearing the stunning frock (designed by my son Kenny) that I intended to wear for dinner I asked her if I might borrow one of her aprons to protect me from 'pavlova splashback'. Did I imagine it or did she go just a tiny bit blank when I made this simple request? She repeated the word 'apron?' a few times rather vaguely and my heart went out to her as I suddenly realised that she, who enjoyed all these wonderful amenities, had probably never rejoiced in the proud uniform of a normal housewife. On her next birthday I sent her a gorgeous 'Venomous Insects of Australia' Irish linen apron with matching tea-towels, hand-crafted in North Korea and a lovely pair of yellow Marigolds.

The meal was, of course, scrumptious but the Australian party couldn't have tasted it since they were too far gone and smoking throughout, even offering ciggies to the Queen who declined with the sweetness of a Saint. I suppose you have to allow for the 'awestruck factor'. After all, this poor little band of overdressed waifs had been plucked out of nowhere and plonked down in a red and gold room with a forty-foot ceiling, Old Masters on the wall, a Royal couple and *me*! Only when my pavlova was wheeled in did they seem to come to life and when the port was passed around it looked as though they might easily outstay their welcome and settle down for the night, droning on and on about the shows they had been to see and the shopping they had done in London at the Australian tax-payer's expense.

I was amazed how my regal hostess managed to listen with seeming interest to the slurred shorthand her guests were talking, particularly when our Prime Minister rambled on about how they had all been to see the Trooping of the Guard and had Her Majesty, by any chance, managed to catch it?

How would she get rid of them? I wondered. As if by magic the answer came. Rising from a beautiful gold chair, the Queen said rather firmly: 'Would any of you care for a cup of coffee *before you go*?' It worked like a charm. Soon the bedraggled little party, their chins still flecked with meringue and passion-fruit, were being poured into their coats by winking footmen, the charming Prince had retired and I was alone with my hostess.

'How can I thank you?' she said, squeezing my hand, her gaze lingering for a moment on the Everage Diamond which blazed on my finger.

'No thanks needed, Possum,' I said daringly, but with sincerity. 'You coped magnificently tonight,' I added. 'How do you do it?'

'All in a day's work, Dame Edna,' she said with a weary smile. 'But it would be nice if Australia had a female Prime Minister one day. A woman of intelligence, dignity, refinement and beauty who could do justice to that wonderful sub-continent.'

'Perhaps,' I said wistfully. 'But where could such a woman be found, Your Majesty?'

The Queen gave me an old-fashioned look and another of her

radiant smiles. 'She may be closer than you think, Dame Edna. Tell me, where do you stay in London?'

'I used to live in suites in some of the big hotels,' I confessed, 'but now I have my own gorgeous penthouse in Mayfair as well as my homes in Montreux, Mustique, Malibu and Melbourne. Why do you ask?'

'I hope,' hesitated the Queen, 'you won't think me forward, but my husband and I would like you always to feel at home in Buckingham Palace.'

I gasped, but the Queen went on, 'It must be a nightmare being always in the public eye as you are, living in a goldfish bowl. My life is private compared with yours. We would just like you to feel free to come and go here at any time of the day or night when the press are driving you bananas. Here is a key.'

Speechless with gratitude I accepted the small gold object and clenched it in my hand, feeling the bevel with my fingers.

'Regard this as your bolthole,' she said, as I slipped into my humanely culled acrylic. 'You can have your own shelf in the fridge.'

We gave each other a little squash and I was off in my limo down the Mall, where the lights of London seemed to shine more brightly than ever before.

Would I tell Madge? I wondered. No way! It would be as good as sending a press release to the *Sunday People*. The golden key in my clutch bag was my secret – *our* secret, I thought, glancing over my shoulder through the rear window of the limo at the receding Palace.

So when people ask me, as they often do, if I have met Royalty I smile a certain smile: Have I met them? Do I know them? Leave it out, do me a favour, you've got to be joking!!

CHAPTER XXVI

Scratches
on the Jamb

W HEN I HUG people – very often women who insist on coming on to the stage during my wonderful shows – they frequently whisper their gratitude and thanks and not seldom follow up with a letter.

I keep some of these, especially if my correspondent has experienced some improvement in a physical ailment or even a mental handicap. Don't run away with the idea that I can heal. What a vain woman I would be if I set myself up as a one-woman Lourdes! But spooky things *have* happened during my performances and barely a night goes by after one of my shows when the cleaners do not discover, in the aisle or under a seat, a pair of crutches, a Zimmer frame or a prosthetic device. I make no greater claim than that.

One of the most regular compliments heaped upon me is some reference to my softness. Men, women and children write saying, 'you were so soft', or 'your softness was a big surprise to our family', or as in the case of one grateful patron 'you were the softest woman I've ever cuddled on stage in front of three thousand people'. People who don't believe me are welcome to inspect all of these letters on microfilm at the Dame Edna Museum in Melbourne, Australia, or the Edna Archive at the University of South West Virginia (ask for Miriam K. Benkowitz).

I think my famous softness really took a big leap forward when my first bubba came along, and I couldn't help thinking of little Brucie as I stood once more in the old nursery at Humouresque

Street. My lovely hazel eyes prickled with tears as I looked around. Yes! There, on the chipped, off-white door jamb, were those little pencil lines where I had marked my children's heights; still there after all those years.

When I saw, scratched on the paintwork, Valmai's name, it was as though a cold hand had entered my breast and given my heart a little squeeze. What a lovely child she had been, I reflected, and to think she had grown up so bitter and twisted. There, just a couple of feet from the floor, was little Kenny's mark. Even then, when he was knee-high to a grasshopper, he would stroke my lovely dresses admiringly, and now he created them! Further up on the doorframe, Norm and I had even notched our heights.

Madge and I had quickly tired of our visit to Moonee Ponds Girls' Grammar. It had changed out of all recognition with the shelter shed demolished and ugly new buildings jutting out into our old playground. Everything looked so much *smaller* too, as things do when you are unwise enough to revisit them, and I thought that if I stayed there any longer, my old memory of the school, and the ghosts who inhabited it, would get blurred and smudged by its hideous present-day image. I popped on a pair of sunglasses and a lovely headscarf the Queen had given me, with horseshoes all over it and red setters with their tongues hanging out. It was my anonymous look. 'Come on, Madge,' I said, grabbing her by the arm and hauling her back to the car. 'I'm sick of this. Let's go to my museum now, it's only a few streets away and I have to face it sooner or later.'

The Royal Edna Museum is one of those special places in Australia and, let's face it, the world.* Tourists love visiting the homes of famous people but they very rarely get a chance to poke around until long after the celebrated occupant has been gathered. I doubt if England's Dr Johnson, the inventor of Johnson's Baby Powder and – I'm almost certain – the Q-tip – would have been too pleased to find a line of tourists traipsing through his lovely period-style home, tucked away behind Fleet Street. Same with Anne Hathaway in Stratford, Goya in Toledo and Elvis at Gracelands. I suppose I must be one of the very few Megastars to have their old home turned into a musuem during their own lifetime. What a compliment.

* I guess it is Australia's answer to Hearst Castle.

As our limo swung into Humouresque Street, I spied once more the enormous silver buses almost dwarfing the houses, and the long line of Japanese tourists snaking up to my old front porch. It was almost as long as the line their compatriots formed outside the Louis Vuitton shop in Hong Kong, and *that's* saying something!

I had not revisited number 36 since Chris Bland at Fennimore and Gerda had set it up as a charitable trust, and it had been officially handed over to the Nation. I had agreed to all this while abroad, and only on the proviso that it was kept pretty well as we left it. After all, Posterity would want to know every detail of how I lived, right down to the contents of the larder and bathroom cabinet, though in the case of the latter I insisted on having a few old items removed from the top shelf which had been there since Mummy's time and would only worry people. The gift shop on the porch was the National Trust's idea, and they sold some of my albums and videos, as well as greetings cards, T-shirts, drinks coasters, oven mitts, and now, this best-seller! The Friends of the Prostate also had a small stall.

In spite of my headscarf and dark glasses, I was recognised at once by a nice woman on the door and discreetly admitted. I must confess that they had kept my home beautifully, with little ropes around the walls to prevent people touching my china ducks and other knick-knacks, and cords across the arms of the chairs as well, in case the Japs wanted to sit there and have their pictures taken, bless them. My priceless sandblasted reindeer doors were protected from accidental damage, or vandalism by maniacs, with a thick shield of bullet-proof perspex apparently identical to the screen in front of the Leonardo da Vinci cartoon at London's National Gallery. There was a photography ban on them because a lovely postcard was obtainable in the gift shop.

In every room in my museum, sitting rather stiffly and slightly bored, was an elderly woman from the Trust keeping an eye on things, and when I visited my old kitchen (what a spooky feeling) one of these attendants snapped at a rather nice little geisha girl for touching the door of my Frigidaire. In our old bedroom, where Norm and I had spent so many happy minutes, the video cameras were really whirring and I noticed some of the female tourists had brought Dame Edna wigs and glasses to wear with their 'I Wannabe Edna' T-shirts. I have already told you of my visit to my children's old nursery, and the evocative hieroglyphics on the door jamb.

'Excuse me, Ma'am!' A rather grating voice interrupted my reverie, and I swung around to see a shortish American woman in a plastic raincoat clutching an Olympus. 'Beg pardon, but are you Maria Callas, only nicer looking?' I politely told her no, inwardly pleased that my disguise was so effective.

At the back of the house, a tasteful little auditorium had been built on the site of our old incinerator and fowl-house, where a long line of people waited their turn to view a continuous screening of a film about my life. Over the fence strange neighbours peered curiously. Nice enough I suppose, but obviously not born on this side of the water.

As Madge and I were leaving, the same little American hurried up behind me panting, and grabbed my sleeve as I was about to get into the limo.

'I'm sorry, Ma'am,' she drawled, 'but you sure do look familiar. Don't I know you from someplace?' I had not realised how emotional I had become visiting that lovely little home of mine which was my home no longer, and I was glad to be wearing those dark glasses as I replied to that pest of a woman.

'I'm no one. I just used to live here,' I said. 'I used to live here once.'

We drove off and I could see her standing there stock-still on the nature strip, her mouth ajar, staring after the limo.

Turning into Puckle Street, we had to pull over to allow another enormous bus-load of Japanese sightseers, appropriately called Pilgrim Tours, into Humouresque Street.

'You'd think they'd won the war,' muttered Madge, not without an unacceptable touch of Nippism. 'Just as well your uncle Vic isn't here, Edna. He's never really buried the hatchet, has he? And if he set eyes on all those little tourists something might snap.'

Something *did* snap. In my brain. *Where was the Butcher of*

Borneo? Hadn't he met us at Melbourne Airport? But when was that? Desperately, I rummaged in my jet-lagged memory, trying to reconstruct the jumbled events of the last twenty-four hours. Events which had grown all the more confused since I had been so vividly reliving my life story. Yes, Uncle Victor *had* met us at the airport, and he had travelled in my limo, bless his heart, all the way out to Dunraven to see Mummy. *But where was he on the return trip?* I had been understandably stressed beyond endurance by those torrid events at the hospital. It's no fun when your own mother doesn't recognise you. I had even fallen asleep at her bedside. Then somehow Madge and I had gone back to the hotel alone. I must have lost my own uncle! Snatching the little car phone off its clip, I jabbed out the familiar code for my mother's terminary. A nurse (was it Ng?) answered and connected me to Sister Choate.

'Excuse I, Sister, but I think it is just possible I mislaid something while I was at Dunraven last night.'

'Nothing has been handed in, Dame Edna,' replied that unappetising woman. 'I seem to remember you had your purse under your arm as you left.'

Hmmm, I thought, trust her to notice that! If I had left my purse behind in that den of thieves, fat chance I would have had of seeing it again! 'No, Sister Choate,' I pursued more directly, 'it wasn't actually my purse I lost, it was my uncle actually.'

'*Your uncle?*'

'That's what I said, woman!' The car phone was making a ghastly crackle, like they all do.

'Wait a minute, Dame Edna,' came Choate's voice through the static. 'We did find a man last night, wandering around the grounds in a confused state. One of the orderlies presumed him to be an escaped patient, heavily sedated him and committed him to the Marilyn Monroe Ward. Come to think of it, he did claim kinship with your good self, but we took that for *folie de grandeur,* a common delusion of our inmates.'

'Well what's he doing now?' I enquired, pretty relieved I can tell you.

'Happy as a sandboy,' replied Sister Choate. 'He's already a firm favourite and settled in nicely.'

A tremendous burst of electrical interference terminated our conversation.

Since Uncle Victor lived alone, I suppose there was no harm in him lingering out at Dunraven for a while. Sister Choate's cheerful tone suggested she had obviously found his credit card. However, it was a big weight off my mind, and I was certainly pleased to clear up that little mystery. I made a mental note to spring my uncle – if he was springable – at an early opportunity, sometime, if I happened to be in the area. It was only as we approached our next destination that it occurred to me that I had completely forgotten to ask Sister Choate how Mummy was.

The low-slung white building designed by famous Melbourne architect Neil Clerehan lay in beautiful grounds amongst gorgeous native trees. As our limo swung in the gate I saw, tastefully incised on a polished travertine plaque, the legend: DAME EDNA PROSTATE FOUNDATION. It was with a sense of pride that I reflected that this revolutionary clinic and its opposite number in London could never have been possible but for me and Ednacare Switzerland, the entity I use for most of my philanthropic projects. A few years had passed since Dr Finzi smoked his last ciggie, and I was greeted on the clinic steps by Professor Colin Morris, Chairman of the World Prostate Bank. There was a touching little guard of honour at the entrance too, of nurses and doctors holding gladdies, and a darling patient in spotless pyjamas and dressing-gown was wheeled up to me so that he could present me with a gorgeous bouquet.

There was quite a procession of us who moved down the long white corridor towards the Norman Everage Wing where my husband's installation was located.

'He's doing wonderfully well,' said Professor Morris. 'In fact he's as strong as an ox and as fit as a fiddle according to his latest printout. Ever since he has been here, Matron Younghusband has personally supervised his therapy and they are almost inseparable. It's a joy to behold.'

I almost stopped in my tracks. 'Matron Younghusband? Is that the nurse who was looking after Lord Everage before I took him home?' I asked sharply.

'Why I believe she is,' replied the Chairman. 'She is a remarkable woman and devoted to your husband's case. Thanks to Thelma, Australia is at the sharp end of Prostate Research.'

We had turned a corner into a large brilliantly lit room, which looked like a futuristic laboratory. A masked orderly holding a pair of tongs issued us all with masks, gowns and gloves, whilst another nurse furnished us with white hard hats out of sanitised polythene bags. Soon we were walking amongst the quietly throbbing machines until Professor Morris stopped suddenly before the large box which housed my husband and his technology. He pulled a remote control out of the pocket of his gown, and pointing it at Norm, punched out a few numbers. More digits in green writing appeared upon a screen. The Professor studied it for a second and chuckled.

'He's really looking forward to seeing you, Dame Edna,' he said. 'If you put your hand in here you can hold his hand.' He indicated an oval-shaped aperture on the side of the box into which I gingerly inserted myself.

I know, Readers, what I should have been thinking at this moment, and what I should have been feeling too; but the thought of that Thelma Younghusband remained persistently in the forefront of my mind. I could still see her as I had seen her last, years and years before, soon after Norm had his first urological incident, standing in the hospital window, staring spookily at my departing vehicle. Now she and Norm were inseparable, were they? She was a 'remarkable woman', was she? 'Devoted' to my husband too. How lovely! *How wonderful!!*

As I sat there beside something resembling an enormous reclining fridge, in the middle of what looked like a gigantic space-age cheese factory, I thought I could smell . . . was it *perfume?* I inhaled the very faintest aroma of a scent I had once squirted on my wrist, and rejected, at the Singapore International Airport transit passengers' shopping precinct. I couldn't remember its name, but it was that one that smells like fly-spray which Sydney women adore. Yuk! It was *her* all right – and not far off either! Probably lurking somewhere amongst all that technology. I would be no sooner gone, and on a plane to London, than she would be sitting where I was now, with her hand in Norm's orifice, fumbling for something.

I hope I'm not a jealous woman. Readers of this book will, I hope, confirm that I never adopted a watchdog attitude to my husband, despite the fact that he was very, very attractive to women, even if they were unaware of it. The incident with Pixie Lambell was an error on my part, which I freely admit, but something was definitely going on here at the Prostate Foundation and if I wanted to keep my husband, I was going to have to do something about it. Fast.

Frankly, I couldn't concentrate on a one-to-one, or more accurately, one-to-machine relationship with my husband at that particular point in time. We would have to wait a little for our moment of intimacy. Now was neither the time nor the place, and I didn't want all these strangers reading his printout over my shoulder. Besides, I think he was asleep.

Back in Morris's office, I delivered my bombshell, and I must say he took it rather well.

'Of course it's feasible, Dame Edna,' he said, making a little church and steeple with his fingers and bouncing it off his lips. 'They have identical technology in London and theoretically it would be a simple matter to charter a jumbo and uplift Lord Norm to our UK facility. I suppose all we would really need to change would be the plugs on his equipment. What are you over there? Three-pin 240 volt or two-pin 210 volt?'

I certainly had no intention of betraying my serious suspicions about Thelma Younghusband, it would have been undignified, and luckily no one asked me why I wanted Norm rushed to London. I suppose they all assumed I wished him to be near me for my first night at the Theatre Royal. And so I did, for heaven's sake!

But Professor Morris seemed to have been reading my thoughts, for as he helped me into my limo outside the Foundation, he said, 'You can be sure I will personally oversee this exercise, Dame Edna. With any luck your husband will be safely installed in Westminster next week, provided British Airways or Qantas come to the party. When all is said and done, the bottom line at the end of the day is only money.'

How true that is, I thought. And still think.

I had a lot on my mind. Let's face it, Possums, when haven't

I? My new show in London, the most important in my career, was looming. My beloved husband was leaving Australia for the first overseas trip of his life, though not a trip which would yield many colour slides, I'm afraid. My daughter Valmai, whom I had hoped to see on this whistle-stop visit, had vanished, and not even her poor husband Mervyn Gittis or the 'girl' on the Trotsky-ite Agit-Prop Women's Switchboard had a clue where she was.

'Basically, we haven't seen her since the last Animal Liberation demo, basically,' said a pretty ordinary-sounding voice over the phone. Why was everything so *basic* with these people, I wondered? And how on earth did they ever string a sentence together before the word 'basically' came to their rescue?

The big issue in my mind, which I had been weighing up for weeks, was Sir Mark's prestigious invitation, and I had decided, after a lot of humming and hahing, to accept it. I couldn't spend the rest of my life jumping around on the stage. I should retire at my peak and pursue an alternative career as a famous diplomat and ambassadress for the greatest sub-continent in the world. There are other stars I could name who keep on doing it 'their way' until they've pretty well got one foot in the grave. Quite frankly a whole new generation has real difficulty in seeing the point of them as they stand up there in the spotlight croaking through their old numbers. Not for me! No way! Do me a favour, leave it out!

Mentally, I was redecorating the Australian Embassy in Strand Street, London, as Madge and I boarded our flight back to England. Some of my beautiful art deco pieces which my antique scouts Big Vic and Edward Clark had scoured the world for, would look lovely in the foyer, and there I would also hang the famous portrait of my younger self by dear old Charlie Eltham. On the staircase . . .

'Edna.'

. . . on the staircase I would put a few of my Jasper Johns lithographs (screwed to the wall just in case), and the little-known David Hockney silkscreen of me . . .

'Edna.'

'For heaven's sake, Madge,' I exploded. 'Can't you see I've got my slumber shades on and I'm wearing my "Don't wake me for cocktails" sticker!'

Madge was waving a newspaper at me and pointing at its front page with more animation than she normally exhibits in a calendar year. The plane had taken off and there was old Malcolm, one of my favourite cabin stewards in his pink blazer, pushing a big trolley of jingling drinks and soggy canapés up the aisle.

"What is it, Madge? You've woken me up, so this had better be good!'

'It's all over the *Morning Murdoch*, Edna. They gave us the papers just after take-off but you had your shades on. It's about your friend.'

I seized the paper and narrowed my eyes to read the small, smudgy print. I needn't have bothered. All I really needed to know was in a huge black headline you could have read a mile off. Naturally I read on.

BARTOK IN BRAZIL

Sir Mark Bartok, the Sydney businessman and financier, chairman of Bartok Holdings, Bartex Textiles, Bartok Constructions, Bartpac Investments and Bartjel, the lubricant empire, who disappeared from his Eastern suburbs mansion last week on the eve of a federal investigation into his affairs, has reappeared in Rio de Janeiro, according to a reliable source. Fears are mounting that Sir Mark may have been directly connected with a huge massage parlour scam worth billions of dollars.

It has now emerged that Sir Mark has been under examination for some time, but was 'tipped off' by an undisclosed Government source in plenty of time to 'clean up his desk' before fleeing the country. The same source claims that Sir Mark, who was a close personal friend of the Prime Minister, never possessed an Australian passport and has lived in this country for years on a tourist visa. Cynics are suggesting that Sir Mark's defection to Brazil, with whom Australia has no extradition treaty, could spare the Government acute embarrassment since the disgraced financier knows, quote: 'where too many bodies are buried'.

I felt stunned, what did it all mean? He seemed so concerned about Australia's image too. Something must be wrong. Then my eye fell on another, slightly smaller headline:

Top Job for Les

Dr Sir Les Patterson, former cultural attaché to the court of St James and Chairman of the Australian Cheese Board, in an over-night decision, has just been appointed as Australia's International Cultural Ambassador world-wide. At his Western suburbs hacienda-Cape-Cod-style home last night, Sir Les was jubilant. He said, 'Shit . . .'

I hurled the paper to the floor and grabbed for the little pocket on the back of the seat in front of me. Madge was spoilt on this trip, travelling first, but normally I used to fill an air-sickness bag with old savouries and have it sent back to her in Economy. This time I was reaching for one of those damp-proof paper receptacles in order to put it to its more orthodox use. The news of Sir Mark was bad enough, but the thought of that yobbo Patterson, whom I had known of old, stepping into *my* job, was chunderous!

Malcolm the steward picked up the scattered pages of the *Morning Murdoch* and scrutinised the front page as I sat hunched and gagging over my paper muzzle.

'Gee whiz, Dame Edna. Old Bartok's gone to the ropes! They caught up with him at last, eh? The word is he was flat broke when he did a flit. Didn't have a dollar to his name.'

Although I was still clutching my bag, nothing was coming luckily; I was too busy thinking of Sir Mark, the pauper. I retrieved my last memory of him watching all those little jumping green numbers on the screen. He must have blinked.

*   *   *

Although I don't rehearse, *per se*, I like to wander about the theatre on the day of a Royal Gala opening night, just to get the 'feel' of the place. They say the Theatre Royal, Drury Lane, has at least three ghosts, and if I ever die, there will almost certainly be four; though I won't frighten people. It will probably be good luck to see me, throwing ghostly gladdies from the stage.

Outside, people were queuing around the block for tickets, and I thought how proud dear old Sir John Betjeman, who had such faith in me in the sixties, would have been to have seen the world and his wife come round to his point of view. As my minders helped me struggle through the crowds to the stage door before rehearsal, I could hear a lot of people calling: 'How's Norm?' and I was pleased and proud to be able to reply: 'He arrived this morning, thank you, Possums.'

They had phoned me from the Foundation when the jumbo touched down, but said that there wasn't much point in my coming out or interrupting my work. Best, they said, to wait until Norman was all set up at his new abode.

At least he's out of that scheming Younghusband's clutches, I thought, as I went through my show-stopping finale number, 'Shyness'. As I sang, I thought how nice it would be if Norm could watch part of my opening night on TV; the celebrities pulling up at the Theatre, and the arrival of Charles and Diana would all be on the news that evening, and it would be wonderful for my beloved invalid to see it all, if only backwards in his mirror.

During the lunchbreak in my luxurious dressing room amongst flowers from Steve Sondheim, Paloma Picasso, Claus von Bulow, Pixie Lambell, the Yehudi Menuhins, Annie Leibovitz, Tally and Gerald Westminster, Pee Wee Herman, Dame Joan Sutherland, Bob Graham and Anjelica Huston, Gian Carlo Menotti, Karl Lagerfeld, Françoise Sagan, Billy Wilder, Bruce and Virginia Beresford, Armistead Maupin, Leni Riefenstahl, John Guare, Madonna, Chuck Heston and Ken Thomson not to mention *you-know-who,* I picked up a phone and called the Foundation.

'Lord Norm's facility?'

'That is correct,' came a woman's voice. 'Who is it?'

'Dame Edna speaking. Who are you prithee?'

'It's Thelma Younghusband speaking, Dame Edna. I'm afraid Norm is not strong enough to chat. He's having a snooze.'

The beautiful flowers in my dressing room all went out of focus for a minute and then back again.

'Good afternoon, Matron Younghusband,' I said, with icy calm, 'I'm very surprised to hear your voice. I thought you were in Australia.'

'He insisted I come too,' came the outrageous reply. 'I'm the only one who knows how to fiddle with his dials. The only one he trusts.'

'Is Professor Morris aware of this?' I enquired, my voice rising, but the line went dead just as my stage director Harriet called over the tannoy: 'Dame Edna on stage please to rehearse finale ballet. Dame Edna on stage, please.'

'Why must the show go on?' I asked Dame Nature aloud, as so many great stars must have asked her down the ages. Quickly I pressed the re-dial button.

'I want Professor Morris.' In seconds he was on the line and the words spilt out of me: 'Professor Morris. Something has just happened which I find almost impossible . . .'

But he interrupted me, 'Steady on, Dame Edna,' he said softly. 'Something has just happened here. We have an emergency. It's bad news I'm afraid. Lord Norm has just gone to his Reward.'

'*Dame Edna on stage please. Orchestra are waiting. Paging Dame Edna. On stage immediately please.*'

'I beg your pardon, Professor? But . . . I was just speaking to that Younghusband woman. He was sleeping . . .'

'It was very peaceful, Dame Edna. None of us could have done anything. He had a lovely trip over and even bought some duty free Brut at Singapore, which we sprayed on his respirator. He enjoyed half an episode of *Gilligan's Island* before he fell asleep.'

Somehow I did the show that night. Somehow I didn't let the Royal Couple see my tears, and the story about Norm only broke later that evening. Somehow I took umpteen curtain calls and was able to put in an appearance at the backstage party too. And somehow I even managed a low-key supper with Chris and Jeremy at Le Caprice. Directly after I heard the news I had called Dr Shardenfreude in case he knew where Valmai was, and he had given me wise counsel: 'Time is a miracle healer,' he had said, 'only time will heal,' and he was *so right*, because five hours later, I felt absolutely marvellous.

When I finally got to the Foundation next morning, the media mobbed me. Kenny had been up all night making me a gorgeous black taffeta number and a lot of women who saw the news coverage were green with envy, I'm afraid. As Madge and I battled our way up the Foundation steps, who should burst out of the crowd but my daughter Valmai looking like goodness knows what and waving a banner which I couldn't quite read, but I think it said: 'Give Prisoners Condominiums' or words to that effect. *'Was that the fruit of my womb?'* I grieved, as she fought savagely with the police cordon in the clinic forecourt. It was ghastly and frightening to behold that attention-seeking monster who had, such a short time before, been a sweet little scratch on the jamb of my nursery door.

Suddenly, from amongst the clamouring journalists, a familiar face appeared, but sadly eroded by age and drink. 'Ed, Ed!' he cried, waving a press badge. It was all that was left of Kevin Farelly. In his efforts to get past my minders, he tripped on the kerb and fell flat on his back. 'Hi, Ed!' he continued unperturbed from a supine position. 'Nice to see yiz in London.'

'It's nice to see you, Kevin,' I replied, looking at the prone journalist in the gutter, 'and in your *natural habitat!*' And I swept for the last time into the Dame Edna Prostate Foundation.

My husband was a generous man, and unbeknownst to us, he had left most of his vital organs to institutions all over the world. When we got to his bedside, he was little more than a dent in the pillow. He had been globally recycled.

I don't really think he'd actually meant this to happen in quite the way it did. As I found out later, he had apparently filled in a card months before and had ticked off: liver, kidneys, brains, tripe, sweetbreads . . . He thought it was the hospital menu! Norm had always been a big offal man. He didn't realise it was his Tissue Donor's Card. I think if you had asked my husband for his tissues in those days, he would have given you a box of Kleenex.

Luckily, I didn't bump into that Thelma Younghusband, but I believe she later appeared on television, dressed up to the nines, suggesting that she was closer to Norm than I was. I leave it to the Readers of this book to form their own judgement of this tragic claim, and in doing so, not to be too harsh on that foolish, deluded nurse. Life is far too short.

We decided against a committal of Norm's remains, since there were hardly any to speak of, and instead, I arranged for something very simple and very dignified to be erected to his memory in the

Melbourne Cemetery. I vowed that as soon as my record-breaking London theatre season came to an end, I would make my long and lonely widow's pilgrimage to that spot and pay my silent tribute to the memory of the soldier, husband, father and medical pioneer, who had shared my life. If only I could cry, I thought. Would this be yet another of those Big Moments in my spiritual journey, when I was seized by some funny old inhibition I could not fathom?

But there *had* been happy times, and plenty of them, I reflected, as Madge and I drove away from the Foundation and I slid my arm behind her little trembling shoulders. On the car radio, the driver was tuned to a nostalgia programme. It was Doris Day singing our song:

> 'Well, what do you know, he smiled at me in my dreams
>   last night!
> My Dreams Are Getting Better All The Time.'

Yes, past happiness is an elusive thing, isn't it, Possums? And recapturing it is as hard as picking up mercury off a carpet. *But how did I know a thing about that?*

*Abschied**

THE LARGE BLACK Daimler rocks opulently as it glides along Royal Parade and swings into College Crescent. It is a perfect Melbourne morning in July and across the road the lawns of Ormond College are immaculately white from the night frost, bruised only by the green footprints of one early jogger.

The Melbourne General Cemetery is not officially open to the public yet, but the black limousine seems to be expected, because a man in jeans and a yellow anorak, his breath a white plume on the morning air, is running out of the Porter's Lodge and heaving open the Gothic cast iron gates. The chauffeur signals his thanks with a wave of one black-gloved hand, and the Daimler rolls up a narrow driveway, flanked by mausoleums and calcified marble sepulchres. At a point about seven hundred yards into the heart of the old cemetery, the car stops and the driver leaps out to open the rear door assisting his lone passenger to alight.

She stands for a moment beside the car, uncertain perhaps of what to do next or which direction to adopt. Then, from the recesses of the car she takes a magnificent wreath of salmon-pink blooms, and with a perfunctory wave to the driver she walks off down a long and neglected avenue of pencil cypresses. Soon her black cashmere coat, black hat and the flash of pink flowers are

---

* As adult education folk will know this is a spooky German word meaning parting.

lost from sight amongst the clutter of tombs and leprous statues.

The young chauffeur lights a cigarette and leans against the car smoking and stamping his numb feet in the gravel. Although it is still early, he has already been up for several hours and there had been a long delay at the international terminal awaiting his employer's flight, and the debouchment of her baggage.

The sky is a perfect blue bisected by one high vapour trail, like a magically attenuating pipe-cleaner. The sun striking obliquely through the cemetery catches the bright chips of mica in the granite obelisks and stone-swagged urns which push crookedly up above the tall and thriving weeds.

The woman with the wreath moves more slowly now, amongst the skeleton weed, lantana and a tangle of blackberries. The area in which she stands, with its vandalised funereal monuments, lopsided stones, and subsiding graves, seems an oddly turbulent and unquiet resting place for the departed. It reminds her of the unruly bed linen of one who sleeps neither deeply nor well. Moreover many of the tombs here have been daubed and desecrated with mindless slogans and expletives.

She has found, apparently, the grave she sought, for she stops in front of a simple marble column and stares at the inscription on its polished plinth. Lichen and obscene graffiti have already, in so short a time, obscured the incised name and part of the epitaph, and the woman seems distressed; uncertain. Then with astonishing speed she runs back to the car, surprising the driver who quickly stamps out his cigarette and replaces his peaked cap. Oblivious of this, she opens the front passenger door of the Daimler unassisted, rummages in the glove compartment, and retrieves a white cloth with which she hastily retraces her steps.

Once more at the monument, she kneels now, and with the rag rubs at the marble plaque, buffing off the lewd aerosol scrawl and the obdurate fans of gamboge lichen and encroaching moss, revealing the inscription:

NORMAN
STODDART
EVERAGE
Beloved husband of Edna
Beloved Father of Bruce, Valmai, Kenny
and little Lois

'Life's a melody,
if you'll only hum the tune.'

She sweeps aside a long-dead wreath of flowers, now sere and cinnamon, and replaces it with her rich chaplet of fresh gladioli. Her work done, she stands for a moment in silent meditation, but before moving back slowly to the waiting vehicle, and the world she must every day confront and reconquer alone, she glances absently at the sullied rag in her hand. Then her heart stops, and with a little wave of grief she sees, for the first time, what it is. A pair of men's Y-front underpants.

Norm's.

Larry Hagman – a Denial

Messrs Fennimore and Gerda, solicitors for Dame Edna Everage and the House of Everage, a wholly owned subsidiary of Ednacare and Ednatainment Plc, Switzerland, wish to categorically deny all rumours currently circulated in sections of the Media, that their client's friendship with Larry Hagman, the Actor of Malibu, California, is more than warmly platonic.

Dame Edna deeply regrets any distress these unfounded and malicious rumours may have occasioned Mr Hagman or his wife and family, and hereby gives notice and due warning to all press and television agencies, that should they give further circulation or credence to these aforesaid rumours, they will be liable to exemplary and punitive damages.

Appendix
Recipe Corner

DAME EDNA'S STRETCH MARK SPECIFIC
Half a cup of good dripping from last Sunday's roast
   (take care to strain out string and burnt fragments of potato
   and parsnip)
One tablespoon of oatmeal or porridge
A generous dollop of Vaseline
One tablespoon of peroxide
Two tablespoons of glycerine
Half a tin of tomato juice

Blend in blender. Perfume with a few drops of your favourite and pour over the tummy taking care that the sheet you are lying on is one for which you have no further use. Ask a loved one (if available) to gently massage the liquid into your s.m. zones for at least fifteen minutes and leave to dry. Chip off later in the shower or tub and repeat daily for three months after delivery.

PAVLOVA
6 egg whites
pinch of cream of tartar
few drops vanilla extract
1 heaped cup caster sugar
1 teaspoon cornflour
1 scant dessertspoon (2 teaspoons) vinegar
arrowroot

Topping
cream
3–4 passion-fruit

Put the egg whites, cream of tartar and vanilla into a bowl and beat well until the mixture becomes firm and snowy. Mix sugar and cornflour together, and fold into the egg white mixture, taking the spoon to the bottom of the mixing bowl each time. As soon as the sugar and cornflour are incorporated with the egg white mixture, add the vinegar and combine well.

Line the bottom and sides of a standard fairly deep cake tin with brown (greaseproof) paper, and sprinkle 2 dessertspoons of both arrowroot and sugar over the paper, reserving a little for sprinkling over the top. Pile the mixture (which should be fairly stiff) into the middle of the cake tin, and sprinkle the remainder of the arrowroot and sugar mixture over the top.

Turn the gas oven on full heat for 15 minutes before putting the pavlova in, then turn it down as low as possible. Place the cake tin on the half-way shelf. If the pavlova shows a faint tinge of brown after 15 minutes the temperature is correct, and the cake should be fully cooked in 1½ hours. If the cake starts to go too brown, turn the oven off completely, relight after 15 minutes and keep an eye on the pavlova.

Remove from the oven and turn upside-down on to a serving plate. Whip the cream and ice the pavlova with this. Scoop out the passion-fruit pulp and place it on top of the cream.

Helpful Hints
Always have the eggs at room temperature, and several days old. New eggs have thin whites, and will not beat up to great volume. A pinch of cream of tartar or a few drops of lemon juice strengthens the protein in the whites, giving it a strong structure. Use half ordinary sugar and half icing sugar, instead of all granulated sugar.